Class, Culture, and the Classroom

American Civilization
A Series Edited by Allen F. Davis

Gospel Hymns and Social Religion:
The Rhetoric of Nineteenth-Century Revivalism
by Sandra S. Sizer (1978)

Social Darwinism: Science and Myth
in Anglo-American Social Thought
by Robert C. Bannister (1979)

Twentieth Century Limited:
Industrial Design in America, 1925–1939
by Jeffrey L. Meikle (1979)

Charlotte Perkins Gilman:
The Making of a Radical Feminist, 1860–1896
by Mary A. Hill (1980)

Inventing the American Way of Death, 1830–1920
by James J. Farrell (1980)

Anarchist Women, 1870–1920
by Margaret S. Marsh (1981)

Woman and Temperance:
The Quest for Power and Liberty, 1873–1900
by Ruth Bordin (1981)

Hearth and Home: Preserving a People's Culture
by George W. McDaniel (1981)

The Education of Mrs. Henry Adams
by Eugenia Kaledin (1981)

Class, Culture, and the Classroom: The Student Peace Movement
of the 1930s (1981)
by Eileen Eagan

Class, Culture, and the Classroom

The Student Peace Movement
of the 1930s
by Eileen Eagan

Temple University Press Philadelphia

Temple University Press, Philadelphia 19122

© 1981 by Temple University. All rights reserved

Published 1981

Printed in the United States of America

Library of Congress Cataloging in Publication Data
Eagan, Eileen.
  Class, culture, and the classroom.

  (American civilization)
  Includes bibliographical references and index.
  1. Radicalism—United States—History—20th century. 2. Student move-
ments—United States—History—20th century. 3. Student strikes—United
States—History—20th century. 4. Pacifism—History—20th century.
I. Title. II. Series.
HN90.R3E15   378'.198'1   81-9415
ISBN 0-87722-236-3   AACR2

For my mother and father

Contents

Acknowledgments ix

List of Abbreviations xiii

Introduction 3

CHAPTER 1
Background of the Student Antiwar Movement 19

CHAPTER 2
Revolt on Campus: Columbia 40

CHAPTER 3
"We Pledge Not to Support the Government of
the United States in Any War It May Conduct" 57

CHAPTER 4
Conflict on Campus: Antifascism and Civil Liberties 72

CHAPTER 5
Students Strike against War 108

CHAPTER 6
Marxism, Progressivism, and the
American Student Union 134

CHAPTER 7
Religion and the Student Peace Movement 153

CHAPTER 8
Students and the Spanish Civil War 169

CHAPTER 9
Collective Security versus the Oxford Oath 183

CHAPTER 10
Movement to War 202

CHAPTER 11
Fire and Ice: Students in the Postwar World 233

Notes 263

Bibliographical Essay 296

Index 305

Acknowledgments

This book had its origins in the antiwar movement of the 1960s and early 1970s. I first learned of the previous student movement while doing a paper for a seminar on the peace movement, at Temple University in 1971. My work on it since then has been shaped by public events and personal influences. The war in Vietnam and its aftermath, the women's movement, and economic changes have all shaped and changed my perspective. What I have written here reflects my own, perhaps contentious, view of the thirties and of recent years, and some of the ideas of friends and colleagues.

As a dissertation, the study was improved by useful (if often contradictory) comments of the members of my committee: Allen F. Davis, James Hilty, and Norman Kaner. Fellow students, especially Marian Bell, Joyce Freedman, Barbara Howe, Barbara Klaczynski, Betsey Lightbourn, Patricia McNeal, Lee Schreiber, and Bill Young, helped me to persist and to finish.

In the course of my research I have been assisted by librarians, archivists, and staff at Temple University, the University of Wisconsin—Milwaukee, City College of New York, the Jane Addams Peace Collection at Swarthmore College, the University of Missouri—St. Louis, and Illinois Wesleyan University. In each case I found helpfulness to be limited only by limited budgets, which in turn reminded me of the importance of economics in history. I am grateful to the ar-

chives and archivists at Vassar College and at the Library of
Congress for their assistance and permission to use the photographs included, and to Tim Garvey of Illinois Wesleyan University for his photographs and for showing me that even in
Peoria, peace sentiment was manifest in the thirties. Carolyn
Colwell and Terry Toll both assisted in my search for photographs and in last-minute research.

A National Endowment for the Humanities Summer Seminar for College Teachers, "The Radical Tradition in America,"
directed by Eric Foner, gave me the time, reading, and exciting discussion of that tradition that encouraged me to think
about the ways in which progressive culture and values can
be maintained and transmitted from one generation of activists to another. All the members of that seminar have contributed to my understanding of the importance of a community
of the left.

I have spoken, formally and informally, over a period of
years to many participants in the student movement and
peace movement of the thirties and of the years since. I am
especially grateful to Molly Yard, with whom I have corre-
sponded and whose politics have led her from the American
Student Union to the National Organization for Women and
the campaign for the Equal Rights Amendment. Even more
important to me than the recollections of the former student
activists have been their continued efforts to create a more
just society. I owe the antiwar movement and the women's
movement a personal and intellectual debt, and their imprint
is on this book. In particular, my work has been influenced
by my friends in the University of Wisconsin—Milwaukee
Moratorium Committee, especially Gene Eisman, Ted Hayes,
George Wagner, and Lois Wilhelm, and by the Women's
Studies faculty at the University of Missouri—St. Louis, especially Kathy Corbett, Marcia Dalbey, Paddy Quick, Christine Roman, and Susan Hartmann, who read and made good
suggestions about the last chapter.

Michael Wreszin contributed substantial and helpful criticism each time he read the manuscript. My editors, Kenneth Arnold and David Perry, were both tactful and sensible. Allen Davis, who by now must know more about the student movement of the thirties than he ever wanted to, has been an ideal adviser and editor, letting me write what I wanted without letting me hang myself (I think.) Throughout my work I have been continually assisted by the comments and discussion and correction of mixed metaphors by A. Theodore Brown of the University of Wisconsin—Milwaukee.

This book is dedicated to my parents because, while they will not necessarily agree with what I have written, they taught me the value of education and of defending one's beliefs. My aunt, Cora Geiger Newald, and others in my family have provided an example of acting upon beliefs. My friends at D'Youville College and some teachers there, especially Sister R. Patricia Smith, Sister Marie Christine, and Richard Gordon, Eleanor Mattes of Wilson College, George Rawick and George Lipsitz of the University of Missouri—St. Louis, Paul Bushnell of Illinois Wesleyan University, and friends and colleagues in Buffalo, Milwaukee, Philadelphia, St. Louis, and Bloomington, Illinois, have all contributed to this book. No one will agree with everything I have written here, and I am happy to take full responsibility for that.

Abbreviations

ACLU	American Civil Liberties Union
AFSC	American Friends Service Committee
ASU	American Student Union
AVC	American Veterans Committee
CME	Committee on Militarism in Education
CORE	Congress of Racial Equality
FOR	Fellowship of Reconciliation
ILD	International Labor Defense
ISS	Intercollegiate Socialist Society
LID	League for Industrial Democracy
NSL	National Student League
NYA	National Youth Administration
ROTC	Reserve Officers Training Corps
SDS	Students for a Democratic Society
SLID	Student League for Industrial Democracy
SNCC	Student Nonviolent Coordinating Committee
WILPF	Women's International League for Peace and Freedom
WRL	War Resisters League
YPSL	Young People's Socialist League

Class, Culture, and the Classroom

Introduction

In the thirties, in a setting of economic catastrophe and international conflict, American radicalism was resurrected. With it rose a student movement that was part of the Marxist, pacifist, and reformist impulses of the period. Although the movement did relate specifically to student issues, the main focus and most successful issue in winning mass student support was the question of war and peace.

From 1934 to 1937 American campuses developed "peace university," though not a peaceful one, with parades, symposia, speeches, and occasional riots. Thousands of students took the "Oxford Oath," swearing never to fight in any war that the United States government might conduct. Tactics varied from campus to campus, with a group which called itself the "Veterans of Future Wars" adding what seemed at the time to be a touch of humor. Banners and placards bore such functional or ideological slogans as "Scholarships, Not Battleships," "Fight against Imperialist War," "Worship Jesus, Not Mars," and "Abolish ROTC." Support for the national Student Strike against War increased with each succeeding year in the middle thirties; in 1936 the sponsors estimated participation by from 350,000 to 500,000 students across the country. Even allowing for normal exaggeration and the fact that this included university-sponsored convocations at some institutions, the inclusion in the protest of schools as diverse as City College of New York, Morehouse

College, North Dakota Agricultural College, and the University of Idaho indicates substantial student concern with serious issues. Although there had been previous episodes of student political activism—during the Revolution, the abolition movement, and the pre–World War I period—the thirties represented the high point for this kind of activity, at least until the sixties.[1]

The primary objects of this study are to trace the origins of the student movement of the thirties, to examine its internal dynamics and reactions to external events, and to trace its legacy. Other themes accompany this narrative of the rise and fall of the movement: the influence on the movement of Marxism, religion, progressivism, and the revisionist view of the Great War; the relationship between government and education and attitudes toward academic freedom; and the development of a new kind of American student, who was to become a model (both positive and negative) for student activists of a later generation.

The economic and social conditions of the thirties made possible a challenge to traditional collegiate culture. The emergence of some students as political activists fostered a new kind of student community and identity. These developments challenged the prevailing view of higher education as a time for preparation rather than action and of the campus as a cocoon rather than a laboratory. For a time, at least, the "ivory tower" leaned a little to the left. When Columbia University President Nicholas Murray Butler declared that it was "the duty of one generation to pass on to the next unimpaired, the institutions it had inherited from its forebears," the student editor of the *Spectator* responded, "It is hardly necessary to point out that if the human race had followed Dr. Butler's advice we would still be living in trees."[2]

Some students clung to a collegiate life of sports and fraternities and sororities and continued to view the university as their ticket to success. This clash between the older culture and the new indicates some of the contradictions of higher education and its relationship to the American economic system. That relationship forms the background for the student revolt.

While religion was important in the founding of colleges and universities, the role of higher education soon became the training of the American upper class. In the nineteenth century a declining birth rate among the upper class and an expanding economy led to the use of higher education as a mechanism to admit new people into the elite. The creation of the modern American university coincided with the consolidation of industrial capitalism at the end of the nineteenth century. Higher education responded to industrialization, urbanization, and immigration by broadening its function and composition. Although this was also true of primary and secondary education, it is in higher education that the role of the new capitalists can be seen most directly. Not only did they create some institutions, as John D. Rockefeller did when he founded the University of Chicago, but their positions on boards of trustees and as contributors gave them substantial say in the development of the modern university (and of other cultural institutions as well). This power has persisted. It entails not so much day-to-day control but power to determine long-term goals of education and to influence the culture and values of society.[3]

In the twentieth century higher education responded to the needs of capitalism for new kinds of workers. It also provided a margin of mobility to relieve pressure that might otherwise have resulted in radicalism. At the same time, however, colleges and universities became more stratified and class conscious. This was partly the result of economic changes and partly a defense against efforts to democratize education with the development of land-grant institutions and municipal colleges.

Before the turn of the century it was not necessary to go to

college to join the upper class. Andrew Carnegie did not
need an M.B.A. to become a robber baron. After World War
I this was increasingly less true. Graduation from the right
school—Harvard, Yale, or Princeton in the East or Stanford
on the West Coast—both certified some as belonging to and
for others provided entry into the upper class. Vocational
professionalism and the need for educational credentials in
industry furthered the selective function of undergraduate
schools and increased the value and enrollment of the most
prestigious.[4]

Specialization in education had not yet matched specialization in industry, but it was headed in that direction. Those
who ultimately controlled education and other economic and
cultural institutions made sure that the stratified economic
system would be served by a similarly stratified educational
structure. The process, through elementary, secondary, collegiate, and professional levels, was increasingly competitive
and selective and encouraged values and behaviors appropriate to a competitive system. Students were becoming the
objects, not the practitioners, of "sifting and winnowing" in
the American university.

This process took place both within institutions and in the
hierarchy that formed among types of institutions: elite universities, liberal arts colleges, normal schools, and schools
serving particular clienteles (women, blacks, religious
groups). Within these types, more such stratification occurred. In urban institutions day schools and night schools
served different groups and different purposes. Sometimes
the intent was openly expressed. At Columbia University,
for example, after World War I, the administration began to
try to limit Jewish enrollment in the college. One proposal
was to create a residential college separate from a preprofes-
sional school. As a proponent explained, this would allow the
university to fulfill its obligation to the community in which
it was placed "without endangering the solidarity and homo-

geneity of the group that must, in a leisurely and thorough manner, absorb the learning of the past and observe dispassionately the events of the present in order to be prepared to meet the tremendous problems of the future."[5] The plan was not carried through, but other forms of exclusion were developed to serve the same purpose.

Students and alumni also furthered division on campus with a system of fraternities and sororities based on class, race, and religious distinctions. These also created useful national networks that lasted after graduation. Efforts to democratize the campus, for example, Woodrow Wilson's efforts as president of Princeton to break up dining clubs, encountered hostility from students, alumni, and other administators.

This stratification was often praised as democratic. President Abbott Lawrence Lowell of Harvard declared: "If, therefore, the aim of democracy, is to develop in each man the fullest possible use of his natural faculties, there must be, not a uniformity of educational methods, but on the contrary a variety of institutions . . . a variety such that everyone who seeks an education desirable to his interest and that of the community, may find it somewhere, in accordance with his natural ability and his aim in life."[6]

Whereas the goal of channeling people into jobs required diversity of educational methods and schools, another major function of higher education required a high degree of cultural homogeneity among institutions of higher learning. This was the effort to transmit to students a code of behavior and a set of common values. A collegiate culture developed, designed in part to promote the assumption of common interests in a milieu of class distinctions. Further, the values of this culture were such as to encourage acceptance and support for capitalism and the belief that the rewards of that system were based on merit, not birth.[7]

Qualities useful to the new industrial order included

competence, discipline, and control. These were encouraged not only in the classroom but in extracurricular activities. Sports, fraternities, and social events helped mold the campus into a closed community, turned inward and with a bond of loyalty. At the same time, these activities also rewarded competitiveness, team play, conformity, and the controlled expression of emotions. As the head football coach of New York University explained in the early thirties, "Football lets off a lot of emotional steam. It we didn't have such a safety valve, we might turn to bolshevism, communism, or some other form of social unrest."[8]

The campus was shaped to act as a family, with the administration and faculty acting as parents. Identity was reinforced "physically, intellectually, and ceremoniously."[9] The architecture of the late-nineteenth-century campus (which persisted until the growth of the multiversity brought a new architectural style), Gothic or Georgian in form and oriented around a quad, indicates the effort to form a respectable and orderly community.

The style was set on the Gilded Age campus, and the prototype was Yale. A caste system developed on campus that was based on the acceptance of the elite by those outside the inner circle but still inside the magic gates. The preservation of distinct status was dependent upon the acceptance of common values. The contradiction grew as nonelite campuses—teachers colleges and land-grant institutions— began to adopt the behavior of the Ivy League. Campuses across the country copied and adopted student clubs, dress, slang, and songs.[10]

The class system and the culture that embodied it were threatened in the period after the Great War. In the twenties increased pressures on enrollment, which included demands from both women and a growing number of second-generation Americans, threatened the homogeneity and structure of college life. At the same time, the economic

demands of the expanding economy required more professional workers, and demands for assimilation of immigrant
groups put new burdens on the college. "Outsiders" were
not always content to restrict themselves to the colleges or
career patterns to which they had previously been assigned.[11]

The basic problem of increasing the number of college
educated to meet the demands of the economy without
threatening the class structure of the university (and potentially of society) would not be solved until after World War
II. In the meantime a conservative solution was found:
selective admissions and its ultimate manifestation—the
quota.

This solution was shaped both by developments on campus
and by the general nativism of the twenties. It was the
period of the Red Scare and the revival of the Ku Klux Klan,
of lynching—legal and illegal. In the North, the execution of
Sacco and Vanzetti represented the triumph of prejudice
over due process. In the South (and other areas) mob action
often had the approval of local authorities. With the passage
of the National Origins Act selective admissions began at
Ellis Island and the Golden Gate. Some thought the door
had closed too late. As higher education became more important and elite schools sought to be national rather than
local institutions, they also came increasingly to represent a
means of social mobility. Increased applications for admissions and actual enrollments threatened higher education
with the specter of democracy.

At Harvard, where the enrollment was approximately 20
percent Jewish in 1920, President Abbott Lawrence Lowell
pioneered in formally declaring his intent to decrease the
number of Jewish students in order to preserve the school's
homogeneity. The specter of sexual equality was similarly
dispelled. Harvard and Columbia law schools refused to
admit any women at all in the twenties, and American medical schools imposed an admission quota of 5 percent for

female applicants. Places that did not impose quotas directly found other methods of exclusion. In the early twenties Columbia and New York University established complex admissions processes including "psychological" or "character" tests that posed as objective means of determining admission.[12]

Blacks, Catholics, and women, all also subject to restrictions to various degrees, formed their own institutions. Ironically, rather than offer an alternative to the stratified education at the elite schools, their colleges mimicked the schools that had rejected them. At Catholic schools both curricular and extracurricular life, including fashions, songs, and sports, resembled that at secular institutions. (One exception to this was the prohibition of sororities at Catholic women's schools.)[13]

Not until the economic structure upon which all these structures rested broke down, and students discarded the tradition of passivity, would the collegiate class system be effectively challenged. In the twenties some students began a rebellion against the old standards and genteel culture. Their rebellion was limited, however, by one continuing shared value on campus: college students, by and large, remained outside of politics.

Throughout the twenties student culture looked inward: "The focus of activity was the campus rather than the world about it."[14] As long as students saw themselves as apart from the world, in a state of limbo, they were unlikely to launch a major challenge either to higher education or to the society that it represented.

This view of student life would undergo substantial change in the thirties. The crisis in the economic structure brought a similar crisis in the institutions that supported it and that it supported. When higher education showed itself unable to perform its function of channeling students into jobs, the values and concept of "gentlemanly behavior" seemed equally irrelevant. An expanded and restive student body confronted college administrators and faculty. Culture and behavior, honor codes, and initiation rites suitable to an elite group at the turn of the century were inadequate in a period of rapid change and social turmoil. The resulting challenge to the homogeneity and culture of the university is part of the history of the student movement.

Education is a two-edged sword. Whatever the intended purpose of higher education, it has room within it for curricular and extracurricular activities that can lead to challenges of that function. Despite the weight of institutional power, some students and some of their teachers have made efforts to shape their institutions to their own purposes and to resist the domination of the schools by outside economic forces. At times, conflict has become overt and student movements have arisen. This happened in the thirties and again in the sixties.

Part of the student movement of the thirties was a reaction to events on campus. The direction that the movement took, however, was shaped by intellectual currents and events off campus. Marxism, religion, and progressive education, and the organizations representing them, helped to shape the pacifist mood on campus—and eventually to divide it.

For students, as for many adults in the peace movement, the major paradigm of war was the revisionist interpretation of the world war. Paul Fussell, in *The Great War and Modern Memory*, describes the way that the war altered people's perceptions and vocabulary.[15] The horror with which that conflict was viewed was the most important influence in creating an antiwar mood on which peace organizations could draw. This was true of students as well as of the general public. Convinced that American entry into that war had been a mistake and a waste, peace organizations and many politicians and publicists pointed to munitions makers and war profiteers as a major cause of war. In ad-

dition, students criticized the role of the universities in supporting the war and the relationship between the government
and higher education.

Condemning jingoism and defending academic freedom,
students challenged values that had increasingly permeated
college life as well as national politics. In doing so, some of
them came to reject, sometimes tangentially, sometimes
directly, the class system that led to war and that dominated
higher education.

The experiences of the Great War revealed both the role
of colleges and universities in supporting the political and
economic system and the fact that not all within the schools
understood the function that they were serving. The faculty,
in particular, had a history of insecurity regarding their
place as intellectuals in a pragmatic society. One result of
this uncertainty was the enthusiasm with which otherwise
rational scholars lent themselves and their institutions to
the government during the war. Historians were especially
eager to rescue history (and themselves) from "implications
of irrelevance."[16]

The pattern was to be repeated in World War II, and the
dangers of this kind of cooperation would become clear
again in the period of the Cold War and McCarthyism. Some
of the former student radicals would see for themselves how
universities could enforce political and economic ideology.

In the thirties some students saw education as a means
of social change and, specifically, as a force for peace. There
is a problem here which became one of the usually unspoken
dilemmas of the student antiwar movement. If education
is a tool rather than an end in itself, what does this mean
for academic freedom? Of course, academic freedom always
has had its limits, and students have been quick to point
this out. In the thirties some Marxist students argued that,
in any case, freedom was a means, not an end in itself. In
the sixties part of the New Left, attracted by Marcuse's dis-

cussion of "repressive tolerance," rejected academic freedom as a false front for conformity and intellectual repression. In fact, however, during both the thirties and the sixties most students and their faculty allies fought to expand freedom on and off campus. They drew on the older radical tradition of William Lloyd Garrison that "a forcible suppression of error is no aid to the cause of truth" and learned from the civil rights movement that freedom was an end in itself, and something to be fought for and protected.[17]

The effort to expand freedom on campus and the opposition that it met were continuing parts of the antiwar struggle. As the second war approached, restrictions on student and teacher expression and activity on and off campus hardened and the response of many liberals shifted to repression and defense of the status quo. This reaction would prove prophetic of postwar behavior. In the meantime, the increased restrictions on student political activity quickened the demise of the student movement of the thirties.

Freedom of expression and political activity was one of the concerns of the student movement. But the major focus in the thirties was the peace issue, as it would be again in the postwar period and the sixties. Other issues have motivated some student activists or dominated at certain moments, but in the United States in the twentieth century it has most often been war and the threat of war that has drawn large numbers of students into protest.

Students contributed to and shared many of the general peace activities of the decade and of the historic peace movement.[18] Some affiliated with groups such as the American Friends Service Committee, the Fellowship of Reconciliation, the War Resisters League, and others, or with youth affiliates of those organizations. Others joined leftist groups that participated to various degrees and at various times in antiwar work. Although the purposes of the American Student Union were broader than simply antiwar agitation, peace was its most successful issue, unifying otherwise contentious groups and attracting support from students not members of or otherwise active with political groups.

Included in the student peace movement were members of the American Student Union, pacifist groups, religious groups interested in peace, radical groups such as the National Student League and the Student League for Industrial Democracy, and national student groups that cooperated with antiwar activities. Unaffiliated students also participated; many shared some of the antiwar views of the organized groups and supported specific proposals or demonstrations. They participated in rallies, signed petitions, picketed, and expressed antiwar beliefs in their writing in student newspapers and literary magazines and in antiwar plays, posters, and debates. Not all these groups or individuals were in the same place in the movement at the same time, but that is the difference between a movement and a party. There was no membership card to sign and no loyalty oath to take.

It is impossible to say how many students were involved in the antiwar movement of the thirties. One measurement is membership in student organizations. Estimates of the members of the American Student Union, for example, range from ten thousand to twenty thousand. Downplaying the extent of youthful radicalism in the decade, Murray Kempton estimates that less than half of 1 percent of high school and college students participated in demonstrations and rallies or signed petitions.[19] This is a misleading figure, since no one claims widespread support among high school students except in a few areas. The activists were certainly a minority of students except at some schools where participation at least at rallies became the norm.

Hal Draper, a former member of the student movement, has refuted one assertion that even at City College of New York activists constituted only 1 percent of the student body. He noted that there were degrees of involvement:

Around the one percent who actually joined a radical student group were concentric rings of influence, embracing different portions of the student body as different forms of commitment were demanded. For every one who joined there were perhaps two who agreed in the main with what the student movement was trying to do but who did not join, either for lack of time to devote to such activity, or for other reasons which did them less credit.

There was another circle of students who were ready to support most of the campaigns or actions which the student organization might launch on a given issue, such as defense of students victimized by the administration. It was probably most inclusive during the annual anti-war actions.[20]

Even those outside the circle could not be assumed to be hostile; many might in fact agree or be won over on specific issues.

A movement is, after all, more inclusive than its leaders or organizations. Its activities affect and include those who may never have signed a petition but who shared common attitudes. Part of the program of the peace movement won broad support from students in general, especially in the years 1934–38. Opposition to compulsory military training, to United States participation in a "foreign war," and to munitions makers probably won the support of majorities of students in the course of the decade.[21] The peace movement was successful in influencing at least some of the opinions of large numbers of people in the thirties, and the student movement shared the peace movement's ideas and propaganda, while it spread its own. Even students hostile to radical organizations such as the American Student Union and the demonstrations that it sponsored often agreed with the antiwar groups' interpretation of World War I and, to an extent, shared a common attitude toward war and peace.

Columbia University is cited at length here because it contained a distinctive combination of radicalism and reaction, with little room for moderation. It also provided the *Spectator*, the student Left's most articulate and uninhibited newspaper. And Columbia would become a focal point of rebellion again in the sixties.

Harvard is cited here for two reasons. Along with Columbia, it provided much of the liberal and power elite of the later Cold War, and events at Harvard in the thirties suggest a background for the world view of the warmakers of the fifties and sixties. Like Columbia, Harvard also reveals the clash between cultures and classes that underlay the political conflict on campus.

This was partly because all the students, in the movement and outside of it, were subject to similar external influences, for example, press coverage of the Nye Committee hearings on munitions and war profiteering. However, student organizations helped to transmit these ideas. People can reject a medium and still get the message. Whatever people thought of radicals and pacifists, they could be influenced by their ideas.

Because this is a history of a movement, I have tried to combine discussion of national organizations with examples of activity on individual campuses. The schools most often cited represent a variety of institutions and of geographic areas: the sparsity of examples from the South is consistent with the general pattern, since that was the area of least involvement. It is true that student activism was strongest in metropolitan areas like New York and Chicago. But for that reason, and because those areas have received most of what attention has been paid to this subject, I have tried to cite developments at schools where students were less politically conscious. Part of the significance of the antiwar movement is that it did cross class, geographic, and ethnic lines. In contrast to traditional collegiate culture it offered a nondiscriminatory fellowship to which many students could respond.

One of the distinctive characteristics of the student peace movement of the thirties is that it was strongest at non-elite institutions (with the exception of women's colleges). Though some Ivy League colleges did contribute to antiwar activity, activism was greatest at municipal institutions and at some of the state universities of the Midwest and West. There was also a tendency for at least a small group of students to be involved in peace activity at religious schools and at teacher-training institutions. I include reports of activities at some of these kinds of schools, in particular, Milwaukee State Teachers College, the University of Michigan, and Catholic schools such as St. Mary's and Loyola of Chicago, although the antiwar activity of Catholic students, primarily in their own separate organizations, deserves separate study.

The perception by students of the university as part of a system of war and exploitation was an important part of student response in the thirties and in the later period. Students saw higher education and the values it promoted as part of a system that they increasingly rejected. But in the thirties students saw the schools not as just a cog in a machine but as a place where people could get together to challenge that machine. Coming together in that effort, they could create an alternative community with its own culture. That effort was driven underground by the war (and fascism) and postwar repression, but it was revived with a new generation of student activists.

It is useful to remember the times when cracks in the educational structure have become gaps, and when alternative student cultures and activities have widened the gap. In doing so, the students have attacked the domination of education by capitalism and the government that serves it. At the same time, student movements have challenged both the passive nature of education and the passive response of individuals to the demands of the state.

The movement of the thirties left a legacy to the others.

In many ways the responses of former student radicals to the Cold War and to the political inquisitions determined the course of the American Left for the following decades. A study of the divisions of the thirties sheds some light on the paralysis of American progressivism in the fifties and its confusion in the sixties. Further analysis of the period could perhaps answer Lillian Hellman's question concerning how people who seemed to share political values in the thirties could take such different paths into McCarthyism and the Cold War and into Vietnam.[22] Divided from each other and sometimes from their children, alumni of the student movement of the thirties might have asked themselves in December 1972, as the United States government sent bombers over Hanoi, the question raised in the film *The Lion in Winter* when Eleanor of Aquitaine is confronted by a divided family: "How from where we started did we get to this Christmas?"

Chapter 1

Background of the
Student Antiwar Movement

In his 1935 introduction to James Wechsler's *Revolt on the Campus*, Robert Morss Lovett noted that young people were influenced by three outside forces: the world war, Soviet Russia, and the Depression.[1] Of these, the last certainly had the most direct impact. Young people in general were hard hit by the economic collapse. They suffered considerably higher rates of unemployment than did other age groups and looked to the future with little hope of improvement. Many young people who were considered, or considered themselves, to be burdens upon their families left home and joined the large population of vagrants.[2] Normal routes to employment through apprenticeship or training programs were denied to them, and they had no experience to offer when, and if, jobs ever did open up. If the present was grim, the future seemed bleak. A poem in *Scribner's* in 1935 made this prediction:

> They will forever wear upon their brows
> This touch of death, this pallor of defeat;
> Though the new years grow prodigal and sweet

Nothing that ever happens can arouse
The bloom of living they were once denied.
Always will they distrust the hand of chance,
Viewing good fortune with the sceptic glance
Of convalescents sternly mortified.
So they will never feel secure content
In sunny days, in laughter, in their work,
In daily bread. This fatal fear will lurk
Within their thoughts until their time is spent.
Even gay pigeons fluttering in a park
Will but remind them of the homeless dark.[3]

College students shared these problems, and a degree
was far from a guarantee of employment. Although students
tended to major in areas that trained them for jobs, they
still faced an economy in which an estimated fifty thousand
engineers were unemployed and in which more people were
training to be teachers than there were positions to fill.[4]
One verse of a popular "Ode to Higher Education" expressed the students' feelings:

I sing in praise of college
Of M.A.'s and Ph.D.'s,
But in pursuit of knowledge,
We are starving by degrees.[5]

Institutions of higher learning also underwent stress
during the period, and changes occurred both in the nature
of the student bodies and in the relationship of the campus
to society. Private schools in particular, where tuition was
high, had difficulty in maintaining enrollments. At municipal
institutions and some of the state colleges, where tuition
was free or relatively low, large numbers of part-time students helped sustain enrollments. Most of these students
paid their way through with part-time jobs (which were

more available than full-time jobs, since they were cheaper for employers). In 1932, for example, 70 percent of Temple University students were working their way through college. This was true for both male and female students, though it was less typical for women. At the University of Michigan during the 1932–33 school year, one-third of the women enrolled were partially or totally self-supporting.[6]

Some observers believed that one effect of the Depression was to raise the quality of the state and community colleges, since they drew students who in better times might have gone away to school. These same observers saw students in general as more serious and hardworking than those in previous periods. Whether this was really true or not, certainly a great deal of attention was paid to analyzing the impact of the Depression on youth and on students in particular, and a great many generalizations, often contradictory, were made. The activities of the students themselves were responsible for part of this attention. National concern with the condition of youth seems to be in direct relation to its obstreperousness. So in the thirties as a student movement bloomed, national magazines featured articles on the problems and deviations of young people.[7]

College students drew much of this attention, partly because of the class bias of the authors and magazines, but also because that group was making itself noticed. If, as has been suggested, students developed a "consciousness of kind"[8] or a kind of class consciousness, it may have been partly as a result of being treated by outside observers as a peculiar and important group to be kept under study. They were the subject of scientific surveys, broad generalizations, worry, praise, and congressional investigation. The opinions, life-style, personality, and future of youth in general were the concern of their teachers, newspaper and magazine editors, and presumably readers, and the federal government, as well as various state legislatures and city councils.

Students were observed from the left and the right. Opinions about them were frequently contradictory and the evidence often ambiguous. Despite these difficulties, and the very real differences among students throughout the decade, certain themes stand out. One was the effect of the Depression upon young people's lives and characters: the motif of the truly "lost generation." At least one writer saw economic insecurity as the main motivation for the student movement, its activities fueled by a "fear that maladjustments in the economic order [would] block the opportunity for advancement, and security."[9]

Concerned perhaps about the youth movements in Germany and Italy, some adults were fearful that desperation here could lead to radicalism. Youth became a concern of the national administration and in particular of Eleanor Roosevelt. Congress also showed concern (though not much inclination to appropriate much money for youth programs). The "whereases" of a bill introduced by Senator David Walsh of Massachusetts indicate fear of the effect of the Depression on "the lives of young men and women emerging from our educational institutions." Walsh suggested the importance of the government's taking care of this group, lest it become "demoralized and disheartened, and thus constitute a dangerous addition to the discontented and radical minded elements."[10] The administration responded with the National Youth Act and the Civilian Conservation Corps. Congress responded with an investigation of "subversive" influences in the student movement.

Fears and hopes of extensive radicalism were not fulfilled, unless one accepted a definition of radicalism by William Randolph Hearst or Martin Dies. However, surveys did indicate an increased interest in international affairs and increased student enrollment in courses like sociology and economics. Perhaps related to this was a general inclination on the part of students toward pacifist positions. These findings show up in national surveys and studies of individual campuses as different as San Jose Teachers College and the University of Chicago.[11]

While college administrators and the press worried about these developments, other people greeted the trend with pleasure and relief. In an article in *Harper's* in 1931, Harold Laski had asked Americans, "Why don't your young men care?" and criticized the lack of political interest on American campuses.[12] Within a few years it became apparent that at least some American young men and women did care. Their concern came not only from external circumstances but from the development of a community of values among the students themselves.

One effect of the economic problems of the period which promoted student solidarity and the development of a new idea of their role was the creation of "depression camps." These were barrackslike dormitories resulting from the colleges' efforts to keep up enrollment. The close quarters presented opportunities for political discussion, and the isolation of the self-governing units gave their inhabitants the experiences and opportunities to develop shared values.

Some of these values were the result of the students' exposure to a newly revived American radicalism. If the Soviet Union proved an inspiration to some of the more radical students, the American Left itself had a more direct influence on the student movement. Both the militancy of the labor movement and the idealism of the peace movement found, and engendered, sympathetic responses on campus. Of the two, however, it was the latter cause that took root most deeply in student opinion and served as the mainspring of student activity. At least until the outbreak of war in Europe in 1939 many students shared with a large segment of the general public an opposition to militarism and a desire to avoid war.

These views had been shaped in large measure by the

revisionist view of the Great War. Disillusionment with the
war began almost with the armistice (and among those who
fought, some time before). Even without the most modern
instruments of mass destruction eight million people had
been killed. The physical havoc was accompanied by psychological destruction, cultural shell shock. The war was the
new lens through which people saw the world. According to
Fussell, that new paradigm was composed of irony and bi-
polarity, the world in black and white, and a skepticism
which came from the destruction of innocence.[13] "The Great
War was . . . a hideous embarrassment to the prevailing
Meliorist myth which had dominated the public consciousness for a century. It reversed the idea of Progress." The
new consciousness was communicated in the poems of former
soldiers Siegfried Sassoon and Wilfred Owen.

In Europe the war left two societies: the survivors of the
war and those who had sent them to the trenches. The
duplicity of the governments during the war, the lies in
the newspapers, and civilian jingoism all contrasted with
the agony of trench warfare and mass slaughter at the
Somme and other battlefields.

A combatant for a shorter time, America was spared much
of this torment. But it too had its victims, both on the
battlefront and at home. Throughout the twenties and early
thirties evidence accumulated that the war and American
participation in it had been a bitter waste. This mood contributed to a revival of the American peace movement.
Groups with their roots in the opposition to the Great War,
such as the Fellowship of Reconciliation, the Women's International League for Peace and Freedom, the American
Friends Service Committee, and new groups like the Committee on Militarism in Education and the War Resisters
League worked together to oppose the revival of militarism
and to try to offer constructive alternatives to war.

These groups and others, whatever their differences,

appealed to and fostered a vein of internationalist peace sentiment in the twenties and early thirties. Faced with a world in which a repetition of world war seemed all too possible, young people in the thirties became a ready audience for antiwar writing and agitation.

Disillusionment with the world war was widespread. It was promoted by both scholarly and popular writers, in literature and films, and through journalistic exposés and congressional investigations. H. O. Engelbrecht and F. O. Hanighan's *Merchants of Death* exposed the power of international arms manufacturers. The historical verdict was given in the works of Harry Elmer Barnes, Charles Beard, Sidney B. Fay, Walter Millis, Charles Tansill, and Bernadotte E. Smith. Kirby Page rendered the story more readable in several books, and John Maynard Keynes provided sophisticated bitterness in *The Economic Consequences of the Peace*.[14]

With variations, the revisionist view generally rejected ascribing all guilt for the war to Germany and saw the war's causes in militarism, nationalism, secret diplomacy, and economic conflict. "A willingness to fight had been a prerequisite" of the war, and this willingness had been fostered by propaganda and appeals to emotion.[15] Within the United States the "Fight for Democracy" had wounded democracy; civil liberties had been suppressed and after the war dissenters had been deported.

The role of the university in the war effort was of particular concern to students. Individually and institutionally, faculties and administrators flocked to the support of the war, turning their services and, finally, their colleges over to the government. It was ironic that historians should play a major part in creating the revisionist interpretation. During the war no group had been as eager to turn its professional objectivity over to the service of the government. With the establishment of the National Board for Historical Service in

1917, historians became "the only social scientists prepared to establish an organized professional body for patriotic service."[16]

As a later historian notes, there is an apparently small but crucial distinction between "service to society" and "service to the state."[17] (Anarchists would point out that the two are not only distinct but contradictory.) Before the world war progressives saw the role of university and of the scholar as one of service (most conspicuously in the Wisconsin Idea: that the public university should provide information and expertise to the state government and extend its services as a "people's university") and envisioned cooperation between the university and the government on behalf of the public interest. On a local level this had some success. In wartime, however, the line between service to society and to the state disappears. This was especially true during the Great War. The universities cooperated with the state in dropping the distinction.

In the twenties and thirties, students and some faculty sought to maintain the distinction between service to society and service to the state. Urging the use of education as a means to social change and to a better society, they sought to preserve the autonomy of the university from the state. In their opposition to loyalty oaths, the presence of the military on campus, and restrictions on academic freedom, the student movement, at least for a time, attempted to avoid and make up for the mistakes, or betrayal, of education in World War I.[18] Students at Columbia University in particular pointed to that institution's war efforts and the accompanying squelching of academic freedom. One of the fathers of revisionism, Charles Beard, had been a prowar professor at Columbia who resigned to protest the firing of two antiwar faculty members.

For the students the revisionist view was a useful symbol and rhetorical device, but it was also part of a system of belief that was important in their world view and influenced both the ideology and the tactics of their movement. Revulsion against the world war cut across divisions within student opinion—it was felt by left-wingers as well as right-wingers, Marxists as well as pacifists, students at elite universities as well as those at normal schools, state universities, and Catholic colleges. A coalition of student groups charged with choosing days for demonstrations against war agreed upon those of the commemoration of the Great War. Thus, students conducted their strikes against war in April, the month that the United States entered the conflict, and held rallies in the fall on Armistice Day to remember the dead.

It was not that students were indifferent to events in Europe or unconcerned about the rise of Hitler to power in Germany. Rather, they, like older observers, saw the growth of facism as the direct result of the terms of peace. Speaking at a student rally at Columbia in March 1933, Rabbi Jacob A. Weinstein declared that Hitler's success was the result of "binding shackles" placed on Germany by the Versailles Treaty.[19] Indeed, events in Europe seemed to justify the belief that the world war had been fought for nothing. The Depression itself reinforced the belief that economics, not ideals, was behind modern warfare.

The futility of war was most dramatically presented in the antiwar films made in the early thirties. Of these the most famous, and perhaps most influential, was *All Quiet on the Western Front*, adapted by Maxwell Anderson and George Abbott from the novel by Erich Remarque. Directed by Lewis Milestone, it came out in 1930 and attained immediate and sustained success. Other antiwar movies included *Journey's End* (1930), *The Case of Sergeant Grischa* (1930) (directed by Howard Brenon, who had made another antiwar film, *War Bride*, in 1916), *The Man I Killed* (1932), *The Man Who Reclaimed His Head* (1935), and *Men Must Fight*. Movies with antiwar implications included two by John

Ford—*Pilgrimage* (1933) and *The World Moves On* (1934)—
and three by Howard Hawks—*The Last Flight* (1931), *Dawn
Patrol* (1930), and *The Road to Glory* (1936)—as well as
Stuart Walker's *The Eagle and the Hawk* (1933).

Many of these were based on antiwar novels or plays, and
sometimes the message was watered down. Lawrence
Stalling's *What Price Glory?* was turned into a virtual recruiting film for the marines. Still, for a time there existed
both a market for antiwar films and producers and directors
interested in making them. That time in America seems to
have ended by 1936, but one more memorable film was to
come, from France. In 1937 Jean Renoir created *The Grand
Illusion,* an attack upon both romantic militarism and class-
bound society.

American writers and painters also contributed antiwar
work. The paintings of John Steuart Curry, the novel *Three
Soldiers* by John Dos Passos, and poems by Archibald
MacLeish and Stephen Vincent Benét all reinforced the
public image of the horrors of the Great War.

Photography also contributed to the pacifist mood. In
spite of the refusal of the United States Signal Corps to
release photographs from its files from the world war, some
were included, along with photos from the French and
German war offices, in a collection that showed both the
war's survivors and their children—*The Horror of It.* Inspired by the graphic brutality, Reed Harris, the editor of
the Columbia *Spectator,* wrote an editorial which expressed
a persistent student attitude toward war. In the absoluteness
of its sentiments, as well as its emphasis on the physical
fact of death rather than on economic or social analysis, the
editorial expresses a strong antipathy toward war and violence as evils in themselves. This emotional response underlay and undercut subsequent debate over the justifiability of
class as opposed to imperialist warfare. The editorial, published March 31, 1932, was titled "Carnage for $1.35."

You can march off to war with your battle flags
whipping in the breeze; you can listen to the warm
cheers of your women as they send you off to defend
the honor of the fatherland; you can start the long,
muddy march to the front line trenches, singing
the songs that lift your spirit; you can take your place
on the fire-step of your dugout; you can surge for-
ward with your companions, shouting hoarsely when you
hear the shrill whistles blow; and you can have
your brains spilled over your face by a burst of machine
gun fire from a tight-lipped gunner across the
way who is fighting for his country and his women as
bravely as you are fighting for yours. All this
and more you can have for exactly $1.35.

The book tells the story simply and powerfully.
Dismembered bodies draped grotesquely over a wire
fence, a sniper dangling from a limb of a tree,
long lines of rotting corpses lying in ditches, dead men
being shoveled like manure into carts, faceless
and formless remnants of the bloody carnival—these are
the things you will see.

Some say it is sweet and fitting to rot in a dung
heap for one's country.[20]

Harris wrote this two days before he was expelled from
Columbia.

In some ways, Harris's editorial was a prose version of
a poem by Wilfred Owen. In it the English poet graphically
described the effect of poison gas on soldiers:

> . . . every jolt, the blood
> Comes gargling from the froth-corrupted lungs,
> Obscene as cancer, bitter as the cud
> Of vile, incurable sores on innocent tongues,

and then concluded that if the reader could see this:

> My friend, you would not tell with such high zest
> To children ardent for some desperate glory
> The old Lie: Dulce et decorum est
> Pro patria mori.[21]

This physical view of war, and the vocabulary that accompanied it, would not be easily erased. The concept that students and others had of war reflected precisely the portrait of trench warfare of World War I. This view would have some consequences. The picture of those horrors made it hard to imagine others even greater. Concern with gas and cannons and unmoving lines obscured the possibility that the impending war could involve a different use of gas—and the bombing of population centers and the destruction of a faceless enemy. Tactics and ethics had trouble keeping up with technology. Like the generals, the peace movement continued to fight the last war.

However, the Great War and the revisionist view of it did create a fundamental change in attitudes toward war. It cast grave doubt upon the honesty of the press and the trustworthiness of governments. A mood of skepticism replaced sentimentalism. The apparent failure of the old system gave impetus to radicalism of both the Left and Right. Students faced with this view of recent history and the existing economic collapse might well decide to take matters into their own hands.

Antiwar materials containing the revisionist view of the war reached a large number of students. Papers on various campuses included reviews of many of the movies and books mentioned above, as well as of *Testament of Youth* by English pacifist author Vera Brittain. Although young people were also reading books like *The Good Earth* and *Anthony Adverse* and seeing movies like *The Scarlet Empress* and *The Thin*

Man, some at least were deeply touched by the antiwar literature. One of these was Eric Sevareid, then a student at the University of Minnesota. He has described the effect of such books and movies on him and on his friends in the student movement:

> We plowed through the pages of Fay and were convinced that there were no basic issues involved and that with a little intelligence and forebearance war could easily have been averted. . . .
> We read with eagerness new books purporting to expose the munitions industry.
> We were excited over newly unearthed and published dispatches from the wartime American ambassador in London, who mentioned the risk to American loans and investments unless we came into the war.
> The conduct of the war itself, with the years of stalemate, the meaningless, slaughterous attempts by bankrupt generals to hang on to their jobs a little longer by sending thousands to certain death in order to gain a hundred yards of mud—all this chilled our marrow and made us, we thought, very wise.
> We read *Three Soldiers,* and *All Quiet on the Western Front,* and *Death of a Hero* with compassion and a sick feeling in our stomachs. We were young, and to those just beginning to taste the wonderful flavors of life the idea of death is a stark tragedy of unutterable horror.[22]

For Sevareid, as for many others, the last war overshadowed the one approaching.

With this background, students were a ready audience for antiwar propaganda and for organization. The setting was right for a student antiwar movement. All that was needed was the development of an organizational basis and the occurrence of a specific incident to touch off student activity. The expulsion of Reed Harris, the antiwar editor of the Columbia *Spectator*, would provide that spark. The organizational foundations had already been begun in activities in earlier years.

The twenties had been a period of rapid expansion in higher education, reflecting the boom period of the economy. Pressures on admissions, plus the nativism of the period, had caused an increasing use of selective admissions policies, especially at the elite universities and professional schools. At the same time, increasing numbers of the children of immigrants looked to college as a means to success and mobility.

Despite some rumblings of protest and talk of a sexual revolution and the new freedom, student life kept mostly to patterns previously established. Of what revolts there were, most were cultural rather than political in an organized or formal sense. Even the cultural revolt was often merely cynicism, which constituted no great threat to anyone in power.

Nonetheless, the period did see the beginnings of a focus on the issues and the development of the organizations that could provide the basis for a movement when conditions changed. In *The American College and Its Rulers*, published in 1926, J. E. Kirkpatrick wrote that although there was no sign of a student movement, there were signs of student activity and students in motion, mostly a "militant minority on campus."[23] Issues that aroused students included censorship, overemphasis on intercollegiate athletics, and compulsory military training. Peace was the concern at student conferences at Princeton and Swarthmore College and in Evanston, Illinois.

According to Kirkpatrick, much of this concern was evidenced in a vociferous student press, especially the *Gadfly* at Harvard, the *Critic* at Oberlin, the *Proletarian* at the University of Wisconsin, the *Saturday Evening Pest* at Yale, and the *Tempest* at the University of Michigan. Other relatively militant papers included the *Dove* at the University of Kansas, the *Blaze* at Antioch, *El Gripo* at the University of Arizona, and the *Issue* at the University of Wisconsin. Particularly important was the *New Student* of the National Student Forum.

A student campaign was waged on various campuses over the issue of compulsory military training. The Committee on Militarism in Education (CME), a group of educators and others active in the peace movement, cooperated with students in a drive against the Reserve Officers Training Corps (ROTC). The efforts met some success. In 1931 the CME issued a report listing schools that had either eliminated ROTC or had made it voluntary: in 1921—sixteen schools; 1922–25—seventeen; 1926–29—nineteen schools; and twelve more between that date and the issuence of the report in 1931.[24] A persistent and sometimes vicious battle went on at Ohio State University, where the anti-ROTC forces were unsuccessful and a sociology professor was fired for opposing compulsory drill. However, a hard-fought battle at City College of New York resulted in victory in 1926, with the elimination of compulsory military training.

ROTC was made voluntary at the University of Wisconsin in 1923. The action received important reinforcement when the Wisconsin Attorney General's Office ruled that while the Federal Morrill Land Grant Act required that the University of Wisconsin (and other land-grant colleges and universities) provide facilities for military training, the act did not require that military training be compulsory for all students.[25] At the same time that ROTC was being eliminated from some campuses, it was being instituted on others, and the battle went on.

Compulsory military drill was also the cause of a student strike at Howard University in Washington, D.C. Following the suspension of students for failure to attend drill regularly, students conducted a successful protest. Although the suspensions were the immediate cause, the roots of the protest lay in the conditions of students at black colleges under paternalistic control, often under white trustees and administrators. Even where black administrators had nominal control, they were usually bound by the financial supporters of the institution and mindful of the racism of the society at large.

Few black students were admitted to nonblack colleges. When they were, they usually encountered conditions that made them conscious of their intrusion into a world that did not welcome them. At about the time that he announced his intention to limit the number of Jews at Harvard, Abbott Lawrence Lowell also refused to allow Negroes into Harvard's freshman dorms.

In any case, the small numbers of blacks who went to college mostly attended "Negro Colleges." There they encountered another kind of dilemma. For if higher education in general was often at cross purposes with itself, the black colleges included even greater contradictions. Besides the conflict over whether education should be primarily vocational or aimed at broader objectives, there was the serious question of the relationship of the black college student and graduate to the black community. (There was a similar question, of course, for working-class students in general.)

Ralph Ellison has described some of the conflict in his portrayal of a southern black college in the period between the world wars in his novel *Invisible Man*. The black colleges provided a small number of professionals and skilled workers, but in the process divided the members of this elite group from their own community. Though the emphasis was firmly vocational (at least at most such colleges) and the curriculum adjusted accordingly, student life and culture were adopted from the elite white colleges, where the "benefactors" had gone.

Describing a meeting in the college chapel attended by white millionaire supporters from the North, Ellison writes, "Around me the students move with faces frozen in solemn masks, and I seem to hear already the voices mechanically raised in the songs the visitors loved. (Loved? Demanded. Sung? An ultimatum accepted and ritualized. . . .) Loved as the defeated come to love the symbols of their conquerors. A gesture of acceptance, of terms laid down, and reluctantly approved." The students were lulled into a sense of their own distinction. "How fortunate to belong to this family sheltered from those lost in ignorance and darkness." College education was "the black rite of Horatio Alger."[26]

But this was not the whole picture, and passivity not the only response. Perhaps given strength by a sense of their distinction, some black students began to make demands on educators. In the twenties, black campuses experienced a series of protests. These were primarily concerned with student conditions, but they also indicated growing militancy against racism in education and society.[27]

Besides the strike at Howard University, there were strikes at Hampton Institute in 1927 and at Fisk in 1924–25. At Fisk the students, with the support of the black community, were successful in getting the president to resign. There was some hope of getting a black president as his successor, but that did not occur. Some of the demands of the students at Fisk and on other campuses were in fact directed at allowing the schools to become more like white campuses and to participate in the standard collegiate culture. Students at Fisk, for example, wanted the right to form fraternities and to participate in intercollegiate sports. They were also demanding the right to an uncensored student newspaper and to more say in their own educations. In that context those were radical demands and led the students to challenge the structure of higher education and of white society. The question raised at Fisk, and among the surrounding community, was whether it was to be a "Negro College" or a "College for Negroes" run by white people.[28]

Although the colleges did produce a black bourgeoisie, they also provided some black activists, both as students and later on as graduates. Howard University remained a center of student activism in the thirties, causing alarm among racists in Congress, who were confronted by rebellious black students in their own front yard. Moreover, some of the black faculty and administrators were sympathetic to the students' militancy. The structure of black education was not without its cracks and life-giving contradictions. Graduates of Howard and other black colleges would lead the attack on racism and especially on school segregation (reflecting liberal faith in education after all).

Although in the twenties these student revolts were isolated on individual campuses, some students began to look to other students for support and to join national organizations. A Howard student was a member of the executive board of the National Student Forum, an organization formed in a merger of the Intercollegiate Liberal League and the National Student Committee for the Limitation of Armaments in 1922. The group's goals were to provide information on student concerns and to foster the development of "a national student consciousness."[29]

The organization never did gain a large nationwide membership, and its major contribution was the publication of the *New Student* from 1922 to 1929. This was a nondoctrinaire journal devoted to student concerns, but with some interest in international affairs, especially peace and disarmament. The *New Student* also published articles on athletics, problems of censorship and academic freedom, and incidents of racial or religious discrimination on the college campus. Although it lacked any kind of integrating social analysis, the *New Student* did serve as a means of student communication on a national level and did foster the idea of a common bond, and a new way of thinking, among students. It also focused on the issue that would remain one of the mainstays of student activism—war and peace. Another organization that also fostered a sense of commonality among students was the National Student Federation of America, which was primarily an organization representing college student governments.

The National Student Forum and some other national student groups, especially those concerned with international affairs, drew much support from women's colleges. Schools such as Vassar, Wellesley, and Bryn Mawr maintained a persistent core of students interested in peace issues. This was a reflection of a general interest among women's groups in peace and participation by women in peace organizations. Although the twenties are sometimes considered a period of a decline in the women's movement, peace was in fact a feminist issue and the focal point of women's organizations across the country, both clubs and overtly political organizations. On women's campuses many of the faculty or administrators were or had been members of groups such as the Women's International League for Peace and Freedom (WILPF).

The *New Student* reported on the International Women's Congress in Zurich in the summer of 1919. There the women swore never to support war directly or indirectly. A similar pledge was then sponsored in the United States by the World Peace Fellowship and supported by the American branch of the WILPF.[30] Despite their own debate over the proper kind of higher education for women (or perhaps because that was a live question), women's colleges and women students had the potential for shaping a student movement and contributing to a new kind of student culture.

Partly because the Socialist and Communist parties were generally uninterested in organizing college students, at least before 1929, the left wing of student activity was represented by the League for Industrial Democracy. This socialist group was not directly tied to the Socialist party, though it was a direct descendant of the Intercollegiate Socialist Society (ISS) founded by Socialist party members in 1905. An organization of college graduates as well as college students, the ISS was renamed the League for Industrial Democracy (LID) in 1921. Many of its leaders and members, including Harry Laidler and Monroe Sweetland, became leaders of the Socialist party in the following years.

The LID was not itself primarily a campus organization, but it had a separate student department, which in 1928 became an intercollegiate council. Sensitive to charges of adult domination, the council became the Student League for Industrial Democracy (SLID) in 1932. This became the parent of the student leftist groups in the thirties and the immediate predecessor of the Students for a Democratic Society in the sixties.[31]

The student segment of the LID conducted mostly educational activities, sponsoring speakers and conferences. Although it avoided the word *socialist* in its title, it did offer an alternative to capitalism and to traditional student views and activity.

The strength and character of the ISS and the SLID varied from campus to campus. It took deep root in New York City, especially at City College of New York. One historian of the student movement has observed that "by 1916 . . . there already seems to have occurred the radicalization of students that made City College unique in conflict between administrators and radical students in the 1920's and 1930's."[32] In 1917, at the demand of the administration that the group remove the word *socialist* from its title, the City College branch of ISS became the Social Problems Club. This would become the major vehicle for the student movement at City College.

In 1931 a group of LID members, including Donald Henderson, an economics instructor at Columbia University, broke off to form the National Student League (NSL), which became the communist-oriented group on campuses, in opposition to the socialist SLID. The conflict between these two groups shaped the student movement until their merger, in 1935, into the American Student Union. This became the major organization for the student peace movement of the thirties.

The background was prepared, a major issue ready, and organizations formed. A specific incident would set off the movement at Columbia University and then in the rest of the country.

Chapter 2

Revolt on the Campus:
Columbia

In the early thirties some students on campus turned their attention from pep rallies to peace demonstrations. While postgame riots continued, they were now supplemented by disturbances of a more political sort. Slowly at first at some colleges, more quickly at others, a dramatic turnabout occurred in the relationship between the student and the campus and society. In this transformation New York City schools led the way.

While activism took hold most broadly and deeply at the City Colleges, Columbia University is worth examining because the first major expression of student discontent took place there. The protest at Columbia in April 1932 set the pattern for further activities. It created a leadership core and an organization for subsequent developments at Columbia and presented a model of tactics and rhetoric that would serve for the rest of the decade. Battle lines were drawn. In addition, the expulsion of Reed Harris, the editor of the student paper, the *Spectator*, meant that authorities were taking seriously the cluster of leftward ideas that were beginning to permeate the thinking of at least a small group on campus. The issues raised by Harris and by his attackers represent a combination of causes that would both provide the student movement with its strength and give rise to serious internal contradictions.

If a "revolt on the campus" was to break out, Columbia was as logical a place as any. Within its walls were progressive educators like George S. Counts at Teachers College and socially conscious theologians like Reinhold Niebuhr and his colleagues at Union Theological Seminary. Donald Henderson, one of the founders of the NSL, was an economics instructor there. (His firing the next year would cause another controversy on campus.) The university had a peace-minded and somewhat pig-headed president in Nicholas Murray Butler and a tradition of faculty dissent that had been sparked by Charles Beard. Most important, the university was located in New York City, surrounded by evidence of the failure of the system, and only a subway ride from Union Square.

In the fall of 1930 Columbia University had an enrollment of almost forty thousand, most of whom were drawn from the area.[1] Of these, 2,400 were in Columbia College and another 1,000 at Barnard. In spite of the rather narrow geographic range of its enrollment, the university had more ethnic and economic diversity than most institutions, particularly its brothers in the Ivy League. The political complexion of the campus also varied. While a straw poll in the fall of 1932 gave student preference to Norman Thomas, the low turnout favored the more zealous and politically aware supporters of the Socialist party candidate, and Herbert Hoover ran a strong second. (As he did on many other campuses, Franklin D. Roosevelt ran third.) Still, there was strong support for Thomas and an active group working for his election. Student results also contrast with the response from 118 faculty, of whom 55 were for Hoover, 35 for Thomas, 25 for Roosevelt, and 3 for William Z. Foster, the Communist party candidate.[2]

During the 1930–31 school year Columbia was mostly quiet and apolitical. However, a Socialist Club existed and the Social Problems Club, which later became the bulwark of the NSL and the Young Communists, invited Thomas to speak. A. J. Muste, then director of the Brookwood Labor College, spoke at an Economics Club luncheon. That fall, Teachers College offered a course for school teachers and administrators on how "to teach universal peace through the medium of education."[3]

In the spring of 1931, Reed Harris was elected editor in chief of the *Spectator*. He was from a well-to-do New York family and had graduated from Staunton Military Academy in Virginia. Harris's career at Columbia had been conventional. He had written for the student paper for three years and had been a member of the news board, as well as a member of the editorial board of the *Columbian*. He was active in campus politics; as a sophomore he had been a member of the Vigilance Committee, and in February 1931 he was elected to the Student Board. Harris was also a member of the Junior Society of the Blue Key and of Phi Delta Gamma. He was, in short, an insider and a successful participant in traditional collegiate culture.[4]

But he had also come into conflict with that culture during his college years. A member of the freshman football team, Harris had soon became disillusioned with the way in which that sport, and other intercollegiate athletics, was conducted. As editor of the *Spectator,* he waged a harsh campaign against the hypocrisy involved in terming collegiate sports "amateur," when in fact the players were substantially, if unequally, subsidized. In an editorial that provoked considerable controversy, Harris described college football as a "racket" and advocated complete professionalization to eliminate subterfuge. Since football did serve some function on campus, he argued, the authorities should hire players just to play the game and not pretend that their activities on the field were incidental to their scholastic efforts.

These editorials, plus one attacking the running of the college dining hall, brought Harris into conflict with the college's administration. On April 1, 1932, the day before he was due to relinquish his post to a new editor, Harris was called into the dean's office and told that he had been expelled. The bizarre timing was typical of the administration's mishandling of the case. Harris was given no formal hearing or avenue of appeal. The sole explanation offered for the expulsion was Dean Herbert Hawkes's statement that "material in the Columbia *Spectator* in the past few days is a climax to a long series of discourtesies, innuendos and misrepresentations which have appeared in this paper during the current academic year." In reporting the incident (on page 1) the *New York Times* noted that as editor Harris had attacked college dining facilities, criticized college athletics, and denounced "narrow minded associations" such as the American Legion and the Daughters of the American Revolution.[5]

Harris quickly gained support. His father, Tudor Harris, of St. James, Long Island, denounced the university administration and declared that he "would regard a diploma received at the hands of a college president who could sanction, let alone direct, such an action for such a cause as a stigma."[6] The American Civil Liberties Union (ACLU) offered its assistance and sent a telegram to President Butler protesting the expulsion and in particular objecting to the lack of due process. Many students at Columbia had disagreed with Harris's views, especially on sports, but student opinion now turned in his favor.

On campus the Social Problems Club and the NSL led the protest. Aided by a stubborn administration and increasing student support, the two organizations called for a one-day student strike to protest the expulsion. On the Wednesday following the dean's action, thousands of students cut class and gathered at a protest rally on the steps of the library. Campus uproar, plus the assistance of the ACLU, led the administration finally to agree to reinstate Harris, who then voluntarily withdrew from the college.

The students, especially the activists, saw this as a victory and as justification for militant action on campus. Clearly, students, whatever their political views in general, could be mobilized around an issue of student rights. The strike captured attention in the city press and at other schools. It became the first sign of "a revolt on the campus."[7] As for Harris, in May the four hundred and fifty seniors at Columbia College voted him "most likely to succeed."

While Harris had written articles on national topics, including his antiwar statement in March 1932, the cause of his expulsion seems to have been not explicitly political controversy but his attacks on a whole series of campus sacred cows, including sports and fraternities. He was challenging the activities and values embodied in traditional college life and beginning to offer an alternative vision of the place of the student in society and on campus. If the alumni, administrators, and athletes responded to his attacks as being a kind of lèse majesté, they were right, for at Columbia, as at other schools, football was king.

There had been previous attacks on the path that college sports had taken since the turn of the century. As early as 1895 educators and some students had condemned the trend toward commercialization and professionalization in college athletics. In keeping with the infiltration of business into the ivory tower of academia, sports had become "a vested interest with a huge capital investment."[8] In the twenties the *New Student* connected the increasing commercialization with the domination of education by the business ethos and by businessmen. Other criticism represented nostalgia for the earlier collegiate culture, including what was essentially an elitist reaction against the decline of gentlemanly sports and the intrusion of talented but lower-class players.

Still, sports maintained the function that they had performed at the turn of the century. As they did in the British system, after which they had been modeled, they continued to inculcate and reinforce a set of values useful to the upper class. College sports did provide a degree of democratization—skill rather than ancestry became a basis for respect—but this varied from school to school. In 1927, for example, the Princeton football squad of forty-four men did not contain a single graduate of a public high school.[9]

A reading of campus papers in the early thirties reveals a picture of athletics and fraternities as the dominant fact of college life. This does not mean that most students went to football games or joined fraternities, but these activities often dominated the campuses, to the exclusion and perhaps alienation of those who did not belong. There were some revolts, using existing campus mechanisms to redistribute power. At San Marcos State Teachers College, Lyndon Johnson used the power of the purse to form a coalition of out-groups in order to take over student government and the student treasury.[10] Harris and later activists at Columbia were not unaware of the possibilities of manipulating power on campus by capturing strategic posts. However, before national or radical political activity could become a major part of student life, it was necessary to attack and to break through the stereotype of what a college student was and to destroy the portrait of student life that had developed during the twenties.

Changes had taken place not only in the nation but in the nation's student body. "Drawn from a wider segment of the whole society than previously, it lacked the common assumptions basic to earlier college life, was more susceptible to the influence of such external events as war and depression, and was, therefore more serious about its studies."[11] Although college youth still formed only a small minority (one writer estimates that in 1930, 12.37 percent of young people between the ages of 18 and 21 were enrolled in some form of higher educational institution[12]), the campus was no longer restricted to the upper-class youth who had nothing to do with his or her time but go to parties and pep rallies. This was true of private colleges as well as of the land-grant schools and other public institutions, which had always been more broadly based. At Columbia and other urban colleges students were entering who had to pay their own way. The new students included members of ethnic and economic groups espousing beliefs and values different from those of their predecessors and colleagues at college. Attacks on "King Football" and on fraternities became a form of revolt against both the deliberate exclusion of groups such as blacks, Jews, and Catholics, and against an entire alien structure.

This attack took place primarily on large campuses, where sports and fraternities were firmly entrenched but where there were also large numbers of students connected with neither: Columbia, the University of Michigan, the University of Wisconson, the University of California, and the University of Chicago.

In the fall of 1930 an editorial in the UCLA *Daily Bruin* called for "open athletic subsidies, openly arrived at" and the end to the hidden tactics that the authorities used to secure support for athletes. Athletics, the editorial continued, were necessary to attract a "colorful" student body, one "which is made up of individuals who are interested in the great game of life not the insane game of learning facts and statistics." The *Spectator* editor (Harris's predecessor) found the latter comment absurd and the idea "weird at best," but he did agree with the concern over deceptive practices in sports.[13]

The controversy was pursued by Harris and continued by his immediate successors. The alumni continued to be angry, and to accuse the "*Spectator* group" of sniping at football. They denied that improprieties such as secret subsidies took place and added that even if they did, "what is wrong with that?" On the other hand, the Student Board voted to investigate the four points in contention: payments to football players, unfair preference given to athletes in obtaining jobs, scholarship aid in unreasonable proportion, and the practice of faculty members grading high to keep athletes eligible.[14]

Nothing much came of the controversy, except the expulsion of Harris and the creation of permanent hostility between the alumni association, college athletes, and the *Spectator*. The dispute did, however, reveal considerable dissatisfaction among students over college priorities, and this dissatisfaction with the role of athletes and fraternities on campus led easily to an examination and rejection of other aspects of the university. In *King Football*, published a year after he was expelled, Harris moved from attacks on the football system to condemnation of the regimentation of thought, lack of academic freedom, and stultification that characterized not only Columbia but most of American higher education. The political direction of Harris's thought is indicated in his article in *Revolt*, the early straightforward name of the journal of the SLID (later renamed *Student Outlook*), titled "College Fraternities—Obstacles to Social Change."[15]

The attacks on athletics caused some concern with what was happening to red-blooded American youth. Some people began to fear that more than their blood was red. At the same time that students were picketing theaters showing *Red Salute*, a film about subversion in academia, Universal was producing a movie called *Fighting Youth* about a "Red plot to undermine college football."[16]

This particular paranoia was based on a partial truth. The young Left did indeed, in its militant period, concern itself with these inequities, especially financial favoritism in a period of depression. The platform of the Communist-dominated NSL included a plank on athletics: "Although

NSL members also participate in sports, we make clear our opposition to the institution as it exists today. We consider the overemphasis on competition between the large colleges harmful because it prevents the mass of students from taking part in sports."[17]

While the idea that college football was an amateur sport was criticized, another major question was its allegedly nonpolitical nature. In a political period it was inevitable that a challenge would be made to the mystique of sports as an innocent nonsectarian activity, outside the bounds of ideological or moral issues. The debate over the purity of college sports reached its highest level of articulation, and of absurdity, in a controversy over whether the Harvard football team should play a game for charity.

In the fall of 1931, Mayor James Michael Curley of Boston proposed on behalf of that city and New York Mayor Jimmy Walker that the Army-Harvard game be played in Yankee Stadium for the benefit of the unemployed in those two cities. Curley indicated that he had approached officials at West Point and that they had agreed to the plan. President Abbott Lawrence Lowell promptly refused Harvard's cooperation on the grounds that it was the college's policy never to play in "public stadiums" and that the proposal would tend to "commercialize" college football. Furthermore, the athletic association, which normally received the proceeds of the games, felt that no game earnings could be spared, since the association was struggling bravely to avoid a deficit. The refusal by Lowell was not unexpected, as Harvard's president had previously turned down a proposal for a postseason game with the proceeds going to "charity."[18]

The decision and continuing refusal set off a dispute at Harvard and between Harvard and Yale, where the student body and newspaper had endorsed such a game. The dispute says something about the collegiate culture at Harvard, that institution's relationship with Boston, and the priorities and values of America's upper class.

The editorials in the *Crimson* supporting Lowell's action emphasized both the inappropriateness of using college sports, especially Harvard's, for purposes other than entertainment and a general antipathy toward anything resembling "the dole." A basic political and social (and economic) attitude underlay the expressed concern with the "commercialization of football." Applauding Lowell's decision, the *Crimson* editorial declared, "President Lowell's refusal to permit Harvard athletes to become commercial dole-subsidizers by the transfer of the Army-Harvard game to Yankee Stadium is the only welcome outcome to an unwelcome proposal."[19] Lowell was, however, willing to allow Boston College and Holy Cross to commercialize their teams, and offered them the use of Harvard's stadium for a charity game. A *Crimson* editorial explained that this was no contradiction, since Lowell's concern was with football at Harvard, not football in general. The decision was admirable, the editorial continued, because it showed that the earlier refusal was caused not by any "lack of sympathy with the needy but by existing conditions in the University."[20]

At schools other than Harvard benefit games were fairly acceptable. The question arose, however, of whom the games were benefiting. In the winter of 1932 a young Socialist at Columbia wrote to the *Spectator* to condemn the use of the basketball team to raise funds for the Seventh Regiment and Armory. This seemed to him to contradict the antiwar sentiment that had been expressed when the ROTC was "laughed off the Columbia campus." The writer noted that "the militarists are trying to build up a preparedness program" and to exploit the war talk in the air. He was careful to add that he often went to the team's games and was criticizing only its use for militaristic purposes.[21]

The major dispute over the relationship of sports to politics came not over campus athletics but over the 1936 Olympic Games, scheduled to be held in Berlin. The controversy reveals the increasing concern of some students, especially those in the student peace movement, with fascism and the deep rift between them and some of their fellow students. It also indicates the clash of values and attitudes between students in the movement and those still attached to the collegiate values of the ruling class.

The proposal to boycott the Olympics because of their location in the heart of the Nazi state challenged the view of athletics as at least apolitical and at best a means of promoting international friendship. It offered an alternative view of sports as, in fact, an instrument of the system in which they existed, whether fascist or capitalist. In this view the athlete was not a neutral amateur pursuing personal achievement but an agent, or pawn, of the system. Much the same challenge was being made to the university, which also claimed to be an objective and neutral institution, outside the boundaries of mundane political controversy. Finally, though legitimate arguments were made about the validity or effectiveness of the boycott, with some antifascists believing that competition could refute the idea of Aryan supremacy, most of the arguments on campus point to a division between those who saw the Nazi state as a horror with which international friendship was neither possible nor appropriate and those who were either unconcerned with or sympathetic to Hitler's policies.

Controversy over American participation in the Olympics was concentrated on the East Coast and on campuses where athletics were of sufficient importance to bring forth vocal proparticipation spokesmen. (It was largely a male issue, which may imply that more was involved than abstract ideals.)[22] Harvard, the University of Pennsylvania, and Columbia were centers of discussion on this issue.

In September 1935 a *Crimson* article reported that Harvard's director of athletics had announced that Harvard would not send representatives to the Olympic games if the German government hindered participation by Jewish athletes. The director added that he was sure no such troubles would arise. An editorial in the same issue noted that the administration had aroused controversy by including an appeal for contributions to the Olympic fund in the mailing of football ticket applications sent to alumni. In the editor's view the only substantive question was whether Hitler's promise to the American committee that no such discrimination would occur was sufficient guarantee.[23]

In a point also made by others, the editorial further noted that Americans should not expect more of Germany than they did of themselves. Before the games in Los Angeles blacks had been excluded from the southern semifinal competition, and the only "colored" athletes had qualified in northern trials. This exclusion had brought forth no protests from foreign delegates at that time. It may be that this comparison, acknowledged or unacknowledged, was a major reason for American hesitation to treat the Nazis as outlaws. In the thirties the American house was built of very fragile glass. This argument, however, posed no problems for the radicals, who were well aware of American racism and spent more time opposing it than did, say, the Harvard *Crimson* or Avery Brundage.

Those students at Harvard and elsewhere who favored the boycott or removal of the games to another country argued both on fact and effect. Clear evidence existed that Nazi athletic policy discriminated against both Jews and uncooperative Christians in training and participation. Advocates of the boycott asserted that American participation implied approval of Hitler's policies and argued that the success of the Olympics would be hailed as a Nazi triumph. As President Jeremiah Mahoney of the Amateur Athletics Union, and a supporter of the boycott, observed, the training of the German athletes was a function of the state, making the games hardly a competition among free individuals.[24]

This was a key question. Did participation in sports competition within a country imply approval of national or even athletic policy? The *Crimson* argued that it did not; moreover, the paper continued, even if it did, why should the boycott be restricted to Germany, when other countries could be similarly condemned. The editor argued, "Should we obey a law, we do not necessarily endorse the law," and continued, somewhat illogically, "Should we gamble, we do not necessarily endorse gambling."[25] According to the editorial, Germany had met all four of the conditions raised by the committee: "Intelligent men with first hand information believe that the Nazi government has fulfilled their pledge" that no discrimination would occur.

Finally, the editor challenged the effectiveness of the boycott as a means of opposing fascism. Its enemies needed not "swords of tin" but "participation in world affairs, willingness to sacrifice economic advantage, and freedom of speech and action." A boycott of the Olympics would produce only "righteous moral satisfaction."

Arguments at the University of Pennsylvania were on a different level. In October 1935 the regular sports columnist of the *Daily Pennsylvanian* termed Germany's invitation to Helene Mayer, "expert Jewish fencer," to compete "a startling rebuke to those who have been spending their days and nights decrying Hitler's attitudes towards Hebrews and its effect on the Olympic games."[26] Echoing the usual argument that the Olympics served to promote international goodwill, the writer declared that "there should be no attempt to use the Games as a spearhead to be aimed at Hitler's theories. . . . 'Sports for sports sake' is an age old motto which might be used to advantage in this respect." It was the old English public school rallying cry.

In response, a student wrote that far from "sports for sports sake" the Olympics would be a "fair for celebration of Nazism."[27] Even aside from the political significance of Germany's success in playing international host, there was immediate danger to non-Aryan athletes. Describing the invitation to Mayer as an effort to ward off international protest, the student cited a *New York Times* article of September 15, 1935, reporting that a Jewish soccer player on a visiting Polish team that had defeated the Germans was beaten to death by a Nazi crowd in Silesia. What, he asked, would happen to a victorious Jew or Catholic on an American Olympic team? The only way to avoid similar trouble was the boycott.

Finally, in a letter that indicates a division within student antiwar sentiment between isolationists and internationalists, a Penn student objected to the proposed boycott and the arguments favoring it as dangerous propaganda that might lead to war.[28] This was similar to the argument that antifascist rhetoric was similar to the anti-German rhetoric before United States entry into the world war and reflected a widespread fear of propaganda resulting from disillusionment with that war. "Whether Hitler's attitude toward the Jews is justified or not remains for speculation. That the German people have overwhelmingly endorsed Hitler's policies is actual fact." In any case, the student concluded, sports had nothing to do with politics.

Student opposition to United States participation in the Olympics was centered in the NSL and the SLID and, after their merger in December 1935, in the American Student Union. This opposition was especially strong at City College of New York and at Columbia. At the latter the *Spectator*, Student Board, and University Antiwar Council all endorsed the boycott.[29] In taking this position the student paper argued against both Germany's sports policies and its national policies. Even judged strictly by athletic criteria, the games would be a disgrace, it said. Discrimination took place not only in the process of selection but in the limiting of participation to athletes belonging to proper sports organizations, which were themselves discriminatory. The editorial also noted the death of the soccer player in Silesia.

Perhaps the most important point that the paper made, however, was that the boycott "would give courage to the spokesmen for political and social democracy and racial equality" inside of Germany. Since American colleges were the main source of the nation's Olympic material, it was up to them to "start the ball rolling." It would not, of course, in itself affect Hitler's policies, but it could show his opponents that they were not alone.

The proposed boycott of the Olympics, along with the criticism of the commercialization of college football, created immense hostility; in some cases attacks on sports aroused more heat than did economic or social debates. At Columbia and other schools the angriest groups were alumni associations and some of the athletes themselves. At Columbia the former group spent considerable effort trying to get the university to censor the *Spectator*. The latter took more direct action. After Harris's editorial challenging the subsidizing of sports, the captain of the football team and another player went to the *Spectator* office and offered to beat up the editor.[30] Other groups shared this distaste for the paper's editorial positions. The Columbia crew men, for example, periodically circulated petitions to limit the freedom of the paper's editor.

This response was not confined to attacks against criticism of athletics. On campuses across the country, especially those with a strong emphasis on intercollegiate sports, the athletes served as vigilantes, often with official endorsement, to break up antiwar and antifascist demonstrations. This was usually done in the name of Americanism, often with the assistance of ROTC cadets.[31] In turn, members of the peace movement and leftist groups rarely participated in varsity sports, though those not devoting all their time to leftist organizations did engage in intramural sports.

If some athletes and their friends resented the behavior and ideas of the leftists, the young radicals often resentfully noted the different treatments meted out to students involved in disturbances at football games and those participating in political rallies. The two forms of activity were not without some resemblance, but the response of authorities, both campus administrators and city police and judges, was quite different. While several Harvard students were sentenced to six months in jail for "loitering" at an antifascist rally in Cambridge, participants in postgame "riots" that involved physical destruction got only wrist slaps and suspended sentences.[32]

This contrast should not be stated too broadly. On many campuses, especially smaller ones where neither politics nor sports aroused complete devotion, pacifism and athletics were not incompatible. The problems arose most conspicuously where sports had come to be an end in themselves and collegiate life and values revolved about them. At schools where the winning team was valued more than either scholarship or the pursuit of social justice, there was between the pacifists and leftists and the athletes and their followers an irreconcilable clash of values.

But even this climate showed signs of change. In successful schools players increasingly came not only from the ranks of the elite (and aspiring elite) but from the talented poor, brought into the university on scholarships. Some of these athletes would be struck by the incongruity of their position. Finally, the economic situation and an influx of new students dampened, to a degree, collegiate ardor for sports, or at least the system as it existed.

Though sports would rise again, there was beneath the debate an attack not only upon athletics but on the people who controlled them, the institutions they served, and values they represented. In particular, their regimentation, disciplined obedience, and unquestioning team spirit were incompatible with many of the assumptions and goals of the antiwar students. Although the question of violence was not often raised directly in discussions of athletics, there was a conflict between such sports as football and the spirit of pacifism. Shortly after the unfriendly visit from the football players, Harris wrote an editorial entitled "Death Stalks the Gridiron," noting that forty deaths had occurred on football fields the previous season, and describing them as "murder."[33]

Again the new paradigm from the Great War came into play. For that war had itself brought a disillusionment, especially in England, with the glorification of sports and the gentleman's code that it represented. In *The Great War and Modern Memory*, Fussell describes the incongruity of the cult of sports and the reality of war. He notes that the British in particular began the war with the idea that war was a game, "strenuous but entertaining," and like sports a test of manhood. One of the more bizarre manifestations of this was the practice of kicking a football toward the enemy lines while attacking. As war went on, the mystique of combat decreased. Fields of mud hedged with barbed wire could not long be confused with the playing fields of Eton. Siegfried Sassoon's *Memoirs* are formed around the irony of the sportsman gone to battle.[34]

The code, of course, had always been a male one, just as battle had been a male preserve, though the death and destruction of war had been a common property. At women's colleges, where sports were less symbolic, and less remunerative, conflict between the two collegiate cultures was less and peace activity broader. Schools like Columbia, however, experienced deep division and a mixture of issues. Out of the conflict came organized activity and student revolt. Although the exact conditions at Columbia were not repeated on other campuses, the groups formed, tactics used, and issues raised would become part of a national student movement and would be emulated on other campuses.

Chapter 3

"We Pledge Not to Support the Government of the United States in Any War It May Conduct"

The Oxford Oath was brought to America in 1933, at a time when antiwar organization was beginning to stir on American campuses. While peace sentiment was not new, the degree to which it was expressed through groups was a clear break with the past and with old student customs. Dormant groups took on new life; religious organizations and leftist clubs found new focus and increased membership. The NSL, for the Communists, and the SLID, for the Socialists, joined with the Methodist youth and the YWCA and YMCA as the basis for a "United Front" against war. These and other groups, conservative and liberal, Marxist and pacifist, came together at a series of campus, national, and international conferences during the first half of the decade.

The first major national student conference was the Student Congress against War, held in Chicago in December 1932 (and following the Amsterdam World Congress in the summer of that year). Although the delegates were mixed, the Marxist groups, with their unity and discipline, dominated the proceedings. However, a substantial number of pacifists and unaffiliated delegates made it clear that a successful movement would require compromise. Though this did not come about immediately, for about five years a tenuous cooperation would exist between students with a common opposition to imperialist war.

Far from being isolationists, the student peace movement shared ideas and activities with international student and youth groups. American students participated in world congresses in Amsterdam and Brussels. With the assistance of Marxist parties and religious and pacifist groups American students planned many of their demonstrations to coincide with antiwar rallies abroad. Students from European or Asian nations were often honored speakers at American meetings. This was especially true as the peace movement began to embody, somewhat precariously, antifascist sentiment and expression.

For American students had no monopoly on antiwar feeling. If the world war seemed terrible to those who had not had their own land touched, the revulsion in Europe was that much the greater. Peace organizations existed throughout Europe, including Germany, at least until Hitler came to power. These groups found strength especially among young people. The most significant contribution of the international student movement to the American movement was the Oxford Oath. The disillusionment of English students with the Great War was profound, a feeling transmitted in the war poems of Wilfred Owen and Siegfried Sassoon. Mixed with religious and Marxist ideology, this revulsion gave the British student movement a zeal and seriousness that caused considerable consternation among politicians and Tory newspapers.

On Thursday, February 9, 1933, the undergraduates at

Oxford Union voted 275 to 153 to uphold the resolution that "this House will in no circumstances fight for King and Country." Similar resolutions were soon passed at other British universities, including Birmingham, Cambridge, and Glasgow. The votes were well publicized and had an immediate impact upon the public and the press. Many people were outraged. Later, some interventionists were to claim that the pacifism of English youth had emboldened fascist aggressors. Winston Churchill claimed to have "actual proof" that the union's vote had had a "direct influence" on Mussolini's decision "to come to Hitler's side."[1]

Writing his history of World War II, Churchill stated: "It was easy to laugh off such an episode in England, but in Germany, in Russia, in Japan, the idea of a decadent Britain took root and swayed many calculations."[2] There is, in fact, no evidence that this was the case, but the claim is indicative of the seriousness with which some in England took the apparent rebellion of those being trained to be the nation's rulers.

The Oxford Pledge was immediately cheered by pacifists in America. Eventually it was adopted at national conferences, and the American Student Union made it the basis for the student antiwar campaign. Rephrased to refuse support for any war that the United States government might conduct, this absolute refusal of support for the government caused division within the peace movement and aroused almost as much hostility among adults as it did in England. Indeed, to many critics of the peace movement this expression of pacifism and refusal to accept national policy seemed even more threatening than Marxism.

It seemed to be a direct attack upon nationalism and a dangerous assertion of individual responsibility over legal authority. Through its wording, the pledge also left open the possibility of supporting wars other than those conducted by the government. Absolute pacifists saw this as inadequate,

but it did provide a compromise to allow support for the
pledge and the antiwar movement by those who, though opposed to imperialist aggression and realizing the horrors of
war, still believed in the necessity and inevitability of class
war.

In 1933 many American students were receptive to the
ideas embodied in the Oxford Oath. As it had in Britain, the
oath found its initial reception at the elite universities. The
first American school to embrace the pledge was Brown, in
March 1933. Declaring in an editorial that "American college
men cannot stop another war but it is in their power to
prevent another repetition of the fatal mistake of 1917," the
Brown *Daily Herald* took the lead to direct student activity
against war.[3]

The student editor drew up a petition to be sent to 145
colleges and universities and eventually to be presented to
President Roosevelt. Its purpose was to "unite the students
of the United States in a drive against war and militaristic
propaganda." The petition read:

>   Whereas, We believe that war is futile and destruc-
> tive and should be abandoned as an instrument of
> international action, and
>   Whereas, We believe that it is to the best interests
> of the United States and other nations that peace
> be maintained, and
>   Whereas, We believe that peace can be maintained
> only by open opposition to the selfish interests that
> promote war, and
>   Whereas, We believe that increasing militarism and
> nationalism in the United States must be opposed
> by united action, and
>   Whereas, We believe that war is only justified
> in case of invasion of the mainland of the United States
> by a hostile power, and

Whereas, We believe that the united refusal of
the youth of America to bear arms, except in case of
invasion, will do much to prevent war,
    We, the undersigned students of _____ pledge
ourselves not to bear arms, except in cases of the
invasion of the mainland of the United States, and to
work actively for the organization of the world on
a peace basis.

The *Daily Herald* campaign was received with enthusiasm
on other campuses. At Columbia University the editorial
board of the *Spectator* circulated the petition and organized
their own campus peace poll. In a rather simple ballot students were asked to indicate the circumstances, if any, in
which they would bear arms for the United States, whether
they would be willing to go to jail for their convictions, and
the basis for their objection to war. The total number of
students responding was 920.[4] Those who responded indicated a widespread reluctance to go to war for any reason
other than actual invasion; indeed, nearly a third stated that
they would bear arms "under no circumstances," and half of
those responding indicated they would undergo imprisonment rather than fight in an unjust war. Similar polls were
taken at the Columbia engineering school and at Barnard,
where the questions were reworded on the assumption that
women would not themselves be called to serve (or, evidently, allowed to volunteer). The pacifist sentiment at
Barnard was significant, since women's colleges would become a major force in the student peace movement.
    The collegiate peace polls received national attention with
the publication of their results in the May 1933 *Literary
Digest*.[5] In an article entitled "Pacifism in the Colleges," the
Digest reported an overwhelmingly antiwar response to the
national survey (which was conducted by the Brown student
newspaper in conjunction with the International Disarma-

ment Council and the National Student Federation). There were some exceptions to the pattern of student rejection of war; for example, all 333 students at Norwich University, "the Military College of New England," signed a pledge to support the government in any war. However, the results in general brought pleasure to pacifists and pain to "patriotic" groups like the American Legion and the National Association of Manufacturers.

While observing that the poll did not necessarily mean that students would carry out their proclaimed resistance to war, pacifists and progressives welcomed the sign of youth's concern for its own future. In opposition to those who complained that students should stick to their books and leave public policy to those "older and wiser," an editorial in the *Nation* applauded the use of such polls to stimulate and express student opinion. Noting the comment of England's foreign secretary Sir John Simon that "the question of war and peace is not one in which the opinion of the uninstructed should be invited," the editor responded: "The instructed unfortunately are just those whose opinions cannot be consulted; they lie beneath the sod in Flanders' field."[6]

A common attitude shared by newspapers as varied as the *New York Times* and the *Dallas Daily News* was that while the antiwar feeling was commendable, it should not be taken too seriously. The editors were sure that when the time came, youth would go to war at their country's call. This particular response, more than opposition or condemnation, outraged the young pacifists. The collegiate editors, whose style was not yet Olympian with liberal certainty, but rather heatedly polemical and often tactless, rejected the confident assumption of common values.

Arthur Lelyveld, editor of the *Spectator*, answered the *Times* editorial in his own, "Rally Once Again."[7] The belief that when the time came youth would "rally round" was the response of "cynical old men to whom youth's ideals are merely safe deposit vaults with nothing of value in them." The attitude was understandable, however, since it was hard to believe that youth had yet fully realized the "folly of war." Many young people took the attitude that it was all right "for the other fellow." "The 'sophisticated' young man will stay at home to clean up," the editorial continued. There was also real weakness in the antiwar movement. Parts of the country had barely been touched by it, and militaristic propaganda was nearly overwhelming. "By every sort of allurement— from shiny uniforms to perky female noses—students are being seduced into thinking of war as something grand and noble." Lelyveld gloomily inquired, "If war broke out the next day where would the anti-war movement be? Some of the leaders would be hustled off to 'slacker' camps to be infused with American idealism. Others realizing the folly of their crusade through subtle proddings . . . would rush off to enlist in 'stay-at-home' units." It might be that protest was futile; but there was another possibility, however slight, that was worth working for:

> Old age may well jeer at those hopeless attempts
> to overthrow a war psychology. They know that
> youth will be swept away amid the hysterical shrieking
> of a war-frenzied nation. Bands, marching, cheers—
> will smother the young bystander with those spine
> shivers so that enlistment will be the natural
> culmination.
> But, sometimes we just hope—perhaps it won't
> work out that way. Perhaps, when our statesmen
> declare another war someday, we'll thumb our noses at
> them and politely invite them to go off and fight
> it out among themselves. Perhaps . . .

Those who look back at the thirties and see the entire peace movement as naive and its members as blind to reality are incorrect. Many saw war as nearly unavoidable. Their analysis recognized that historical forces were almost inevitable. But the "nearly" and "almost," the place in the back of their minds that insisted that "perhaps," made the effort worthwhile. It is, after all, just this hope that arouses people from apathy to challenge evil and the status quo, to create the possibility of change. Perhaps genocide and racism and napalm are not inevitable. Perhaps "they'll give a war and no one will come."

Certainly there were those who feared this pacifism, however fragile. When students at Southern Methodist University took the Oxford Oath, veterans' organizations denounced them and organized a counterpledge. The dean of CCNY refused even to allow a poll to be conducted, fearing that adverse publicity resulting from the predictable antiwar vote might "threaten the life of the institution." This concern was not without some basis. As a result of the Brown student newspaper's sponsorship of the peace poll and its editorials on the subject, the Rhode Island state legislature launched an investigation intended to root out a connection between communism and the peace movement. One state representative described the Oxford Oath as "treasonous."[8]

Among students in the peace movement there was debate over whether the pledge went too far or not far enough. Some argued against such a forthright refusal to fight and urged a clause to allow for a defensive war. Pacifists argued with Marxists over whether limiting the oath to wars "which the government might choose to conduct" amounted to sanctioning class war. There lay a conflict with no real resolution.

The latter issue was fiercely debated on individual campuses and at national conventions. At the latter, Communists and their allies often, through discipline and numbers, carried the day. But the pacifist contingent was always large enough to ensure a battle. With a revealing, if biased, outlook, a young socialist described the division at the second

Student Antiwar Congress in Chicago in December 1933. He noted that the young people at the convention had surprised the older people in the peace movement by their militancy, as they "swept away disarmament, the League of Nations, the World Court, the piles of treaties in existence, as useless acts of well-meaning innocents or as a deliberate means of deceiving the masses and hiding imperalist adventures."[9] J. S. Matthews, who would prove the Talleyrand of the American Left, was still secretary of the pacifist Fellowship of Reconciliation, but already, in fact, a Marxist (which he would desert in turn for a career testifying before the Un-American Activities Committee). At the convention he won the enthusiasm of the group by proclaiming that he and they were not opposed to a war that would destroy capitalism.

Carrying the convention was one thing, winning the campuses another. The supporters of class war were a minority even on those campuses where they were strongest. At many schools the struggle was between liberal and conservative pacifists and those who saw any tinge of pacifism as subversive. For most students the revulsion against war was stronger than the appeal of any positive program to change society. The call to support a class war as a way to end all war had too many echoes of Woodrow Wilson.

The postwar disillusionment of the twenties remained. This feeling was given force by an awareness that all was *not* quiet on the Western Front. A typical student editorial began, "Fifteen years after the war that ended war, . . . the world is once again an armed camp."[10] Noting a rising tide of world armaments the student editor asked, "What will the college man do when the drums roll and the band begins to play?" Would he rush off to enlist, intoxicated by propaganda? Would he "forget the knowledge of a generation"? The action of the English youth at Oxford Union was a hopeful sign that history might not repeat itself. Explaining the purpose of the peace poll, with a rhetoric and emotional imagery that were not untypical of other student writing on the subject, Lelyveld wrote: "Civilization once more stalks blindly toward chaos. The upheavals precipitated by the last war have made no lasting impression on statesmen. But a rising note of pacifism, if sounded long and loudly enough by this generation, may somehow penetrate the ears of those who, it seems, will never learn to see."

Antiwar activity received impetus from academic studies by anthropologists and sociologists as well as historians. Pitirim A. Sorokin and N. N. Golovin, both Harvard sociologists (and Russian emigrés), reported the results of a study of war through the ages.[11] Based on five criteria, namely, size of armies, duration of battles, casualties, proportion of the warring population to the general population, and the number of countries involved, they concluded that modern war was 2,100 times worse than war in medieval times. All past wars together were insignificant compared to World War I. According to the authors the evidence "refutes the theory that war tends to disappear with the progress of civilization." Anthropologist Ruth Benedict, while denying that substituting one economic system for another would eliminate war, also denied that the impulse toward war was instinctive or ineradicable.[12]

The military establishment also provided ammunition for the antiwar movement. The standard manual for ROTC provided a variety of lessons that seemed to clash with the purposes of higher education and of a peaceful society. To refute the suggestion that military training taught good citizenship, the *Spectator* published an excerpt from the 1925 manual: "To finish an opponent who hangs on, or attempts to pull you to the ground, always try to break his hold by driving the knee or the foot to his crotch and gouging his eyes with your thumbs. This inherent desire to fight and kill must be carefully watched for and encouraged by the instructor."[13]

It was a violent world. In addition to military wars, there was economic conflict and exploitation. One student asked, "What does it matter if human suffering goes on endlessly? We have billions of dollars to throw into the gaping jaws of a war machine, which destroys and destroys; and, yet, for masses, starving, undernourished, without hope we have pleasant smiles, vague promises."[14]

To evils of this magnitude many proposed solutions proved inadequate. The movement itself offered many, and sometimes contradictory, proposals. The old liberal standbys included free trade, reduction of armaments, and international organizations. Typical of this approach was a program offered by the Columbia faculty at a peace convocation in April 1933. They endorsed an eight-point program to curb "rampant economic nationalism and individualism."

1. Removal of barriers to international trade
2. Nationalization of the manufacture of munitions and an embargo on the export of munitions.
3. Cancellation of war debts and reparations.
4. "Genuine and effective disarmament."
5. Abandonment of all military intervention in affairs of other countries.
6. Abolition of conscription, military training, and ROTC.[15]

Radicals believed that war could be ended only through the elimination of capitalism. The profit motive in its various manifestations was the cause of war, and imperialism was the ultimate form of capitalism. It was the ruling classes who made war on behalf of their economic interests. Consequently, to end war it was necessary to create a classless society, and in the meantime to create solidarity among the workers of the world.

This position dominated the Amsterdam World Congress in the summer of 1932 and the Chicago meeting that December. At the latter the first resolution passed endorsed the antiwar pledge of the Amsterdam congress, which included statements against armaments, war preparations, "the imperialist powers that rule us," "imperialist capitalism," "chauvinism," and the exploitation, oppression, and massacres of colonial peoples. It called for students to "fight with all forces and with all the means at our command against imperialist capitalism."[16]

In response to attacks by pacifists supporters of the resolutions declared that the fight against imperialism did not necessarily imply violence. According to the Socialists at least, resistance might take the form of a general strike. The Communists, however, during the early years of the thirties, insisted on the inevitability of class war. One *Spectator* editor, Arnold Beichman, whose editorials in a year went from the pacifist to the Communist position, declared that the proper response to the next world war would be not a refusal to fight but a revolt against the capitalist class. General strikes and passive resistance would be useless, as they would be crushed. "Only by overthrow of the class which has made war can we insure permanent peace. . . . The world war to come should be our salvation and not our doom."[17]

Pacifists were beginning to work out a positive alternative. In Boston, in 1931, a follower of Gandhi who had been with him on his salt march to the sea talked to the students about the Indian leader's approach to peace and revolution.[18] Inside the student movement, as within the peace movement in general, pacifists engaged in debate and struggle with advocates of class warfare.

This conflict was particularly strong at Columbia. But it occurred on many campuses and especially at national congresses. The debate surfaced in the pages of the *Spectator* in the fall of 1932. Lelyveld, the editor in chief, continued Harris's tradition of socialist sympathies and forthright pacifism. His insistence that the antiwar congress in Chicago should oppose all kinds of war drew attack from a young communist. Pacifism was "idealistic" and futile, the student insisted. The experience of the world war showed that when war approached, mere pacifist opposition disappeared. Furthermore, pacifism failed to deal with the causes of war: capitalism and imperialism. Finally, it was unrealistic to believe that people could be convinced to renounce the use of force.[19]

Lelyveld responded in an editorial entitled "Dirty Idealist." It was ironic, he said, that the word *idealism* should be used as a pejorative. The term and concept were once respected. Idealism and pacifism were not unrealistic, at least no more so than communism. Although it was true that some pacifists went to war in 1917, the failure of individuals did not prove the falsity of the belief. In any case, war was not imminent, and time remained to prepare for it.

The editor challenged the idea that winning support for communism was more likely than winning it for pacifism. Why, he asked, was it any less likely that through propaganda and mass movements pacifists could "make the ideal of peace so strong and compelling that war [would] be impossible" than that through the same instruments communists could convince the masses of the necessity of class war and a worldwide communist society? The idea that the day would arrive when people throughout the world would hold the same political and economic beliefs was also "idealistic." "The revolutionary state will still be faced with the necessity of carrying on constant warfare with its own enemies within and without."

While agreeing that specific wars did have economic causes, Lelyveld and other pacifists saw the cause of war as lying deeper than economic necessity. Wars are born in the assumption that "bloodshed and killing are necessary to the attainment of ends." The pacifist objection is not merely to imperialist wars or to fighting on behalf of the rulers. "His objection is fundamental. He abhors the killing of man by man." He believes that the way to attain his ideals is not by violating them, "that the last way to stop the killing of man by man is to kill the killer." He declared that "only by infusing the mass of humanity with these ideals can war be effectively stamped out."

The division between pacifists and Marxists was not clear. The Socialist wing, which followed the lead of Norman Thomas, the party's presidential candidate and an opponent of World War I, participated in pacifist organizations like the Fellowship of Reconciliation (FOR) and the War Resisters League (WRL). In turn, many pacifists were opposed to capitalism.

A group of students from Columbia's Socialist Club participated in the WRL Conference in Washington in April 1933 and worked there to incorporate their own understanding of the economic causes of war. (The WRL was a secular organization founded in 1923 "to unite political, humanitarian, and philosophical objectors to war.") James Wechsler reported that the group played a significant role in carrying the conference further to the left than the WRL wanted it to go. The 220 young people in the youth section of the WRL accepted a clause calling for membership "to work to uncover and end those economic conditions and group prejudices which promote war."[20]

The FOR was a religious pacifist organization with a fairly leftist leadership. The FOR section on Columbia's campus consisted mostly of members of the Socialist Club. In October 1933, J. B. Matthews spoke to the group to urge them to join the campus "united front" against war.[21]

Socialists on campus, like those in the party, were divided as to tactics and responses to war. This ambiguity was to become greater during the Spanish Civil War. In the meantime, however, the socialist appeal was strong, and many students not affiliated with any Socialist party youth groups considered themselves both socialists and pacifists.

To an extent, of course, the debate was moot. In the early

thirties imperialist war, not class war, was threatening. It was possible, therefore, to form an antiwar coalition of those opposed to that specific danger. For this, the Oxford Oath proved an important unifying device. Its popularity drew upon a broad base of youthful skepticism about government and business. This legacy of the Great War led some students to take refuge in irony, as in one Columbia student's proposed "Contract between the United States Government and an Anti-Militarist." Describing the expected horrors of war, the student pledged to fight only if civilians would be paid at the same scale as the men in the army, there would be no profits for any war industry, and such industries would be run by the government. He would go to war on the condition that "the man on my right shall be the son of the then President of the United States, the man on my left shall be the son of the House of Morgan, the man in front of me shall be the son of the Rockefeller philanthropic and oil trusts, the man behind me shall be the son of the then Secretary of War."[22]

To the Communists the next war would be a "harbinger of revolt"; to pacifists it would be a "harbinger of chaos." All saw it as a repetition of World War I. What none of them predicted, however, was a war that would fit none of their categories and that would pose particular problems for both leftists and pacifists. The advent of fascism at home and abroad would raise new questions for the peace movement. It would also provide a spur for antiwar and antifascist activities on campus. Debate over the proper sphere of student activity and the proper tactics would exacerbate the clash between the new student culture and the old and create a real, if fleeting, "revolt on the campus."

Chapter 4

Conflict on Campus:
Antifascism and Civil
Liberties

War was not the only issue that concerned students. Developments abroad increasingly made fascism a serious test of their belief in pacifism. How to meet fascism became a major debate within the movement. This debate reflected both arguments in society in general and in the Left in particular and also the young people's own experiences on campus. Attitudes toward civil liberties, like attitudes toward pacifism, revealed a division between idealism and instrumentalism, and between those who saw freedom or nonviolence as ends in themselves and those who considered them means to the end of a better society.

Arguments over methods and tactics also reflected the continuation of discrimination and class division on the American college campus. Conflict occurred among students and between some students and administrators and faculty members. Students' views of fascism abroad and the means of combating it derived in part from their experiences with bigotry and violence at home.

While the Left in America professed to see little differ-

ence between the imperialism of England and France and
the expansionism of Japan and Italy, it was beginning to see
fascism as a distinctive phenomenon. Marxists rather opti-
mistically saw fascism as the last stage of capitalism, but they
responded to it with an intensity that belied their theory. As
Hitler's racial policies became increasingly clear and his
practices increasingly extreme, many in the Left and in the
peace movement began to see the existence of the Nazi state
as an evil more intolerable than war. During the first half of
the decade, however, this remained subordinate to the
peace issue. Opponents of fascism spoke in general terms,
declaring it to be inevitably linked to expansionist policies
and therefore a major cause of war.

Particularly on the East Coast students and student peace
groups began to join the cause of antifascism to the cause of
peace. Members of the NSL and the SLID participated in
demonstrations in New York and Boston and organized campus rallies to bring the issue home. The focus of demonstrations varied from campus to campus. At Columbia controversy surrounded the alleged presence of fascists in the Casa
Italiana and on the faculty of the Italian department. At
Harvard students protested the presence at commencement
of Hitler's press agent. In addition, the appearance of the
German ambassador, Hans Luther, at several universities at
the invitation of the administrations provoked students to
reaction, as did the visit of a group of Italian students, most
notably at City College of New York.[1]

These demonstrations raised a question of the focus of the
student movement and created a new controversy over the
choice of tactics. Although the debate sometimes appeared
to be a clash between Marxists and traditional liberals, the
division is not so clear; liberals, in particular, could be found
on both sides of the argument. Like the Left in general,
students were divided over the meaning of freedom.

As one historian has noted, it was an argument between

idealism and instrumentalism. The heart of the problem for defenders of civil liberties was whether they were ends in themselves or simply useful instruments for social change.[2] The question divided civil libertarians and especially the ACLU. Those who defended First Amendment rights primarily as a means of attaining desired ends believed that "the new social and political order that they sought depended upon wider boundaries for radical agitation." Roger Baldwin, a founder and director of the ACLU, wrote in 1933 that "civil liberties, like democracy, are useful only as tools to social change."[3]

This was also the position of some students. To others there seemed a contradiction between the demand of some radicals and leftists for freedom for themselves and their insistence that similar rights be denied to fascists. Specifically, demonstrations and disruption of speeches and the insistence that right wingers be eliminated from the faculty seemed to be an attack upon academic freedom. In May 1934, for example, the Columbia Student Conference against War and Fascism approved a resolution calling for the denial of civil liberties to "fascist organizations." By a slim majority the NSL, the Young Communist League, and other affiliated groups overrode the opposition of Socialists and liberals. According to the resolution, fascism was the "final degenerate attempt of decaying capitalism to maintain its rule," and its supporters deserved no freedom. In February 1935 the Columbia Anti-Fascist Council urged expulsion of three professors from the Italian department on the grounds that they were supporters of Mussolini.[4]

Both communism and American liberal relativism provided a rationale for subordinating civil liberties to political and economic objectives. This view was made appealing by the evident failure of liberalism in Europe and the emotional intensity of student reaction to fascism. Its development can be traced in the editorial positions of the Columbia *Spectator*.

In the fall of 1933 a *Spectator* editorial opposed the city's refusal of the use of the 165th Regiment Armory for a meeting of the United German Societies. It described the move as an "adoption of Nazi methods of suppression" and expressed the fear that the refusal set a dangerous precedent. Noting a Communist demand that the Nazis be deported, executed, or imprisoned, the editors suggested that the radicals "should look back on their own history in this country and remember how insecure their own liberties are."[5]

By March 1935 the paper's position had changed. In a long editorial entitled "Notes on Freedom 11," Wechsler analyzed the origins and meaning of liberty and concluded that absolute freedom was a myth used by oppressors to control the majority, that freedom was a means to an end, not an end itself, that those struggling against oppression should use it to accomplish their own objectives, and, finally, that this of necessity required the denial of freedom to those who were the agents of oppression.[6]

With perhaps intentional irony, he based his analysis on Walter Lippmann's writings, using liberal relativism as a weapon against the liberal idea of freedom. He also struck at the heart of the liberal dilemma. If it was no longer possible to believe in freedom as a "divine gift" or a natural right, then what was it but the creation of the state? But the state is the instrument of the controlling economic groups ("Economic power and political power are identical"), and under the domination of modern technological capitalism labor had no freedom. A redefinition of freedom in the modern world was needed. Wechsler quoted Thomas Carlyle: "Liberty, I am told, is a divine thing. Liberty when it becomes the liberty to die by starvation is not divine." To speak of political freedom in the absence of economic freedom was an absurdity. How could the worker, dependent for his livelihood upon the whims of his boss, exercise freedom?

It was time, Wechsler insisted, that the majority seized

upon freedom and used it as their own weapon. It must be used, he continued,

> not by those in whose hands the mass of wealth is
> constituted, and who employ it to further their own
> interests, but by the many who are being deprived of
> the basic necessities of life by the system of free
> business enterprise under the profit system. . . .
>
> Liberty is a weapon . . . ; it must be used in
> the modern age to recast society for the promotion of
> the interest of the majority who are now oppressed,
> not by a hypothetical state, but by the powers
> inherent in concentrated wealth. . . . The further grant
> of liberty to those who are bent upon oppressing
> mankind, and the advance armies of fascism are always
> of this nature, is utter suicide.
>
> It is to shape the outcome of social conflict and
> to safeguard the stakes involved—nothing else—which
> is the function of liberty today. The test will
> come, not in Philosophy Hall, but in far more decisive
> spheres.[7]

Perhaps Wechsler's most important point was that freedom was not an end but a means, and had always been so. Turning to the supposed apostles of freedom, the editor saw all of them as excepting groups from their guarantees: "From Plato to Hoover, from Milton to Hitler" they had "paraded under the banner of absolute liberty" (this might have been a surprise to Hitler, as well as to his opponents), while in fact they were concerned not with liberty itself but with "specific ends, the attainment of which liberty could serve."

> Plato would give liberty to all but slaves; Milton,
> despite his stirring plea for liberty of speech in the
> "Areopagetica," introduced a reservation in the

case of "Popery"; Locke, Tom Paine, and the founders
of the American constitution professed freely their
love of liberty, the ideal, and their hatred of usurpa-
tion of liberty by the state, yet all of them wanted
liberty only for free economic enterprise, unlimited
use of private property, with the restraint of the
state. Professor Beard, in his *Economic Interpretation
of the Constitution,* has proved this beyond question.

This editorial continued a debate that had been going on
in other editorials and in letters to the editor. One student,
who signed his letter "One Who Would Rather Live," added
another argument for limiting the rights of fascists. Pointing
to Hitler's use of freedom of the press, speech, and assembly
in Weimar Germany, the writer declared that extension of
civil liberties to fascists was "suicide" because an uneducated
public could be won over more easily to a simple emotional
program than to a complex analysis of society. "A polite debate before an educated audience is one thing; harangues
before fickle mobs quite another." Replying to those who
challenged the Soviet Union on grounds of political oppression, the writer responded that while he did not see Russia
as Utopia, he had "seen enough of Russia's progress to make
up [his] mind without further debate on that score." Answering those who said that free expression of all views was necessary for people to weigh both sides, the student declared
that "debate without decision is stupidity, to put it mildly."[8]
The reference in this letter to "fickle mobs" and "ignorant
masses" sounds inappropriate from an apparent Marxist, but
the spectacle of public support for fascism in Europe raised
serious questions about trusting "the people" as a force for
social change and made the concept of an educated "vanguard" more acceptable and seemingly inevitable. Later, the
comparative reliability of a leftist elite was less obvious, as
the role of the leadership in the Soviet Union, in the Ameri-

can Communist party, and even in the student movement raised questions of the utility as well as the morality of control by a small group. In the thirties, however, the militants tended, with some justification, to take an apocalyptic view and to see war and fascism as imminent and therefore justifying drastic action.

Most of those who defended academic freedom for all groups attacked the *Spectator* position as inconsistent. Some critics challenged the editors' sincerity in defending freedom at all. To many observers the refusal of civil liberties to the Right seemed to contradict the paper's previous statements on academic freedom. This was partly caused by the omission of discussion of the relativity of freedom in previous statements, which had read as though the paper's editors regarded the Bill of Rights as an absolute. The most common reaction therefore was to ask the *Spectator* and the Communists, "How can you demand rights for yourselves and others who think as you do and at the same time demand suppression of those whose theories you oppose?"[9]

Opponents attacked the *Spectator* position on both moral and tactical grounds. By adopting the methods of fascism the editors were becoming like the enemy they fought; this, their opponents continued, would lose them support among those who were similarly opposed to fascism but who believed that suppression of freedom was as wrong on the left as on the right and who believed that such suppression should be censored, "whether in Germany or in Russia."[10] The inconsistency alienated support in the same way that moderates rejected the peace movement at Columbia because of the Anti-War Committee's support for the American League against War and Fascism, a Communist-dominated national antiwar organization, and tolerance of class war. Finally, by declaring the relativity of freedom, the leftists were providing a rationale and ammunition for those who wanted to suppress them. If academic freedom were restricted, the Left would be bound to lose.

Another student noted that if the editors did not believe in absolute freedom, they did seem to believe in absolute truth and that they possessed it. If this was the case, then they should be confident enough that their position would win others and they should have no need to suppress other ideas. Particularly in a university, he continued, the radicals should have more confidence that their fellow students could sift truth from falsehood and discount the lies of fascists.

> Liberty is not a weapon but an end in itself. Liberty
> is not being used to accomplish some purposes.
> It is the suppression of liberty which is being used.
> Again, I say that you are in no position to "grant"
> liberty to those who are "bent on oppressing mankind."
> It is suicide to give them a philosophical justifica-
> tion for their misuse of liberty. Rather we must fight
> for that interpretation of it which will not permit
> the powerful few to take advantage of the many.

The writer concluded: "I have thought long and hard over this attempt at a categorical refutation of your editorial, but want to say that I heartily agree that now is the time to make clear what we mean by Liberty."[11]

The debate was prophetic. Although it was possible to respond, as some supporters of the *Spectator*'s position did, that the Right needed no justification for repression and would clamp down when it could in any case, the radicals' arguments came back to haunt them. Before the decade was over, liberals were using the same instrumentalist arguments to restrict the rights of Communists and pacifists. The passage of the Smith Act in 1940, the first peacetime sedition law since 1798, and the expulsion of Elizabeth Gurley Flynn from the board of directors of the ACLU on the basis of her Communist party affiliation were the logical culmination of the instrumentalist view of civil liberties.[12] It was fitting that Baldwin should play a key role in the purge of the Civil

Liberties Union. In congressional investigations in the thirties and the postwar period leftist students experienced the results of their belief in the relativity of freedom. When antiradicalism and civil liberties came into conflict, it was the latter that went out the window.

In any case, in the thirties the issue of the limits of tolerance created a division that at some schools limited the success of the student peace movement. At Columbia, especially, the antagonism between Communists and moderates shortened the life of the antiwar coalition.

While some of the problems confronting efforts to create a united front were ideological, others involved personality and style. Much of the criticism of the student peace movement focused on the students' supposed emotionalism, extremism, and lack of decorum. Although the student strikes seem a mild form of protest, especially when many of them were approved by faculty and administrators, the use of a tactic that smacked of labor tactics aroused considerable hostility. Brushing off the proposed student strike of 1935, Columbia President Butler saw the tactic as futile and inappropriate: strikes were themselves "a form of war," he declared. In a letter to the preparations committee, Butler stated: "Mere emotional outbursts and declarations against war are quite futile, no matter what momentary satisfaction they may give to those who make these demonstrations. Experience proves that they will melt away like snow before the heated passions which the war spirit arouses when it once gets underway."[13]

The same kind of criticism was directed toward outdoor demonstrations, picketing, and any activity that took place "in the streets" instead of in a lecture hall. Students were accused of being unduly upset, of being in poor taste, and of being rude and boisterous.

Although some of this criticism was a cloak for disagreement with the objectives of the protests, much of it seems to reflect the fact that the activists were not conducting themselves like ladies and gentlemen. Since a major function of higher education was to transmit a code of behavior reflecting the values of the upper class, this seemed to be a threat to the stability of the university and the power of those who controlled it. The activists did not fit the stereotype of the well-behaved student, sowing his wild oats on the proper occasions but generally knowing his place. The response reflects a kind of fear similar to that of the Boston Brahmins confronted with nineteenth-century immigration. Standards were being lowered. The assimilation that had been so successful in accommodating some students from outside the alumni list was beginning to fail. Indeed, in some cases, the outsiders were winning over, subverting, and contaminating the children of the elite.

It was a class and ethnic phenomenon. Not restricted to criticism of radical students, it also, in many universities, led to an intensified quota system aimed primarily at Jewish students.[14] This conflict also brought a reaction against the behavior and style that students brought from working-class homes or adopted in imitation of the working class. While found on many campuses, this criticism of behavior and style was strongest at elite institutions, the bastions of civilized behavior. Harvard presents an example of the opposition that activists met from liberals as well as conservatives and the debate that occurred over the relative importance of issues and tactics. Like the debate over academic freedom, under whose guise it sometimes appeared, it reflected a real conflict of values and a division of opinion over the purpose of higher education.

Harvard was quite a different place from Columbia. In the 1934–35 school year, the total full-time enrollment in the university was 7,301, about half of whom were in the college. Although the university enrollment was about one-third that of Columbia, Harvard College had a thousand more students than Columbia College. Like Columbia, Harvard drew its students mostly from the surrounding area: over half (55 percent) were from New England, while another 24 percent were from the Middle Atlantic states. The remainder included 16 percent from the Midwest, 2 percent from the South, and 3 percent from the West. Of the total enrollment, 40 to 50 percent were from public high schools, the rest from private academies.[15] The surprisingly high percentage of public school graduates can be attributed to the contribution of the elite Boston Latin School, which provided the largest single group of incoming students.

Although Harvard students experienced some impact from the Depression, it was certainly less than elsewhere. The graduates of the college and the engineering school early in the decade were three times more successful at finding jobs than were students elsewhere. In October 1933, 38 percent of the class of 1932 were employed, compared to about 15 percent from other colleges.[16] Not surprisingly, then, despite the Depression Harvard maintained its enrollment. In fact, the college had its largest freshman class to date in 1932–33.[17]

A *Crimson* editorial in the fall of 1931 expressed concern that the school and its students suffered by being shut away from reality and noted that "the problems of strikes and the unemployed lose their poignancy when viewed from the vantage point of Harkins easy chairs." There was a striking discrepancy between the sheltered college and the world outside. Many undergraduates, "particularly those holding scholarships, . . . will find swift disillusionment when they learn that their earning capacity in the first years after graduation is insufficient to maintain the inflated standard of living to which they have now become accustomed. The Liberal Arts College, in teaching their sons to live, teach them too well."[18]

Reading about Harvard in the thirties, it is clear that the Depression was not a common experience for all Americans or for all students. In 1936 the *New York Herald-Tribune* conducted a poll of students on their attitudes toward Social Security. By a vote of 545 to 431, Harvard students joined their colleagues at Yale and Princeton in opposing old-age insurance. While the Columbia *Spectator* was attacking the New Deal as washed-out reformism, the *Crimson* editors applauded the results of the poll at Harvard as a victory for the American Way. At the same time, the editors congratulated the Harvard administration for its refusal to accept National Youth Administration (NYA) aid for students. The *Crimson* declared that acceptance would be "hardly conducive to academic freedom because a recipient of favors is invariably obliged to the donor." A University of Pennsylvania editorial described the Harvard position as "false pride."[19] It was more accurately an expression of pure class interest.

Harvard was not, of course, the monolith that it appeared to be. Along with religious and, to an extent, class variations, there was the usual split between residents and commuters and divisions among the residents which reflected the differing character of the houses.[20] Still, the image of the Harvard man did reflect some reality. For if the student body was diverse, the power structure was not. Clubs and houses maintained a social hierarchy that reflected the traditional elite. This was true at other colleges, where fraternities and sororities (or eating clubs in the case of Princeton) played a dominant role. They were consistently selective, exclusive, and discriminatory and organized the student bodies into significant subgroupings.[21] Because many of these institutions were self-perpetuating, they were largely immune to any real change and reflected a social order untouched by upheaval.

This was also true of the student paper. The Harvard *Crimson* presents a picture not of the total Harvard body but of the segment of it that could calmly assume its rightful place, first, on campus and, then, in society. The paper's former members included Franklin D. Roosevelt, who described his experience on the paper as "the most useful preparation I had in college for public service."[22]

Because each staff selected its successors, background and ideology were remarkably consistent during this period. Unlike the *Spectator*, where with a similar method of succession the editors and staff were predominantly Jewish, the Cambridge paper was an Anglo-Saxon preserve and might well have been titled the Harvard *WASP*; exceptions to English or German backgrounds among the paper's staff tended to prove the rule. Among the editors in 1935–36, for example, were David Rockefeller and Casper Weinberger. (The large editorial staff made possible the inclusion of an unusually large number of persons without being so large as to make the office meaningless as a sign of prestige.) Editorials reflected this makeup with phrases like "we, as Anglo-Saxons. . . ." This homogeneity was in accordance with the intent of the administration and alumni of Harvard. The quotas established in the twenties continued throughout the thirties. The *Crimson* did not write about these restrictions.

Indeed, in editorials opposing the idea of geographical quotas to ensure a more diverse geographical draw of students (and to limit the number of students from large urban areas), the *Crimson* declared that quotas interfered with "natural selection." "Darwin has shown conclusively that the struggle for existence is the cause of natural selection. Such should be the case in the colleges. . . . Natural selection contributes to the progress of education as well as to the improvement of the natural universe."[23] Like their mugwump grandfathers who crusaded for the civil service system, the editors placed their faith in the triumph of merit over circumstance. In life as in sports, the best man would win.

The *Crimson* carried on an ambivalent tradition, combining provincialism and internationalism, conservatism and liberalism, cynicism and idealism. Early in the decade the paper began giving international events the most complete coverage of any student newspaper. Coverage of national and local news, however, showed some peculiar lapses. An article about a ceremony honoring a famous Harvard legal scholar was headlined "Birthday of Justice Van Dyce is honored." It repeated that spelling in the article, and it was not until the next day that the famous Harvard legal scholar was revealed to be not Justice Van Dyce but Louis Brandeis.[24]

Throughout the decade the *Crimson* downplayed the role of students in political movements. Editorial response to student activism tended to be patronizing. Radicalism was not in tune with the *Crimson*'s desired image of humor and sophistication. Nor did it seem in tune with the editors' views of conditions in America. In January 1932 the editors saw youth's political interests being channeled into "model Leagues of Nations, model Congresses, model conferences," all of these "doubtless very pleasing intellectual exercises," but really useless. According to the editor, such conferences were handicapped by unrealistic idealism, the students' lack of "practical experience." An example was a recent congress in Buffalo where, an editorial noted, students expressed hope that the Kellogg Pact "might become reality." According to the *Crimson*, "It is this kind of idealism which stunts the political influence of the undergraduate when he becomes a citizen and blinds him to the difficulties of governing which even reason cannot pierce." The "prosaic nature" of American issues precluded the role of student as revolutionary in America, since there was no place for "gestures of defiance."[25]

The idea that the student was not yet a citizen was implicit in the common argument that students should leave politics to older people. This was coupled with the argument that colleges were a place for training and reflection, not action. As the *Crimson* expressed it, "College men . . . who are destined someday to take over the reins of government may use their undergraduate days for better advantage in sideline preparations on major problems than in front rank agitation on minor problems that becloud the day."[26]

This was not exactly the idea of disinterested scholarship. The assumption, a reasonable one at Harvard, was that education was a preparation for the power that would come naturally in the course of things, and for which there was no need to struggle. Here, then, is probably the major reason why radicalism found little support at elite institutions in the thirties.

Still, if students were best not involved in politics, the same did not hold for the student press. Although its positions were usually well to the right of the Columbia *Spectator* and the tone calm assurance rather than anger, the editors shared the assumption that the student press should comment freely on current events and mold student opinion rather than reflect it. (The *Crimson* preferred the word *thought* to *opinion*.)

In the fall of 1931 an editorial described the role of "the liberal college press." Liberalism was defined as "essentially a training in the ability to choose." The college paper, the editorial stated, was in a peculiarly independent position, especially as compared to the commercial press. "The college journal owes no debt to any class or institution, save to the university which supports it. Its financial debt is to the student body." The place of the press was in the world as well as in the college. "Its liberalism consists in the evolution of first principles behind collegiate structure, whether it be athletic, academic or social." The university was unique in its role of defender of liberal principles. "The luxury of liberalism . . . exists only in the university or among the idle rich. The outlaws cannot afford to be liberal; they must be radical."[27]

The history of the *Crimson* itself refutes an assumption of this liberalism. While the student press at Harvard seems to have been relatively uncensored in the thirties (except the humor magazine, which is another issue), the debt that it owed to the university was quite as binding as the debts that a commercial press owes to its advertisers. The very composition of the editorial staff ensured that "the ability to choose" would be meaningless in a world where few alternatives were taken seriously. Within its limitations, however, the *Crimson* did consistently defend the student press from administrative or faculty censorship.

Perhaps the *Crimson*'s form of liberalism can best be described in its position on the treatment of black students at the university. In an editorial condemning the refusal of the United States House of Representatives dining room to seat black students who were there with a congressman, the Harvard editor wrote: "That all men are created equal is untenable. But all are entitled to equal rights with attainments limited only by their own inherent qualities."[28]

Another brand of liberalism on campus took a more positive attitude toward student activism and gave birth to the student peace movement on campus. Eventually, the Liberal Club became more or less identical with the NSL, but early in the decade it was a diverse group offering an alternative to *Crimson* conservative liberalism. Officially, at least, it even maintained some of the rhetoric of more traditional liberalism. In the winter of 1934, when adopting a new constitution to prevent a takeover by the NSL, the club prefaced its program with a quote from Alfred North Whitehead: "A race preserves its vigor so long as it harbors a real contrast between what has been and what may be; and so long as it is nerved by the vigor of an adventure beyond the safeties of the past." They added "with active participation in the political and social movements of the time, and constant adventure in new thought."[29]

The members of the Liberal Club constituted a contrast to

their fellows at Harvard. The five officers were from five different states, none of them Massachusetts. Thomas Quinn, the president, was from East Warwick, Rhode Island; Vice-President Griffith B. Washburn, from New Jersey; Secretary Victor H. Kramer, from Cincinnati; and Treasurer George Clifton Edwards, Jr., from Dallas. Raymond Dennett, committeeman-at-large, was from Washington, D.C.

The differing definitions of liberalism and of the role of the student were paralleled by differing attitudes toward war and peace and the student antiwar movement. Unlike student papers that took the lead in organizing and promoting peace conferences and strikes, the Harvard paper adopted attitudes that ranged from humorous superciliousness to Red baiting. The tone varied according to the personality of the editor and the degree of provocation. Editorial comment on war and peace took two apparently contradictory directions, both of which resulted in acceptance of government policy, whatever it happened to be at the moment. According to the "realistic" critique, pacifist ideals were worthy but impossible of attainment. Commenting on Gandhi's warm welcome in Britain and the subsequent failure of the Round Table Conference, an editorial expressed doubt that independence would come to India anytime soon. Gandhi's tactics were bound to fail. "People are usually ready to accept an idea in theory long before they apply it in practise, and the principle of non-violence in particular is one for which men are not yet ready. History indicates that such messages must be sealed in blood before they are accepted. 'The fathers stone the prophets and the sons build their sepulchres.'"[30]

The acceptance of the inevitability of bloodshed was carried further by an editor in April 1934 who came close to the pre–Great War romantic attitude. He asserted that war was necessary because ideals were more important than life. Citing the American Revolution, the writer contradicted the pacifist claim that war never settled anything. "Fundamentally it is a question of which is more important: abstract ideals or human life." Life without ideals was meaningless, he stated, and continued:

> Do we live for the sake of living or because we
> in some way attempt to justify our existence? It appears
> that without the daily impulse of certain ideals
> and aims our lives would be drab and worthless.
> Individuals will fight to the bitter end for ideals they
> cherish and nations will continue to do so by any
> means they see fit. If Nazi Germany finds her ideals
> threatened by unsympathetic neighbors, she will
> not hesitate to defend them and her great fuhrer will
> see that she does.[31]

The editor drew a contrast between generations. Youth opposed war because it loved life for its own sake. "The old men . . . for them living for the sake of living has lost its value and only because of loyalty to some ideals do they press on toward a goal and wait patiently for their short span of life to end." In any case, the *Crimson* editor concluded that war could be fought for an ideal and that "a war between eastern and western civilization may easily be of this nature."

But if war abroad was permissible, war on campus was not. The same Harvard gentleman's code that placed athletics beyond politics also set firm rules on student political conduct. Hospitality, decorum, and good manners all forbade excesses of feeling or in tactics. The methods of street protests and mass demonstrations were not in keeping with Harvard traditions. As one young man put it in a letter to the *Crimson*, "The methods which obtain in Union Square fail sadly here. . . . A Washington Square harangue will always be met with a certain derision in the Yard; bad grammar will ever meet tutorial reprimand. . . . The progressive organization is, too, possessed of an unfortunate type of speaker . . . hardly felicitous of accent or manner. Until this group offers men a bit more representative of the student body as a whole, serious attention will surely be withheld."[32]

The clash between two styles, two sets of values, two worlds, can be shown in three episodes in which radical tactics aroused more comment than did the substance of their proposals. Armistice Day, 1933, is the first of these. The second involves antifacist protests centered on the *Karlsruhe* Affair and the Hanfstaengel controversy. Finally, the activity of the Michael Mullins Chowder and Marching Club in the antiwar strike in April 1934 indicates the degree to which criticism of tactics represented a more deep-seated clash.

Armistice Day, 1933, brought the first antiwar demonstration at Harvard. It also brought the Harvard-Army football game. The coincidence seemed to the Liberal Club, the NSL, and the SLID to present an opportunity to focus on militarism in American society. They planned to rally near the parade of the cadets and to distribute peace literature along the route to the stadium.[33] The plan aroused a storm of protest on the grounds that such a demonstration would be offensive to the visiting Army team and a breach of hospitality. Such "harrying of the guests" was not in good taste, the *Crimson* pointed out.[34]

Faced with internal dissent, the Liberal Club revoked its support for the demonstration, but the NSL and the SLID carried on. (The Liberal Club did continue its cooperation with plans for a pacifist rally on Boston Common that weekend in conjunction with other area college and peace organizations.)

President Conant then refused permission for a demonstration in the Yard that morning and suggested use of the steps of Widener Library between 9:00 and 9:30 or any other building during the day. The plan was then revised for a ral-

ly on the steps of Memorial Hall at noon. In announcing the
meeting, Edward M. David of the NSL and Lewis S. Feuer
of the SLID declared that the rally was not intended as an
insult to the cadets but rather as an occasion to raise an issue
in which they, the cadets, had some interest.[35]

Both the football game and the rally went off without any
great problems, but the controversy did reveal and add to
the antagonism between those who saw sports as beyond
politics and those who saw issues such as war as transcending
traditional good manners. At the rally, speakers from the
SLID, the NSL, and the Episcopal Seminary denounced war,
the Roosevelt administration, and the *Crimson*.

In the spring of 1934 militancy increased on the part of the
Left in general and in the student movement. Escalation in
both tactics and numbers brought an increasingly stern response from vigilante groups and official agencies. In May
1934 the German warship *Karlsruhe* came into Boston harbor. Its officers and cadets were treated as "guests of the
city." They were also invited to the Naval and Military Ball
at Harvard.[36]

Antifascists on campus and in the city were outraged at
this official reception of military representatives of the Nazi
state. A demonstration was organized in protest, and a crowd
of about a thousand, including protestors, spectators, and
hecklers, met in City Square in Charlestown. The police
proceeded to break up the gathering, beating people indis-
criminately and arresting twenty-one persons. These included three Harvard students, who with the others were photo-
graphed, fingerprinted, finally released on a one-hundred-
dollar bond, and charged with "inciting to riot." For others
bail was set at one thousand dollars and was raised by the
International Labor Defense (ILD) and a group of Harvard
faculty members.[37]

The demonstration, which had been sponsored by thirty
organizations, including Harvard's NSL, had been entirely

legal, and the police behavior stirred considerable criticism. While observing that "the activities of shouting 'Red' or other agitators who insist on making themselves obnoxious must be curtailed in the interest of good sense . . . since courtesy must be extended to the visiting ship," the *Crimson* condemned the police tactics as a violation of free speech. "Any nation espousing a belief in free speech will not submit to a subjugation of it under the tattoo of horses' hooves. The brutality and officiousness demonstrated yesterday are to be deplored."[38]

A student-faculty committee was formed to investigate police tactics and to defend the three students involved. It was composed of leftists and traditional liberals, but its report, which substantiated the misuse of police power, did not convince everyone. The *Crimson* changed its position and denied that the police had broken up the meeting without due cause. The editors' attitude toward the committee, which included representatives of a number of nonpolitical campus organizations, is indicated by a private demand by a representative of the paper that as a condition for the *Crimson's* support the committee include no Jews.[39]

The jury likewise found sixteen of the defendants guilty of inciting to riot. They were sentenced to six months in the house of corrections. Of these, one was a Harvard graduate student. Another student was fined one hundred dollars and given a six-month suspended sentence. Although all appealed, the convictions were ultimately upheld.[40] This response to "premature antifascism" could not have enhanced the students' belief in impartial justice or codes of gentlemanly behavior.

While liberals and moderates supported the demonstrators and opposed police violence, more direct antifascist activity was greeted with horror. Allen R. Philbrick, secretary of Harvard's NSL, was arrested while attempting to stuff bundles of anti-Hitler leaflets down the blowers of the German

warship. He was caught by a German sailor and turned over
to a United States Marine guard and then to the Boston police; after spending the night in jail, Philbrick was released
after questioning.[41]

Again, Harvard's sense of hospitality was offended. To attempt to propagandize United States cadets was bad enough;
to trespass against foreign visitors was intolerable. So at least
a vocal group, including the *Crimson*, believed. An "anti-
NSL club" was formed, composed mostly of ROTC men, to
"prevent further demonstrations" against the ship. An editorial, "Off the Track," declared that Philbrick's action was "not
only an act of discourtesy but lends the League [NSL] a
radical tinge." A letter to the editor from a student named
Nixon de Tarnowsky described the act as "despicable" and
expressed indignation that anyone should be "coarse enough
to stoop to an act insulting to guests on our shores. Common
decency and respect for the most elementary laws of courtesy should have restrained Philbrick from committing such an
ungentlemanly act which reflects not only on himself, but
the entire University as well."[42]

There were other antifascist protests that spring. The presence of Ernst Franz Hanfstaengel, an aide to Hitler and
graduate of the Harvard class of 1909, at the 1934 commencement exercises led to student disruption of the ceremony. The German press agent was invited by the chief
marshall to be an aide at the reunion and an official at the
exercises. He was welcomed both as an alumnus and as a
prominent foreign official. As two students said in a letter to
the *Crimson*: "He is a graduate of Harvard College, an educated man, and a world figure, and Harvard should be glad
to have him return for the commencement."[43]

Others were less proud to have a Nazi leader at their graduation. The NSL protested that his presence condoned the
acts of his government and gave him an opportunity to engage in propaganda. In the latter charge, at least, they were

quite correct. For while Hanfstaengel turned down the position at the reunion, he opened a new controversy by offering
a one-thousand-dollar gift for a scholarship for a student to
spend six months at any German university. Since the German government was conducting a public relations campaign
at the time to combat the negative publicity elicited by Hitler's internal policies, it is likely that the offer was not simply
that of a grateful alumnus.

Ultimately, after pressure from some alumni and students,
the Harvard Corporation turned down the offer. President
Conant explained in a letter to Hanfstaengel: "We are un-
willing to accept a gift from one who has been so closely
associated with the leadership of a political party which has
inflicted damage on the universities of Germany through
measures which have struck at the principles which we believe to be fundamental to universities throughout the
world."[44]

This position was opposed by the *Crimson*. "That political
theories should prevent a Harvard student from enjoying an
opportunity for research in one of the world's greatest cultural centers is most unfortunate, and scarcely in line with
the liberal tradition of which Harvard is pardonably proud."[45]
An earlier editorial urging that a Nazi official be given an
honorary degree had observed that "as long as [Germany]
keeps her experiments within her borders, it is no concern
of this or any other country."[46] At Columbia the *Spectator*
praised Conant's decision. In an editorial entitled "A Liberal
Who Takes a Stand," Wechsler suggested that President Butler should take note and compared the rejection with Butler's reception of German Ambassador Hans Luther and a
group of Italian students.[47]

In June 1934 students at Harvard took action against Hanfstaengel's participation in the commencement. As a result of
their protest seven persons were fined twenty dollars each
and sentenced to six months at hard labor in the Middlesex

House of Corrections. At Conant's request charges were dropped against two women who had chained themselves to benches and fences in the Yard and, as the *Crimson* reported, "temporarily secure from police intervention repeatedly interrupted Conant's speech with 'Down with Hanfstaengel.'"[48] The use of city police and city courts to handle the situation indicates the cooperation between the the university and the precinct house.

Opposition to radical tactics and demonstrations culminated in disruption of the antiwar strike in April 1934. There vigilantism wore the face of farce. Harvard's most notable contribution to the history of the antiwar movement of the thirties was a bizarre attack upon it by the Michael Mullins Chowder and Marching Club. Oddly enough, the group exhibited all the characteristics so deplored in the radicals: lack of courtesy, ungentlemanly behavior, poor taste, and intolerance of the rights of others, yet it found favor among those who attacked those qualities on the left.

Early in April 1934 the Harvard chapter of the NSL voted to join the national student strike against war scheduled for April 13. With the cooperation of the SLID the group planned a walkout from classes and a mass demonstration. In response, the Michael Mullins Chowder and Marching Club, a "long defunct organization," was revived with the intention of disrupting the meeting. On the day of the rally, the *Crimson* printed a front-page article about the group, which stated in part: "Incensed by the N.S.L.'s protesting against all future wars, a second organization in the college will today stage a second demonstration at the same time to agitate against future peace." The paper continued, "The feeling is running high against the steps taken by the Communist organizations, and many students seem eager to counteract the drive for peace by engaging in favor of war."[49]

The *New York Times* reported the ensuing riot. Hostile students threw eggs, oranges, lemons, onions, and grapefruit at the antiwar speakers, while the club paraded in Nazi uniforms and gave the Nazi salute. Students also interrupted the antiwar speakers by booing and blowing a bugle. The police finally cut off the supply of weapons in the kitchen of the Freshman Union and led the students out to the Yard, where traffic was disrupted for an hour. In contrast to the treatment of the commencement disrupters, no action was taken against any of the members of the club or the spectators.

Having promoted the disruption, the *Crimson* blamed the riot on the antiwar forces. It proved "the uselessness of emotional demonstrations to end war." Almost all students were opposed to war, it continued, but the question was how to prevent it. "Emotional appeals" were not the answer. The editorial proposed that "young men who are used for cannon fodder refuse to follow the martial music and stubbornly demand that differences among nations be settled in a more rational civilized manner." Antiwar organizations should avoid "marching around displaying placards or shouting anathemas against war, especially in such a conservative stronghold as Harvard."[50]

The same idea, that the antiwar, antifascist students took things too seriously, was expressed in an editorial in the *New York Herald Tribune*, which commented favorably on the actions of the Michael Mullins club. It was reprinted in the *Crimson*. According to the editors, "in the bitter seriousness of these [antiwar] young people lies their chief menace to the world." Germany would be better off, they said, if it had such groups as the Michael Mullins Chowder and Marching Club instead of their political youth. "So long as students see the dangers and absurdities alike in parades for peace and in the forceful militarization of the youth of a nation we need have little fear in this country of 'revolution' or 'Fascism.' Long life to the Michael Mullins Chowder and Marching Club."[51]

Not everyone agreed. The riot received wide publicity. Antiwar students on other campuses had been heckled and thrown at, but it appears that only the Harvard students had had the ingenuity to pose as Nazis. Noting the *Crimson*'s appeal to the antiwar movement to be rational and constructive, the *Spectator* observed that the Michael Mullins club must be very reasonable, since the *Crimson* had encouraged its efforts. "The Michael Mullins Chowder and Marching Club marches on rationally and constructively," it said. The *Daily Princetonian* also commented on events in Cambridge. Despite the "high quality of liberal thought" at Harvard, "there has nevertheless been a strong reactionary spirit there." The editorial noted earlier attacks on Harold Laski, the kidnapping of an NSL member, and the latest affair. "It is not the lackadaisical conservatism which so often shows itself at Princeton; it is active, intolerant, and reactionary." While the NSL did not always behave in the best possible way, the paper continued, it had a right to conduct meetings and to free speech. The reaction to it indicates "a resurgence of intolerance and bigotry. . . . It would be ironic if Harvard, claiming to spiritual descent from the revolutionary fathers, should turn out to be the intellectual seat of American fascism."[52]

If there was indeed a "resurgence of intolerance and bigotry," Harvard certainly had no monopoly on it. American collegiate life was based upon conformity to hierarchical structure and a code of behavior that enforced that structure. This was accompanied by the exclusion of some groups from the university altogether and by the use of internal institutions to control student behavior.

The American campus both reflected and perfected the intolerance and bigotry of American society. This included discrimination against blacks, Jews, Puerto Ricans, Mexicans, Italians, and, of course, women.[53] Racism was a constant principle; segregation was still firmly entrenched, even in

the North. In 1940, of the only 1.3 percent of the total population of blacks who had completed a four-year college
(compared to 5.4 percent of native whites), only 15 percent
had graduated from integrated institutions.[54]

The university's response to Jews was more flexible. They
were channeled into certain institutions and fields and admitted into others in limited numbers. As their percentage
of the total student enrollment increased, these restrictions
became more rigid, so that during the thirties anti-Semitism
on campuses reflected administrative policy.[55]

These practices applied to the faculty as well as to student
bodies. Until World War II, most major American universi-
ties and colleges were staffed almost entirely by old-stock
Protestants. At most institutions the faculty and administra-
tors shared common background, values, and class interests.
The exceptions seem indeed to prove the rule. Of Lionel
Trilling's appointment as instructor at Columbia in 1932,
Diana Trilling writes: "If it was [the] intention to test a Jew,
Lionel made a good gamble both in appearance and name.
Had his name been that of his maternal grandfather, Israel
Cohen, it is highly questionable whether the offer would
have been made."[56]

In 1936, Trilling was briefly dismissed from the Columbia
faculty on the grounds that he did not fit in because he was
"a Freudian, a Marxist, and a Jew." His Marxism was short
lived, and in the summer of 1939 he was appointed an assistant professor. His values proved to be as sound as his diction
(and his erudition); he became an eloquent defender of Culture, and of its institutions. In the thirties, however, Trilling's
position was tenuous and the virtue of institutions of higher
learning not so clear. Referring to his appointment as instructor, Trilling later observed that "for some time my career in the College was complicated by my being Jewish."
The ambivalence of the relationship cut both ways. Writing
of the experience of the thirties, Diana Trilling notes that "to

all Jews and maybe to most non-Jews, too, certainly in New York, the university had an authority not unlike that of the state: remote, virtually absolute."[57] It was rather a citadel to be conquered or captured than a shelter for liberal values or politics.

It is not surprising that the actions of radical or antiwar groups, which seemed to threaten the values and interests of the previously dominant groups, would meet with hostility from administrators and faculty, as well as from some students. It is true that at some schools administrators supported the peace movement and that at most places at least some of the faculty cooperated with and encouraged antiwar and antifascist students. They often played a key role, but they were a minority, usually junior faculty and instructors who had grievances of their own as a group and little power within the university.

In some cases administrators found themselves in conflict with the majority of the student body. This was most conspicuously true at the city colleges of New York, at Hunter and Brooklyn, and especially at City College. There the conflict had begun before World War I when the large numbers of Jewish students admitted to the colleges confronted administrators (and alumni) who longed for the return of the WASP majority and who perceived the new group as "lowering standards." In the twenties and thirties the students, and some of the instructors, differed in background, ideology, values, and humor from City College President Frederick B. Robinson and a large part of his faculty. In *Revolt on the Campus*, Wechsler gives a pertinent, if somewhat jaundiced, picture of the extended conflict.[58]

One incident may describe the distance between the president and the students. Against considerable student opposition, President Robinson held a reception for a group of Italian students traveling as official representatives of the Italian government. Wechsler described the results:

As the fascist students strode to the platform, a
chorus of hissing broke out in the audience, to
be followed by more vigorous exclamations when
Robinson rose to speak.

Less than two years before the President of City
College had been seized with uncontrollable fury. On
that occasion, he had used an umbrella; this time,
fortunately, he was unarmed. All that he could deliver
was a frantic expostulation, sonorously delivered:
"Guttersnipes. . . . Your conduct is worse than guttersnipes."

A few days later the campus blossomed with buttons proclaiming "I am a Guttersnipe." The administrative response
to the incident was to expel twenty-one students, disband
the student council, and conduct an investigation of student
publications.[59]

City College was not a place easily mistaken for an ivory
tower; its site belied its aspirations. It had lately been moved
uptown to 137th and Convent, and its traditional collegiate
architecture, turned inward from the street, did not hide the
view of the neighboring tenements. Memoirs of the period
describe the students trudging uphill from the IRT Seventh
Avenue subway stop and arguing politics in the cafeteria al-
coves. It was not exactly an island of serenity in a heartless
world.

Nor did the students fit the conventional middle-class
model. The university's influence was limited to the time
that the students spent there. Most worked in outside jobs
and lived away from the campus. Most of them, too, attended the evening or night school. In some ways the night
school was a separate institution, and the teaching was done
largely by instructors who were usually not much older than
the students.[60]

Student loyalty to old values and institutions could no

longer be assumed. Consequently, the administration and the state legislature devised other methods in an attempt to produce conformity. A classic example is the "pledge of loyalty" that students in the city colleges were required to sign upon entering. "As some small recognition of the gift of education which, in the American spirit of freedom and self-government, is now offered by the College of the City of New York" the student pledged allegiance to the Constitutions of the United States and the state of New York, to abide by the disciplinary codes of the school and the Board of Higher Education, and "to preserve all public property now or hereafter entrusted to my care and protect its value."[61]

There were other efforts to shape the students into the image of the conventional good student. A report of the Strayer Commision of the state legislature indicates as much about the goals and values of those in power as it does about the students.

The report first described the family and economic background of City College students. Almost 80 percent were Jewish or "of Jewish derivation." A large majority were first- or second-generation Americans; of freshmen entering in 1938 only 17 percent of the fathers and 22 percent of the mothers had been born in the United States. More than three-quarters of the students held outside jobs during summer vacation, and a large majority worked during the school year.

The report then cited what the school's personnel counselors considered to be the "social handicaps" of City College students. It is clear from the description of the students' "maladjustments" that the kind of student desired would be one much easier to deal with, one who would fit into traditional collegiate culture and into American society.

Our students are markedly lacking in social skills,
the ability to meet people and to get along with them.

> They frequently feel ill at ease in a social group and cannot engage in conversation in other than argumentative fashion.
>
> Our students are constantly being frustrated by financial difficulties, by their immaturity, by their social awkwardness, and by their lack of practical and social experience. Even their drive, persistence, and competitiveness, by offending others and especially employers, operates to frustrate them.
>
> They . . . lacked most the important opportunities possessed by students in residential colleges to acquire social poise and self-responsibility.
>
> Their record of high scholastic achievement in lower schools and the constant pressure placed on them by their parents to succeed scholastically, resulted inevitably in an over-emphasis on intellectual values to the detriment of other vital areas of personal development.[62]

In short, they were poor, smart, and obstreperous, hardly the image of the Harvard gentleman. Although the concern expressed is for the students, the fear seems to come from other interests. Psychology, as well as coercion, could be a weapon against nonconformity and radicalism.

Indeed, psychology became a new instrument of social control. Psychological tests began to play a larger role in college admissions. Following their development during World War I, IQ tests and "character tests" were adopted by such colleges as Columbia, Barnard, and New York University. They were a particularly sore point at Columbia, where Edward L. Thorndyke, a key figure in their development, taught in Teachers College.

Many observers attacked these tests as a way of hiding ethnic and racial discrimination behind the mask of science. An article in the *Nation*, "The Degradation of American Psychology," criticized their use. The author noted that "many complaints have been raised by Jewish, colored, and other 'undesirable' students that colleges are using the mental tests not only as a 'measure of personality' but as a method of discrimination against them."

Since some psychologists contended that the tests were not subject to environmental influences, they were increasingly used in the nation at large as a justification for nativist theories of a hierarchy based on intelligence. They became an "objective" way of defending the existing culture in the university, as well as in the nation.[63]

These techniques were perceived by some students as "fascist." In fact, they were conservative attempts to preserve the status quo in the university and in society. But if this exclusionism was hardly the same as fascism, it did constitute a threat to the student movement and pushed many of its members to the left. While much of the peace movement's impetus came from events abroad, it received additional impetus, and bitterness, from developments at home. The antiwar movement and antifascism met increasing opposition from right-wing and vigilante groups on campus as well as in the community.[64] If the students, and the Left, seem sometimes to have overreacted, it was in the context of violence abroad and at home.

A right-wing response was developing in the nation and on the campus. Much of the "vigilantism" and disruption of meetings may have been knee-jerk antiradicalism, although in some cases it appears to have been organized by campus authorities. But there were efforts to turn this to political purposes.

Most of the right-wing students were not profascist. Ideology was vague, but it was usually characterized by superpatriotism, not by admiration for other societies. The City College ROTC club paper, the *Lavender Cadet* sounds somewhat beleaguered and bewildered by the Young Communist League and its paper, *The Red Menace*.[65] On some campuses many of the right-wing students (rather than the merely conservative) were sympathetic to Germany, and many, especially at Harvard, were of German background. The anti-NSL club had opposed antifascist demonstrations because they might have "antagonized the German people against the United States."[66]

Some extreme right-wing organizations attempted to recruit students. The Black Legion, based in the Midwest, required members to "exert every possible means for the extermination of the anarchist communist, the Roman Hierarchy, and their abettors."[67]

More common was the creation of ad hoc groups on campus, often with the backing of conservative groups in the community. On some Ivy League campuses, in particular at the University of Pennsylvania, students formed chapters of the Liberty League, and at Penn the group initially had considerable membership, exceeding that of the leftist groups. Its reputation was damaged, however, when a newspaper article linked its financing to Irenee Du Pont of the munitions, General Motors, and chemicals family.[68]

Anti-Semitism, however, seems to have characterized and perhaps motivated much of the right-wing student activity. Because a substantial part of the Left and of the student movement was Jewish, antiradicalism and anti-Semitism often merged. Sometimes the sentiment was cloaked, sometimes overt. During student protests at Columbia over the firing of a leftist teacher, one of the counterprotesters gave a speech in front of the library in which he reportedly stated: "You American Jews are wondering why Hitler has permitted atrocities in Germany. You have the reason right here today. Agitation of this sort makes men of Hitler's sort." His comments were reported in the *New York World-Telegram* and in the *Spectator*.

In a letter to the editor of the student paper the speaker tried to set the record straight, saying that he had been misinterpreted and his words taken out of context: "In my six years at Columbia I have come to the conclusion that a certain element among the Hebrews has a marked propensity for making itself unpopular. One reason, I believe, is to be found in the undue activity of a considerable number of this race in agitation of the type that has been disrupting the campus during the past two years." He declared that it was well known that in time of economic troubles leaders looked for a scapegoat. That had been the case in czarist Russia and was behind Hitler's actions in Germany. "Who knows what the future has in store for the United States?" he concluded. "My words were not intended as a general criticism of all Hebrews—that would have been obviously absurd. Nor were my words to be taken as endorsing the atrocious and short-sighted policies of Adolph Hitler."[69] This was in the spring of 1933.

Anti-Semitism was a force on campus, both in administrative policy and in student and faculty attitudes. Like racism, it was a concern to many students in the antiwar movement and the Left. In 1935, Wechsler called anti-Semitism a key part of campus vigilantism.[70]

Although anti-Semitism was most formalized at elite institutions, it was present elsewhere as well. An editorial in the student newspaper at the University of Chicago noted the "militancy and reactionary trends of state colleges," where racial and religious lines were enforced in fraternities and sororities. It also cited the example of students discouraged from entering an English department with the hope of teaching unless they were Anglo-Saxons. After a student election in which all Jewish candidates for office were decisively defeated, campus leaders at the University of Wisconsin met to oppose the apparent "race prejudice." The University of Michigan *Daily* expressed disappointment and surprise that the campus at Madison, "supposedly the most liberal in the country," should be characterized by such bigotry.[71]

Still, the state schools should not be singled out. Implicit in much of the criticism of the NSL at schools like Harvard and the University of Pennsylvania was a criticism of the religious and ethnic background of its members. This was in spite of the fact that in most cases a majority of members of peace and leftist groups were not Jewish. A letter to the editor of the Harvard *Crimson* attacked the actions of Philbrick in the antifascist demonstrations and stated that the government "had gone too far" in allowing Communists and "other traitors" to "gnaw from within." He urged the university to expel Philbrick and all other known radicals. He declared: "The German Consul-General, cringing before the opposition of a noisy semitic minority has chosen to ignore yesterday's escapade, and the N.S.L. publicity seeker is free again. He should have been shipped over to Germany, where they know how to handle his breed, and sterilized as undesirable. Then perhaps there would be less Communist martyrs ready to follow his example."[72]

Having experienced some of its manifestations themselves, Jewish students had an additional reason to oppose fascism. Facing opposition from some, and apathy on the part of many other students, the antifascist movement turned to more drastic tactics. But the issue went beyond tactics or good manners to the heart of American nativism, as represented by the university and its traditions. In its own way the student movement was a struggle for a redefinition of America and Americanism. The students' attack on war, racism, and anti-Semitism was a repudiation of the existing collegiate culture and the hegemony of the ruling class.

Exposure to the vigilantism of fellow students and the brutality of police in handling labor strife led some students to look to dangers at home and to call for radical means to combat them. Eric Sevareid later wrote of the effect of police tactics during the Teamsters strike in Minneapolis: "Suddenly I knew, I understood in my bones and blood what Fascism was. I had learned that lesson in such a way that I could never forget it, and I had learned it in the precise area which is psychologically most removed from the troubles of Europe—in the heart of the Middle West. I went home as close to becoming a practising revolutionary as one of my non-combative instincts could ever get."[73]

Attitudes such as these were to shape the future course of the student movement. For a time the antifascist and antiwar movements ran together, and gave strength to each other. Such would not always be the case, but in 1934 and 1935 this made possible the creation of a strong student movement and of the great 1935 Student Strike against War.

Chapter 5

Students Strike against War

Between 1934 and 1936 the student peace movement grew in numbers and intensity. Antiwar feeling centered on two issues: munitions and militarism. In Congress, Senator Gerald Nye chaired a special investigation of the arms industry; Nye allowed the lobbyist of the Women's International League for Peace and Freedom to select the committee's chief investigator.[1] Student interest focused on the munitions hearings and on the place of compulsory military training on campus. ROTC and munitions became the two issues that provided unity among the antiwar forces. Marxists, liberals, and pacifists could organize and demonstrate around these; along with the Oxford Oath, they formed the basis of the peace programs of 1934 and 1935.

Throughout the spring of 1934 student newspapers across the country reported and commented on the revelations of the Nye Committee. The hearings reinforced the revisionist view of the world war as the product of economic competition and an armaments race. In Milwaukee and Michigan, in Cambridge and New York, students came to view profit making as the major cause of war. In response they supported proposals to nationalize the munitions industry and to set limits on corporate profits during war. At Ann Arbor, the *Michigan Daily* noted with approval an amendment to a naval appropriations bill that would limit to 18 percent the profit of builders in naval construction. Regretting that those opposed to construction itself as well as the profits had not been more successful, the editorial observed, "There is patently no reason why an expansion should line the pockets of ship and plane makers at the expense of the American people."[2]

An editorial reprinted from the *St. Louis Post-Dispatch* had "made clear the fact that greed for profit is one of the chief causes for the maintenance of expensive military systems." Another student editorial offered, "for those who still believe the World War was fought to make the world safe for democracy," figures cited at the hearings that compared the profits of four years of peace time to four years of war: U.S. Steel increased profits from $10 million to $239 million; DuPont increased from $6 million to $58 million; Bethlehem Steel and Atlas Powder Company had similar bonanzas. The editor of the *Daily* hoped that those figures would help to forge a negative answer to the question "Would youth give in so easily the next time someone handed them a flag and herded them across the sea to fight an imperialist war?"[3]

This sentiment was not confined to the Midwest. For once the *Spectator* and the *Crimson* were in agreement. Supporting the hearings, the Columbia paper cited, and the Harvard paper reprinted, an article in *Fortune*, "Arms and the Men: Prominent German, English, and American Manufacturers." When President Butler joined the outcry against the companies, the *Spectator* expressed the hope that this denunciation would "hasten the nationalization and government control of one of our many 'public utilities.'" A *Crimson* editorial urged controls on the international sale of war materials. Urging this not as a "cure-all" but as a necessary step,

the editorial declared that only enough should be produced
for a nation's defensive needs; "further production should be
regarded as a crime against civilization."[4]

Although a criticism of capitalism was implicit in the condemnation of war profits, the Left failed to broaden the
attack. The simplistic nature of the rhetoric and debate allowed people later to brush off the legitimate points and to
retreat from the recognition of economic interests as basic
to international war. Still, the issue did provide the student
movement with a unifying issue and a potentially radical critique of the American system.

Another unifying theme was opposition to compulsory military training and to the use of the schools for that purpose.
Expansion of military training in the public schools beginning in the 1880s had coincided with increasing jingoism and
the romanticizing of military values. (It had also coincided
with the development of collegiate culture based on the
system of sports and fraternities.) Disillusionment with the
Great War and with glorification of battle brought with it
reaction against the intrusion of the military into education.
Beginning in the twenties and throughout the early thirties
efforts were made to remove compulsory military training
from the high schools and colleges. The campaign was carried out by students on individual campuses and by the
peace movement in general, especially the CME. In the
thirties, ROTC became a major issue for the national student organizations and for the American Student Union.[5]

The results of all this activity were mixed. In 1926, with
the leadership of Felix Cohen, the editor of the *Campus*,
students at City College, won repeal of compulsory drill. In
this effort they had the support of the young editor's father,
Professor Morris R. Cohen, who shared the eastern European immigrant background of many of his students and saw
compulsory ROTC as a form of conscription. He later wrote,
"It seemed to me that conscription had thrown a pall over

European civilization and brought in train many hideous manifestations of nationalism and intolerance." Compulsory military training in the schools, "the seed-beds of American democracy," might have similar results.[6]

Other schools at least temporarily eliminated their requirements, and some dropped their units; others acquired units and made them compulsory. However, the agitation did call attention to broad issues of militarism in American society and the relationship between the schools and the military. Like the debate over the Oxford Oath, the ROTC controversy raised the question of the right of individual conscience versus the demands of the state.

The attack on ROTC was on two levels. Most of the opposition was to the compulsory aspect, and peace groups supported legislation aimed at making military training optional. But other protest aimed at eliminating all military training from the schools; underlying the opposition to compulsion was the assumption that ROTC was inherently undemocratic and authoritarian and contradictory to the aims of liberal education.

The action of individual resisters gave reality to the debate. In January 1934 seven students at Ohio State were suspended for refusal to participate in military training. At Minnesota a sophomore with sixteen credits of As and two of Bs was expelled for failure to attend a ROTC course. At UCLA that same semester, two students, Albert Hamilton and Aronzo Reynolds, requested exemption on religious grounds. This was refused; the Board of Regents declared that compulsory military training was "merely good physical exercise." The students were both Methodists, and Hamilton was the son and grandson of ministers. They based their refusal on the opposition of their church to killing. They asserted that military training was not exercise but a way of teaching young men to kill.[7]

The issue became one of religious freedom and rights of

conscience, and the students received support from many individual clergy and some of the churches. A Methodist church committee headed by Bishop James Baker hired a lawyer for the students. On this issue religious conviction became the heart of the peace movement's position and agitation.

The expulsions created controversy on campuses across the country. Antiwar and leftist organizations took up the cause, and the students involved spoke at colleges to explain their position and to win support. On December 3, 1934, however, in *Hamilton* v. *Regents of the University of California,* the Supreme Court ruled in favor of the Regents and denied that the requirement of military training violated the due process clause of the Constitution. In the decision the judges declared that "since the ROTC was part of the Armed Forces of the United States, it was the responsibility of Congress, not the courts, to provide exemptions."[8]

Legislation, specifically the Nye-Kvale Bill, thus became the focus of the anti-ROTC activity, and the peace movement at large and student groups turned to lobbying and applying public pressure on Congress. Both the NSL and the SLID adopted planks condemning compulsory military training and the expulsions and planned demonstrations against the Supreme Court ruling.

The Senate hearings on the Nye-Kvale Bill became a forum for attacks on the existence of ROTC in the schools. Students, teachers, and religious leaders spoke against both the element of compulsion and the connection of education with militarism. Although the hearings were supposed to be confined to the issue of voluntariness, George Edwards, speaking for the American Student Union, outlined the arguments against the whole idea.[9] According to Edwards, ROTC prepared students for the war through military propaganda, took away money from education, was "antidemocratic and anti-American," was "a center of class prejudice and reaction," and represented the whole system of "profit war."

For Edwards and the student union, as for many of the liberal educators and clergy, ROTC did represent the intrusion of war onto the campus and an effort to brainwash students into accepting military values and attitudes. The ROTC handbook instructions on how to kill and the definition of democracy as "mob rule" were often cited as examples of the potentially fascist indoctrination involved. While they probably exaggerated the influence of ROTC classes, there was some cause for concern. The War Department manual on citizenship did raise real questions about the content of military training and its compatibility with traditional democratic values.[10] The use of ROTC cadets as vigilantes seemed to show that the antidemocratic theory was put into practice.

Military training was also condemned for glorifying war and ignoring its reality. A handbill given to freshmen in the dorms at the University of Pennsylvania noted that in the classes and the parades, "there is no suggestion of muddy trenches, poison gases, mutilated bodies of fellow students."[11] The military balls and dress-up parades had no resemblance to the Western Front. The glamour and pageantry used to attract students to ROTC. added to the distrust of emotionalism and parades.

The role of women in promoting ROTC aroused particular criticism, most of it from men. Although there was a real basis for condemning "the exploitation of sex on the campus as a recruiting device," critics sometimes used the argument that women push men into battle. According to Robert Morss Lovett, a teacher at the University of Chicago, "When an officer of the United States Army praised a student corps and predicted its success because it had 'such a pretty honorary colonel', the degradation of the honor of the soldier was complete."[12]

Congressman Maury Maverick introduced legislation "to prohibit female citizens from wearing the insignia of male soldiers." As he explained in an article in the *Student Advo-*

cate, his purpose was to "stop this business of girls dressing up in fancy uniforms and prancing up and down the streets with ROTC units. . . . If the girls want to learn about war . . . they can do well by going into a hospital and scrubbing floors, and doing other menial tasks which they will have to do during a war."[13] (Women were, apparently, unfit for other than menial tasks.) Women were not, in those days, required or permitted to join ROTC and evidently few of these observers foresaw the role that women would play in the next war, serving in their own uniforms. In the meantime, however, women did participate in the campaign against military training in the schools.

The role of the churches and religious groups added strength to the peace movement. In addition, regional and national antiwar conferences gave students a sense of common interests and valuable contacts and organization. Gradually, the political fervor and ferment in the nation at large found its way onto the campus. All that remained was to find a dramatic means to mobilize it. For this, students looked off campus.

The thirties were a period of labor uprisings. Left-wing students, like the Left in general, looked to the labor movement as the major force for change. In March 1932 a bus load of eighty students from the New York City schools, Harvard, Smith, and the universities of Cincinnati and Tennessee left Columbia for a trip to Harlan County. Their proposed investigation of the living conditions of the miners never occurred. As they drove into Kentucky, they were stopped by local law officials and a mob and were forcibly escorted out of the state. The episode was, as Wechsler later observed, "a revelation which no text book ever carried. . . . The students had, as individuals, experienced memorable contact with the institutions of their land."[14]

Some students saw a connection between the struggles of labor and the antiwar movement. Marxists viewed the student antiwar activity as auxiliary to the strength of the working class. Students needed to realize their "common bond" with "the factory worker, mill hand, white collar slave. . . . Before a united American student opposition and a united opposition on the part of the wage earning classes no banker, imperialist, or demagogue will dare to embroil the country into any war."[15]

The union struggles inspired some students to militancy of their own and offered tactics and vocabulary (and songs) for their campaign. Mass demonstrations and marches offered students an opportunity to participate in a movement for social change, to be actively involved rather than passively attending a lecture or conference.

The adoption of the Strike against War as the major form of demonstration thus offered both practical and ideological advantages. It was visible and active. It connected the student movement with the movement of the workers. By the use of a tactic that was used with increasing effect by labor, the peace movement was identified with a military and successful national force.

In the eyes of some students, especially the Socialists, the strike also served as a "dress rehearsal for war." It was still the hope of part of the Left that if another war threatened, the workers would refuse to participate and would forestall war through a general strike. Students would join in that refusal. Much of the discussion of the April demonstration was of its use as an illustration of what would happen at the outbreak of the next war. The student strike was aimed, then, not at the schools but against war itself and the system that produced war. Responding to criticism of the strike as a tactic, Wechsler declared in a front-page editorial on April 13, 1934, the day of the first strike, that the walkout of classes would be "the most dramatic, effective, unmistakable testimony of our strength" and the best way to send the antiwar message "into the chambers of finance and the smoke-filled rooms of government."[16] It would make the country wake up and take notice.

And indeed it did. On the appointed day, demonstrations, like spring flowers, burst out on campuses all across the eastern seaboard. Winter was over, and the students were coming back to life. At Smith College the students planted white crosses on the campus as a reminder of those killed in the Great War, and of those who might be killed in the next. At Vassar, President Henry McCracken, trustees, faculty, and three hundred students marched through the streets of Poughkeepsie. It was the school's first public demonstration since 1917. "In that year students marched for war. Today they marched for peace," noted the *New York Times*. Norman Thomas spoke to a peaceful assembly at Yale, and at Williams the students listened to the college's president, Harry A. Garfield, and Carl Rogers, of the class of 1934.[17]

There were other demonstrations. At Syracuse, where the rally was aimed primarily at ROTC, several hundred students listened to speeches against imperialist war. The strike was not observed in every case. At Wellesley, "because the administration and faculty are so much in sympathy with the peace movement," a mass meeting was held after classes.

Activities were not restricted to the East Coast. At the University of Chicago students participated in a peace parade, a symposium, and a two-day antiwar conference. As part of the activities, William Randolph Hearst was burned in effigy.[18]

Still, most of the participation was in the East. Of the twenty-five thousand students estimated to have taken part, fifteen thousand were in New York City. There the strike was largest and most controversial, though the only actual disturbance was at City College. At New York University fifteen hundred students heard speakers including philosopher Sidney Hook. At Hunter, where President Eugene

Colligan attempted to prevent the demonstration, three hundred women met to condemn war and the school's administration. In Brooklyn a combined demonstration of students from Brooklyn College, Seth Low Junior College, and Long Island University attracted large support and left the classrooms of Brooklyn College "virtually empty."[19]

The largest single demonstration was at Columbia, where the university, sensibly, had dismissed classes. Wechsler presided at a rally attended by perhaps two thousand students. Among the faculty speakers was Reinhold Niebuhr of Union Theological Seminary. Students at the law and medical schools had their own meetings, while radical students went off campus to picket the German, Austrian, and Japanese consulates, the offices of the National Civic Federation, and the home of J. P. Morgan. Five hundred students attended a counterdemonstration convened by Eugene S. Daniell, Jr., who had previously been convicted of placing tear-gas bombs in the New York Stock Exchange and who was currently accusing the antiwar demonstrators of being communists. His rally featured the singing of the "Star Spangled Banner."[20]

In some places the strike aroused a strong reaction. Student vigilantes, college authorities, and city police responded with anger and apples, arrests and expulsions. The antiwar forces were accused of using "warlike tactics" to oppose war and of tending to antagonize rather than attract people to the peace movement.[21]

The attention that strike attracted was in itself a mark of its success. The protest stimulated a debate in letters to the editor of the *New York Times,* including a defense of the strike by the president of the New Jersey Youth Federation and an attack upon it by General James C. Harboard, who found the strike "discreditable." The *New York World Telegram* congratulated the students on their activities; it was fitting that those who would have to fight a war, should it come, should join in opposition. Other newspapers played up the violence and horseplay, but the *World Telegram* saw the movement as serious and deserving of respect, "a challenge to reactionary educators, munitions makers, politicians."[22]

Most important, perhaps, the strike was a sign to students on campuses across the nation that the antiwar movement was alive and growing. At schools where there was no strike, other forms of activity expressed student concern with the same issues. After the strike, student papers discussed it, and groups began to organize on inactive campuses. The national publicity provided the movement with a means to bring in students who were isolated from the main centers of activism.

During the rest of the spring of 1934, students on the more active campuses maintained their involvement through antifascist, May Day, and antijingoist demonstrations. International events of the summer served to deepen concern about an impending conflict. Teachers who had gone abroad brought back ominous reports. Clyde R. Mills, director of the Bureau of Educational Services at Columbia's Teachers College, reported after a tour of Europe that most European observers expected war to break out within five years, adding that the only thing delaying it was the "recent understanding between France and Russia."[23]

In the fall the students returned to campus, and a new round of organizing began. The second United States Congress against War and Fascism met in Chicago in September, where some moves were made toward unity on the left. But the most important events occurred on individual campuses, where new antiwar coalitions grew up, usually focused around Armistice Day demonstrations.

At the University of Pennsylvania plans were undertaken for a November meeting. In late October an executive committee of a new peace league was created consisting of ten members representing campus groups: Avukah, Newman Club, the Student Association, the Jewish Students Association, the *Daily Pennsylvanian*, and the *Bennett News*, the paper of the women's college. This was especially important at Penn, since previous demonstrations had been largely the work of the NSL, which, on a conservative campus, had been isolated and ineffectual. The new coalition did not hold together permanently, but the religious groups (with the exception of the Newman Club, which soon withdrew) added substantial support to the peace movement there.[24]

While these and similar developments were going on at various colleges, changes were occurring on the left. The American Youth Congress, formed in August 1934, became the first manifestation of the popular front in the youth movement. It was to become one of the sponsoring groups of the next April peace strike. The hard line of the Communist party had been softening throughout late 1933 and 1934, and this began to be reflected in its youth groups. Indeed, to an extent these groups anticipated the change. At the same time, some of the young Socialists in the Young People's Socialist League (YPSL) and in the SLID had been moving leftward. As Hal Draper, a member of YPSL in the thirties who became an ally of the Free Speech Movement at Berkeley in the sixties, has observed, by April 1935 "the political orbits of the Socialist and Communist students were at a perigee." Their paths "were crossing each other as they went in opposite directions."[25] For the moment, therefore, cooperation was possible.

In January 1935 a world congress met again in Brussels, sponsored by the International Student Committee against War and Facism.[26] Five hundred delegates from thirty-one nations heard reports on conditions in individual countries. Ten students from the United States participated. The political makeup of the group was heavily Marxist, and more Communist than Socialist. The American students came back from the conference with an increased sense of urgency and of the need to form strong student opposition to war and facism. Throughout the winter organizing continued.

On April 12, 1935, a cold rain fell on much of the country, covering the Ohio River Valley and the Great Lakes region, and extending from the Carolinas northward to New England. Across the nation, up to 175,000 students left their classes in a strike against war. Placards mingled with umbrellas as students listened to speakers and marched in the rain. Under a variety of banners they suggested to the country that they were neither fair-weather radicals nor merely sunshine pacifists. At large universities and small "cow colleges," at religious schools and technical institutions, students joined in the first truly national student protest.[27]

At some schools the day brought convocations or indoor meetings sponsored by the administration. At others, classes were officially canceled. In some cases conflict between radicals and moderates resulted in competing meetings. Nevertheless, some form of participation occurred in at least 150 institutions, and in all sections of the country.

Again, the greatest support was in New York City, where the sponsors estimated that thirty thousand students were involved. At Columbia the strike moved indoors to the university gymnasium. There the students attacked war "vociferously but not barbarously" and listened to Baldwin, Wechsler (at his last major demonstration before graduating), Ellspeth Davies, of the class of 1936, of the Barnard Peace Council, and Niebuhr (still a pacifist), as well as representatives of the groups and colleges that had endorsed the strike: Julliard School of Music, Union Theological Seminary, Jewish Theological Seminary, Teachers College, and the NSL and SLID. Loud applause greeted John Stafford Cripps of the British University Labour Forum as he urged the solidarity of world student bodies. The gathering was not entirely unified itself: the reading of the Oxford Oath brought a mixture of cheers and boos, and banners declaring "life is short enough" were answered by the rather brief unfurling of a swastika.[28]

Two thousand struck at New York University, and in Brooklyn once again the students of Brooklyn College, Seth Low Junior College, and Long Island University joined for a peaceful and nearly universal observance of the strike. At City College, where the dean had forbidden the gathering the previous year and the police had come on campus to break it up, the student council conducted the strike with the dean's approval (obtained when President Robinson was on a trip to California). Voting on resolutions there resulted in 1,544 students supporting the Oxford Oath and 186 rejecting it; 1,694 condemning the Hamilton decision of the Supreme Court and 53 defending it; and 1,393 voting for the firing of President Robinson and 237 for his retention.[29]

While administrative pressures had eased temporarily for the City College men, conditions had worsened for their sisters at Hunter. There, President Colligan forced the peace movement off campus. Prior to the strike he had disbanded the peace council and suspended three students for their antiwar activities. When a group of students went to his office to protest the suspensions, he suspended three of the delegation. In order to prevent the appearance of unwanted speakers at Hunter, Colligan stationed police on the campus. The police were apparently members of the Alien Radical Squad of the City Police Department. In spite of, or perhaps because of, this administrative behavior, twenty-two hundred Hunter women met for a peace demonstration at a midtown hall.[30]

There was also rain in Cambridge. This time, however, the speakers at Harvard did not face a barrage of vegetables, and the strike was largely peaceful. The same was not the case at MIT. Despite support from the school paper and some other organizations, as well as the NSL and SLID chapters, the 500 students at the rally were nearly matched by 350 hostile onlookers, and students in ROTC uniforms attempted to break up the meeting.

A week before the strike a group had obtained a set of keys to the dormitory rooms and had proceeded to beat up the two antiwar leaders, one a member of the NSL and the other a member of the SLID and chairman of the Boston Strike Committee. In the process they shaved the head of the former and, after partially shaving the other, cut a swastika in the remaining hair. The college authorities made no effort to find out who was responsible; the president of MIT confined himself to a warning against further violence.

That radicalism should have even penetrated that bastion of the corporate structure is an indication of both the seriousness of the Depression and of the strength of the student movement. In any case, MIT, along with Boston University, Emerson, and other Boston colleges, added to the strength of that city's antiwar forces and the success of the student strike.

Activities throughout the rest of New England indicate the variety of responses of individual schools and groups of students. More than in other sections administrators and faculty either endorsed the strike and participated in it as a unit or held their own school-sponsored convocations. This was the case at Bennington, Brown, and Wesleyan. At others peace meetings were substituted for the strike. The women's colleges, in particular, showed support for the antiwar activities. New England was also an area in which religious groups were important, and the movement drew on old tradition of opposition to war.

Next to New York, Philadelphia was probably the city with greatest participation, and the strike's composition reflected an uneasy alliance of groups whose sole point of agreement was that imperialist war was hell. The presence of the Quaker colleges added a pacifist force that was sometimes missing in New York and on campuses dominated by Marxists or conventional liberals. The NSL and the SLID had initiated the student movement in Philadelphia and dominated it through 1934. This was especially true at Temple and the University of Pennsylvania. By early 1935, however, pacifism had penetrated the Main Line, and the suburban colleges began to stir.

In February, representatives from twenty-three colleges and peace organizations met at a conference at Haverford College. They were welcomed by the college's president.[31] The featured speaker was Norman Thomas. In addition, Dean Helen Taft Manning of Bryn Mawr spoke on the Quaker approach to peace, Frederick J. Libby of the National Council for the Prevention of War discussed the economic aspects of peace, and Dorothy Detzer of the WILPF analyzed the Nye Committee hearings. The conference provided an opportunity for the pacifists and latent pacifists to organize and to prepare a program for the April demonstrations. The result was that both the demonstration in downtown Philadelphia and those on individual campuses reflected a true, if temporary, union of radical, liberal, and pacifist forces, which had the ability to mobilize a large number of their less ideological colleagues.

As the *Philadelphia Bulletin* noted with some surprise on April 12, "an army of Philadelphia youth, with school books instead of muskets, today wrote their generation's protest against war."[32] At both Temple and Penn classes were officially canceled, and at both, Thomas spoke to large crowds. Two hundred students listened in the rain outside Mitten Hall on the Broad Street campus as he attacked profits and nationalism and called for more "guts," "color," and organization in the fight against war. After the Socialist leader drove on to Princeton for his next rally, thirteen hundred students met downtown at an all-city rally at Rayburn Plaza. The speakers were students from Temple, the University of

Pennsylvania, Haverford, Bryn Mawr, and William Penn High School.

Despite the weather the mood was militant, as the students swore together not to fight in any war that the government might conduct. Banners and placards indicated the diverse makeup of the crowd. "Down with Imperialist War" and "War Breeds Fascism" mingled with "Worship Jesus, Not Mars," "Disarm Now," and "War Is Un-Christian." The omnipresent "Scholarships, Not Battleships" was joined by "Education, Not Armaments." The real fear underlying the demonstration was expressed in two slogans that no one there could have quarreled with: "No More War to End War" and "1914 Again?"[33]

The strike was successful because it had wide support among students and faculty at area schools. In contrast to the situation in New York some of the Philadelphia high schools officially participated (though others took strong measures against a walkout). In a sense this broad support was possible because of the minimal ideological content of the rallies. The common sentiment that drew the students together was expressed by an editorial in the *Bennett News*, endorsing the demonstration at the University of Pennsylvania. In a front-page editorial the women's paper urged students to join the fight for peace: "As the people who will be most affected in the next war we owe it to ourselves to fight and fight hard. Let us fight as hard for our lives as the few will fight for their millions. And let us use their methods. Let us be militant, let us use propaganda, and above all, let us be heard."[34]

Washington, D.C., was another center of activity. At American University, Jeanette Rankin addressed the student body, while at George Washington University, in spite of the opposition of and some trickery by the administration, nearly a thousand students struck. At Wilson Teachers College four hundred students attended an administration-sponsored meeting. Perhaps most significant was the protest at Howard. Continuing the tradition of opposition to military training begun in the twenties, six hundred students marched around campus, after being denied the use of the school's facilities. The administration's caution was not entirely unjustified. Under the rather fearful view of the federal government and racist southern congressmen, Howard had become a center of black scholarship and activism. The faculty, especially in the social sciences and in the law school, were turning the school away from its role as the educator of a black elite and into a force for change. The students, too, were attracted by this activism and sympathetic to the Left. As a historian at Howard later noted, the role of the Communists in the Scottsboro case and the apparent absence of racism in the Soviet Union led some students to active opposition to war and fascism and to an unwillingness to engage in criticism of communism.[35]

One result of this activism was a series of investigations of Howard by congressional committees and federal agencies, including the Department of the Interior. This investigation included a wiretap on the phone of Howard President Mordecai Johnson, apparently with the knowledge of Interior Secretary Harold Ickes.[36] Later, a witness before the Dies Committee (the predecessor of the House Un-American Activities Committee) complained that Ickes had ignored the results of this investigation and evidence that Johnson had praised Russian communism. A black congressman from Illinois urged a study of Communist influence in Negro universities. Clearly, the activism of some black students and faculty, and their association (however exaggerated) with the Left, was striking some nerves. The antiwar activity at Howard, and at a number of other black colleges, including Morgan in Maryland, Morehouse in Georgia, and Fisk in Tennessee, indicated that, to some extent, the movement was successful in crossing racial barriers.

The participation of schools in the South represented another breakthrough. In 1934 there had been no strikes in that part of the country, although there were peace organizations on some campuses, notably Southern Methodist University in Dallas, where a small but stubborn group promoted the Oxford Oath to the consternation of local flag wavers. One of the campus pacifists, George Edwards, went on to Harvard to do battle with the Michael Mullins Chowder and Marching Club and then to become head of the American Student Union.

By 1935 activity had spread to other southern schools, including Texas Christian, Southwestern, where a joint meeting drew an estimated fifteen hundred students, and State Teachers College at Murfreesboro, Tennessee, where ninety students protested. The peace movement was especially strong in North Carolina; Duke could boast a pacifist cadre, and a demonstration at Chapel Hill received the approval and encouragement of President Frank Graham.

In the Great Lakes region and the Midwest participation was substantial. In Ohio it was the small, often religious schools that showed the most interest—colleges like Oberlin, Fenn, Muskingum, Antioch, and Wittenberg. On the other hand, while there was a fair amount of support at Ohio University, the strike supporters themselves claimed only four hundred (at most) at Ohio State. On another Big Ten campus opposition was overt. A large group led by a number of ROTC cadets broke up the antiwar meeting at Michigan State and threw several students into the river. The situation was more peaceful at Ann Arbor, where two meetings were held: a strike a eleven o'clock sponsored by the NSL and a faculty-student meeting in the late afternoon.

Chicago again saw much activity, but it was Wisconsin and Minnesota that indicated the persistence of progressive feelings on state campuses. At Madison the strike was controversial, but successful. The conservatives in the campus peace movement had attempted to persuade President Glen Frank to hold an official convocation to avoid the strike, but he refused. The *Daily Cardinal* opposed the strike because of the leadership of the NSL: the editors may also have been irritated at being outmaneuvered by the radicals. Nevertheless, between one thousand and two thousand students attended the rally, and many took the Oxford Oath.[37]

Eastern colleges had no monopoly on antiwar sentiment or on an economic interpretation of the world war. Throughout the early thirties, student editors of the Milwaukee State Teachers College paper, the *Echo Weekly,* took positions against ROTC and armaments and in favor of student freedom of expression. With the support of President Frank Baker antiwar feeling was especially strong. This was indicated not only in the paper and student polls but in the selection of antiwar plays by the school's dramatics club and the frequency of antiwar themes in the student literary magazine.

Still, the radicalism was muted, though a traditional socialism was implicit in much of the discussion and activity. It remained for the campus NSL to support overt demonstrations and, in particular, to organize the strike. In 1934 the *Echo,* in an editorial endorsing the elimination of compulsory ROTC, noted the demonstrations on eastern campuses.[38] By the next April the school was ready for its own.

In an effort to involve as many students as possible in planning the program the planning committee circulated the proposed platform and requested students to indicate what points they were most in agreement with.[39] An emphasis on democratic planning and decision making was particularly strong at the college; the influence of progressive education was reflected both in course content and in the running of the school. The peace groups on campus had wide support and encountered little overt hostility. The absence of a Big Ten football team, a ROTC unit, and an entrenched fraternity system (those Greek organizations that did exist often supported peace activities) meant that the school was without the most obvious or organized sources of reaction—or distraction. It was possible for the sports editor of the paper to be on the planning committee with members of the NSL.

On the day of the strike 650 students gathered at eleven o'clock in the morning to listen to speakers including President Baker, representatives of the strike committee and the local branch of the WILPF, and J. Martin Klotsche of the school's history department. Baker described pacifism as necessary for the preservation of civilization:

> We will be charged with lack of patriotism. My answer
> is that it is my patriotism that makes me a pacifist,
> that I love the democracy established by the Declara-
> tion of Independence, and today we see a world in
> which democracy trembles in the balance. We will be
> called cowards, and we will be challenged to be
> "he-men" and prepare to fight and kill for our country.
> I say that war must be banished from civilized soci-
> ety if democratic civilization and culture are to be per-
> petuated.

Baker added that to be peaceful, people did not need to be "super-human"—"We need only to stop being savages."[40]

The tone of the meeting was more pacifist than Marxist, though many of the proposals were mildly socialist. These included the nationalization of the munitions industry, elimination of war profits, and complete disarmament. Speakers urged the use of the social sciences in the schools to teach the causes of wars, and they urged the elimination of those causes, including the economic conditions that could lead the unemployed to prefer the battlefield to the breadline. The antipathy of youth to armed conflict was represented by the reading of Mark Twain's "War Prayer," and Isabel

King of the class of 1937 declared that the national strike was just a dress rehearsal for what would happen if war were declared.

Meanwhile, downtown at the University of Wisconsin extension, 240 students crowded into a hall and another 200 were turned away. At the same time, 500 students at West Allis High School in an industrial suburb of Milwaukee walked out of classes and assembled in the school's football stadium, where they were addressed by student speakers. There was also a walkout at Milwaukee Vocational, where the director had urged students to fast instead of striking.

The strike in Milwaukee was remarkably successful and left in its wake improved organization and increased support for the peace movement. As the Young Communist League, district 18, noted, with only slight hyperbole, the students had shown "a sense of responsibility and an aptitude for organization that had dumbfounded the authorities."[41] In addition to hatred of war the movement drew upon deep-rooted democratic feelings and the real concern of people to control decisions that directly affected their lives. Responding to an American Legionnaire's assertion that his definition of Americanism was the Preamble to the Constitution, a student asked, "Who is to determine what is best for the general welfare? . . . The decision, to be consonant with democracy, cannot be left to one group."[42] However contradictory or unsophisticated the ideas of the student movement, its existence was in itself proof of the determination of its members that public policy, and foreign policy in particular, should not be left to the control of an economic elite or to the dictates of politicians and statesmen hiding behind the screens of national security. In the Midwest the movement seems to have tapped the old populist tradition, which gave the movement there its own character.

The University of Minnesota provided further evidence of this. There, in spite of the administration's opposition, a large rally took place, which included an address by the state's governor. Floyd B. Olson was the bearer of the state's radical traditions and a man who "hated the stuffed shirts of the university as much as he hated them anywhere."[43] The governor was the particular hero of the campus "Jacobin" group, which included Eric Sevareid and Richard Scammon, and they all enjoyed the embarrassment of the university president, who had refused the use of the school's auditorium and who, from his office overlooking the rally on the building's steps, could hear every word of the governor's speech.

Sevareid, Scammon, and their colleagues cooperated with the campus Communists, but looked on them with some disdain; their opposition drew on the eclectic traditions of midwestern reform. Though they made economics the basis of their analysis, they tended toward pragmatism. "Philosophically socialists," Farmer-Labor in state politics, and for Roosevelt in national politics, they embodied many of the liberal-leftist ideas of the time.

Their ideas on war and peace reflected the strong revulsion against the world war. As Sevareid later wrote, "Of all the instruments designed to uphold the existing order, I think we most hated the military establishment." With their allies, the Jacobin group carried on a successful campaign to make ROTC optional, and they incorporated the Oxford Oath into their antiwar platform. Their attitude was summed up in a speech by one of the group before the large crowd at the 1935 strike. Lee Loevinger "smacked palm upon fist and shouted, 'And next time, when they come and tell us we must invade the land of some other innocent and misguided people to "defend our wives and sweethearts" we know what we will do—we shall defend them by preserving our lives, by staying at home with them. We will not listen to the scream for slaughter.'"[44]

This sense of war's futility and of betrayal by politicians bound together students across the country. It gave a common program and common rhetoric to midwestern populists and eastern radicals, religious pacifists and New Deal Democrats. It was reflected in the lining of the walks of the University of Kansas with white crosses "in memory of the tragic betrayal of 1917"[45] and by the appearance for the first time of large rallies on the West Coast.

Student activity at UCLA and Berkeley was certainly linked with the presence of the militant Left in San Francisco and other parts of the state. Students were caught up in the industrial welfare and class conflict of the longshoreman's strike in 1934, but they were also concerned with asserting their own rights to political activity against an administration determined to keep the lid on student radicalism.

Following controversy over the activities of members of the NSL on the UCLA campus, lines began to be drawn between fraternity members and engineering students, who provided members for antiradical vigilantism, and the moderate and liberal students, who rallied to support the suspended NSL members. At Berkeley a student rights association was formed to obtain and defend freedom of speech and the right of all student groups to meet on campus and in opposition to "vigilante groups and every form of violence."[46]

The issue of student rights unified otherwise diverse groups. The NSL, the SLID, and the students rights group joined together to oppose a bill introduced into the state legislature to "prevent the formation of student organizations for the purpose of resisting or interfering with the management of educational institutions by the governing authorities."[47] Anti-Semitism at UCLA and the hiring of students as informers by the American Legion aroused other students and increased political activity on campus.[48] These all generated support for the April strike.

At UCLA on the day of the strike three burning crosses appeared on the campus, and some handbills were passed out calling for students to "unite and drive off the menace of Communism," but the peace meeting was carried out peacefully. At Berkeley, President Robert G. Sproul posted the regulation against mass meetings, but made no effort to enforce it. He issued a statement noting that he had not given permission for the meeting, but "neither had permission been granted to break it up." He warned students that they could cut class with the usual penalties, but might neither interfere with the work of the university nor disturb its peace, either as "strikers" or as "vigilantes." Despite the opposition of the student newspaper and the student association thirty-five hundred students met on city property outside Sather Gate.[49]

Like that of the year before, the student strike of 1935 brought a mixed response across the nation. Hamilton Fish, the American Legion, and the *Chicago Tribune* were appalled. Fish, a right-wing congressman from New York, was particularly concerned with the role of "crackpot professors." He warned, "Our younger generation, sent to college by fathers who made their money under the capitalistic system, are taught by pink intellectuals that our system is wrong." And he suggested that "if the alien communists do not like our country, . . . all they have to do is go back home." It was all the fault of Protestant ministers, who were urging students "not to defend their country, our homes and our flag from invasion from a foreign power."[50]

More serious reactions occurred at the Columbia College of Physicians and Surgeons and at the University of Michigan: six students at the former and four at the latter were expelled for their part in the strike. At Columbia, the president of the New York Board of Aldermen refused to attend commencement in protest against the dismissal of the students without a hearing. President Alexander Ruthven at Michigan showed more tactical sense than his colleague at Columbia. He waited until summer and the demobilization of the activists to notify the antiwar leaders of their dismissal.[51]

The student organizers were jubilant at the support that

the strike received, but were quick to note the need for continued action and cooperation to combat just this kind of reaction. They realized that support was hardly unanimous and that many who did participate were not fully conscious of its meaning. As Wechsler observed, "To believe that 175,000 who joined from coast to coast were declaring their hostility to the existing order is a grave delusion, [but] they were manifesting their opposition to one palpable procedure of that order—imperialist war." This opposition came from all parts of the country and from all segments of the student population. There was, it appeared, a need for an organization that could draw upon this broad support, that had no ties to any adult organization, and that displayed no political exclusiveness.[52]

Though there continued to be opposition to the founding of such a group, that opposition could not long hold. The trends of student politics, and of events in Europe, were leading to the creation of the American Student Union.

Chapter 6

Marxism, Progressivism, and
the American Student Union

As 1935 ended, 450 delegates from approximately two hundred schools met in Columbus, Ohio, to determine the future of the student movement. There, a coalition of Socialists, Communists, and liberals created the American Student Union (ASU). The creation of the ASU and its subsequent history reflect the influences of Marxism, progressive education, and religion on students of the thirties and on their opposition to war.

Organizationally, Marxism had the greatest impact. The formation of the union was the result of negotiations between the NSL and the SLID, as the United Front gave way to a Popular Front. Many of the Socialists entered the union with reluctance, and their skepticism was proved prophetic before the new organization was two years old.

In the meantime, however, the ASU was received with enthusiasm on many campuses; it grew to be proportionately the largest and most influential such organization in American student history, achieving a peak membership of around twenty thousand and conducting strikes in 1936 and 1937 that doubled the numbers of the 1935 strike.[1] For three years it was the key unit of student antiwar activity, and its successes and failures parallel the growth and collapse of the student movement itself.

The steps leading to the creation of the ASU reveal the interplay of campus developments with international events and left-wing politics. The success of the 1935 strike had indicated that a substantial number of students were receptive to antiwar organization. Events of the summer and fall of 1935, including the Italian invasion of Ethiopia, made the mobilization of that support even more urgent. Still, it was clear, even to the most fervent NSL or SLID partisan, that neither organization had been able to make inroads into basically moderate student bodies. As the NSL journal, the *Student Review,* noted in calling for the creation of a broad "nonpartisan" group, the combined membership of the two leftist organizations in 1935 was no more than eight thousand.[2]

It was also clear that the organization would have to be based upon a few generally agreed upon positions which could attract the widest possible support. As the secretary of the NSL observed, although some students would work with Marxists in antiwar coalitions, a permanent national organization would have to be clearly distinguishable from the SLID-NSL United Front. Only a group with no connection to a political party could attract students who had steered clear of Red-tinted organizations.[3]

To an extent, this was an unrealistic hope. Although non-Marxists were in the majority at the founding convention and shared in power both nationally and on the campuses, the role of the Left was obvious and duly noted. On some campuses broad support was achieved, but in most places membership was not for the squeamish or for those who preferred their politics in a more somber hue. (Even when the ASU made the change to New Dealism and collective security, some critics of the students, like Martin Dies, saw in the patriotic bunting only the red.)

In practice, however, the real conflict was not between liberals and Marxists but between left-wing Socialists and the rightward-moving Communists. Indeed the suspicion of the YPSL members that a popular front with the Communists would prove to be a paper tiger (or a stuffed bear) was the main obstacle to amalgamation. They were afraid that the Young Communists would come to dominate the organization, and that their concern for peace would be subordinate to their concern for the security of the Soviet Union. That concern could destroy the union's effectiveness as a student organization.

The Young Communists' enthusiasm for union received official sanction at the Communist Party World Congress in August 1935. In response to increased fascist aggressiveness, the congress declared that collaboration with progressive bourgeois forces was not only permissible but imperative. This happily coincided with the inclinations of many Young Communist League members and NSL members, whose own experiences on campus had convinced them of the need for allies.

In mid 1935, the Communists' cajoling of the Socialists in the United Front gave way to a new call for unity not only among radicals but with all antiwar and antifascist students. After the April strike, the NSL submitted a proposal to the national executive committee of the SLID. Members of both groups met to work out a plan for union.[4] There were serious disagreements on both sides on the relationship between students and the labor movement and on issues of war and peace. The most important difference involved the best means of avoiding war. The creation of the ASU was primarily the result of successful cooperation on this issue, yet there lay the source of eventual conflict. The very policy that led the Communists toward cooperation was also leading them in the direction of support for military preparedness and collective security. For the time being, however, the Oxford Oath won out as the basis of the student union peace plank. As the *Student Outlook* noted, "In spite of the position of some communists to the contrary, after prolonged discussion the N.S.L. gave assurance that it will 'refuse to support any war which the government of the United States might conduct' and with no reservations whatever."[5]

The ratification at the convention brought into existence an organization that had more than the usual amount of talent. The first president was George Edwards of SLID, and the two co-editors of the new journal were Joseph Lash and James Wechsler. Their selection was for political balance, but a longtime collaboration ensued (and Lash shortly became a Communist). Celeste Strack came east from Berkeley as a representative of the NSL, and Molly Yard, from Swarthmore, represented the SLID.

The ASU began consciously to form a new kind of student community, both nationally and on individual campuses. As Lash noted, political activity was not enough. The ASU needed to develop cultural activities, including dance, art, music, literary, and philosophical groups. . . . We must set about creating new symbols of loyalty to replace the old ones." The ASU was to be to its members what labor unions have been to many organizers: home, school, and family. Joseph Starobin, an early leader of the NSL and later foreign editor of the *Daily Worker*, has noted that the Communist party played a similar role for many of its members.[6]

Irving Howe, a young Socialist and student at the City College of New York in the thirties, has described "the Movement" as his "home and passion," "a school in both politics and life."[7] It provided a sense of belonging and meaning, and its Marxist perspective gave him a way of looking at the world that was in tune with his own experiences. Given the clear failures of capitalism and the threats of war, young people required no great leap of faith to adopt Marxist analysis. It made sense and gave people a way of under-

standing what was happening around them. Further, as
Howe notes, Marxism involved "a profoundly dramatic view
of human experience."[8] It provided a sense both of history
and of the future and guaranteed a role in its shaping.

The old order was breaking down, in the world and in the
university, and those students who had no stake in that order could see freedom and their own futures in the destruction of hierarchy and the breaking down of the old barriers.
In England, middle-class and upper-class youth rejected
what they perceived as a decaying society and welcomed the
chance to participate in creating a new world. John Cornford, a young Communist at Cambridge, wrote:

> Time present is a cataract whose force
> Breaks down the banks even at its source
> And history forming in our hand's
> Not plasticine but roaring sands,
> Yet we must swing it to its final course. . . .
> We are the future. The last fight let us face.[9]

Marxism provided the sense of a "final conflict" (or, as
Jessica Mitford took it, "a fine old conflict") within grasp.[10]
The previous generation fought a "war to end all wars."
Students in the thirties sought to combine peace with revo-
lution.

Socialism for some young people was an inheritance, part
of a world in which they already lived. Alfred Kazin has
written of being a young radical in New York that he was
a socialist as many Americans were Christian; it was part
of his environment, not a conscious choice.[11] But for others
radicalism did require a break with their upbringing and
represented conflict, not continuity. Stirred by the team-
ster's strike, Eric Sevareid declared to his father that if it
was revolution then "maybe we'd better make the most of
it." His father was shaken, and as Sevareid later wrote, "I

had not understood that to some people like my father the institutions of public order, no matter what kind of social system they reinforced, were endowed with a religious sanctity."[12] Muriel Rukeyser, an editor of the *Student Review,* wrote in the mid-thirties: "We focus on our times, destroying you, fathers in the long ground: you have given strange birth to us who turn against you in our blood needing to move in our integrity, accomplices of life in revolution."[13]

Student activists and other leftists lived political lives that broke down barriers between the individual and the group, work and play, school and society. Just as the Great War had intruded into the private lives of another generation, public events of the thirties defined the lives of the young Marxists of that period. Sometimes the balance broke: the political crushed the personal; other conflicts were subsumed in class conflict. But the initial effect was to make connections and to open up the future. Some of this hope was to be short-lived. The Marxism of many students was also short-lived, but it left its mark. Howe writes of the movement: "For most it was an experience both liberating and crippling, beautiful and ugly."[14] Reaction to, or against, Marxism would shape attitudes toward the next generation of young radicals.

Another movement breaking down the walls between school and society was progressive education. It, too, was influential in shaping the student movement. In the classroom students encountered both its theory and practice. In turn, many of the participants in the student antiwar movement went into education and furthered the progressive education movement in the schools. The idea that schools could play a part in creating a new social order had strong appeal to students who wanted to participate in that process.

Throughout the decade the Left debated the role of schools and education in bringing about social change. Believing in the primacy of the working class in efforts to overthrow capitalism, Marxists tended to downplay the role of educators and intellectuals. The Communist party, especially in the early thirties, emphasized its own educational programs and pointed out the control of education by the ruling class and its role in preserving the status quo. As party leader Earl Browder noted in an article in the January 1935 issue of the progressive educational journal *Social Frontier,* "Bankers and lawyers make up about 95% of all controlling boards in the educational system and it is utopian to expect to change the situation fundamentally until bankers and lawyers are in general expelled from seats of power."[15]

What was true of the public schools was also true of colleges and universities. Studies of the boards of trustees testified to the domination of higher education by business interests. In *Revolt on the Campus,* Wechsler cited the position of the trustees as representatives of business at the top of the academic hierarchy. Upton Sinclair in *The Goose Step* and Thorstein Veblen in *The Higher Learning in America* had described the function that colleges played in the economic hierarchy. Progressive educators like William Kirkpatrick showed how the values of the ruling class permeated institutions of higher learning. Events of the thirties, including the imposition of loyalty oaths for teachers and the firing of dissidents, strengthened the picture of the schools as captives and agents of the status quo.[16]

Nonetheless, some educators and students argued that the schools could be instruments of social change. At a minimum they were one battlefront in the revolution; at a maximum the schools could be a major agent in fomenting change and constructing a new society. According to one writer the question was not "Dare the schools build a new social order?" but "Dare Education fail to contribute to a new social order already under way?"[17] Others, less optimistic, thought that educators and students could at least struggle against the efforts of reactionaries to dominate the schools more completely. According to Browder they could do this by making alliances with progressive forces outside the schools. A writer in the *Communist* in 1937 noted the contradiction between the ruling class's desire to keep the masses ignorant and its need for literate workers. The Left could call for democratic control of school administrations and the inclusion of students on school boards. Schools could be one arena of struggle.

The Communist party largely confined itself to organizing teachers as workers and to its own educational activities. They opposed the idea of trying to impose a postrevolutionary cultural revolution on a prerevolutionary structure. In practice, Communist teachers separated their political activity from their classroom teaching. It was left to non-Communist radicals and educators to carry their ideas into the classroom and into educational reform.[18]

While acknowledging the relationship between the colleges and capitalism, students like Wechsler and others retained some faith in the power of education. This faith was shared by many in the peace movement, including students and educators active in opposing militarism in the schools. Education could be useful in two ways: eliminating favorable attitudes toward war and presenting positive instruction in the cases of war. Student activists (and others in the peace movement) therefore opposed military education in the schools and proposed instead courses on war and peace. The Committee on Militarism in Education, composed of progressive educators and old progressives—Jane Addams, John Dewey, Carrie Chapman Catt, and Norman Thomas—sought both to defend schools from outside forces and to use them to their own ends.[19]

There was an inevitable contradiction in efforts to protect academic freedom and to use the schools as an instrument for collective purposes. Eventually, many of the same educators who sought to use the schools for peace sought to turn them into schools for good citizenship during the war.

In the thirties, however, the struggle was often to protect such freedom as existed within the schools and to promote the rights of students and teachers. Consequently, the battle against loyalty oaths for teachers and students and against censorship of the student press and political activity on campus was important in defining the role of education in the student peace movement.

In contrast to a later generation of students, those in the thirties had a largely positive attitude toward colleges and universities. They were critical of some of the uses to which education had been put and of the relationship between the university and the government during World War I, and they were critical of specific university administrators. The *Student Advocate* ran a series of articles entitled "Academic Napoleons," for example, President Ruthven of the University of Michigan.[20] But in general students still saw education as a means of both personal and social betterment.

This was especially true of course of students at teachers colleges or in education programs. At many schools there was a clear relationship between students in education and in peace activities. At Temple University, for example, a high percentage of ASU members were in education, and ASU members were on the staff of the *New Horizons*, the journal of Temple's secondary education association. It was also clear at Milwaukee State Teachers College that issues of peace and education were closely related. It was a rare teachers college, however small or remote, that did not have at least some antiwar activity during the thirties.

In turn, ASU chapters at some schools, such as Temple and Bryn Mawr, concerned themselves with educational issues. They opposed for both economic and ideological reasons tendencies toward educational retrenchment. Regarding efforts to cut back teaching staffs, one student noted, "The final resting place of all good teachers is the Department of Public Assistance." Another student described as fascist efforts to cut back on college enrollment and declared that education was the enemy of the "entrenched minority" and that efforts "to convert high schools into vocational schools, eliminate general education and prepare students for their 'proper' place on the factory beltline" would "stultify American life."[21]

Other students condemned the separation of college from the outside world and of education from daily life. The content of education should reflect the problems of society, they said. The faculty should not isolate themselves in an ivory tower. One student wrote this, entitled "Lines to a Professor":

> I sought to be a wonder in men's eyes.
> Flanked by the merits of a Ph.D.,
> I sought the field where greatest learning lies
> And prayed the young would come and learn of me.
> The molecule would be my single art—
> One branch of science in a special way—
> And through the years I kept my soul apart,
> And taught my students molecules each day.

Just this, while the world went on "and war cries rang, and souls were hungry still" and "the unemployed marched daily on to hell."[22] In ten years the relation of science to society would be displayed more vividly and another generation of students would confront their teachers with the question of an intellectual's responsibility for the product of his research.

Peace education was one issue that could unite students from various schools and factions. Students demanded, and sometimes received, specific courses on the causes of war and methods of peacemaking. An article in the *Catholic Educational Review* discussed peace and the college curriculum. A student at Marquette urged students to unite to prevent war and emphasized the need for education for peace.[23]

Concern with education derived in part from fear of propaganda. Explanations of World War I stressed ideological factors as well as economic. Writers emphasized the effect of private and public propaganda in stirring up war fever and the possibility that if war began once again, emotions were bound to be played upon, allowing the government to suppress civil liberties and destroy opposition. Education was essential to aid people in sifting truth from falsehood and to enable reason to overcome emotion. In addition, students boycotted militaristic films and condemned the Hearst newsreels as propaganda for war. Still, students were not overly optimistic about the possibility of combating war propaganda and emotional appeals. They knew that appeals to "national security" and "national defense" were strong. Realizing the power of propaganda, they used their own and tried to give peace some of the emotional appeal of war.

Implicit in the emphasis on propaganda and education was a belief in "the will to peace," that somehow the people could refuse to go to war. It was a rejection of determinism. For many in the peace movement, support for proposals like the Ludlow Referendum, which called for a popular vote before war could be declared, indicated their belief that the people were less likely than political or economic elites to favor war and that public opinion could and should play a major role in foreign policy. A general will to peace could prevent "a warlike attitude on the part of the government. . . . For governments draw their sanction from the consent of the governed."[24]

An educated public needed freedom of information and discussion. If truth and reason were to bring about peace, openness was essential. For students freedom of press and of discussion were goals that needed to be not only defended but achieved. They also had reason to fear that another war would destroy the gains that had been made. On many campuses freedom of assembly and from administrative or faculty censorship of student papers were the issues that crystalized student sentiment.

Freedom for the student press was a major issue. Richard Neuberger, later a senator from Oregon, described his experiences as student editor at the University of Oregon. He maintained that the paper was hampered by pressure from administrative officials, alumni, fraternities, and local business interests. A survey that Neuberger made of college newspapers showed that restrictions were nearly universal, the papers at Columbia and Chicago being notable exceptions. Issues that tended to arouse pressure or censorship included criticism of professionalism in "amateur" athletics, "condemnation of campus social inequalities and snobbery," "digs at militarism and fascist tendencies," and generally "any liberal tendency."[25] The City College of New York *Campus* was frequently in trouble with the administration and hampered by "alumni editors."

Students in the peace movement also defended the rights of teachers, both in higher education and in the secondary and elementary schools. The issue was sometimes personal: they intended to become teachers themselves. It also involved their right to information and to teachers who were unhampered by governmental and private pressure or prohibition. Some students also knew that if restrictions could be placed on teachers, they would be placed more formally on students. This was especially true of loyalty oaths.

Following World War I, the antiradical hysteria had culminated in the demand for loyalty oaths by teachers and other public employees. In the mid-thirties this campaign revived with demands that teachers sign or swear that they would be faithful to state and federal governments and uphold the constitution. Such acts in Massachusetts and New

York provoked opposition (but still went into effect). The Ives Act was passed by the New York state legislature in August 1934; it required an oath from every teacher in all public and private tax-exempt educational institutions throughout the state. Although many who did not like it felt it was not a serious matter, opponents (including George Counts of Teachers College) saw it as discriminatory against teachers because it singled them out and implied their disloyalty.

In response, a group of educators, including Counts and Morris R. Cohen, of City College, signed a teachers' "Pledge of Pupils," declaring teachers' highest loyalty to be "the promotion of the health, material well being, cultural growth, and happiness of the children in our charge." They also declared their intent to "do our share in protecting the school children from the horrors of war by opposing war propaganda and war preparation, especially in the school."[26]

In turn, students in the movement made opposition to loyalty oaths part of their program, and students protested the firing of teachers for their political views. This interest in education was especially strong in women's colleges, and so was the peace movement. The role of women in the student movement illustrates the degree of conflict and contradiction in collegiate culture and higher education in the thirties and the conflicts and contradictions of women's role in the Left and in society.

In many ways women in coeducational schools and in women's colleges reacted to the same experiences and influences that moved men. Certainly the news from abroad, the memory of the world war, and the impact of the Depression influenced all students. Although women were spared the need to compete on the playing field and to prepare to join "old boy" clubs, they were subject to definitions of proper feminine campus behavior. Even in women's colleges, or, perhaps, increasingly at women's colleges, the idea of education as a means toward developing (or acquiring) so-

cial graces and getting a husband served to keep the educated woman in "her place." The elite women's colleges also
practiced the same discrimination in admissions that their
male cohorts practiced. Bryn Mawr, for example, in addition
to the usual request for the applicant's religious affiliation,
also asked for the names and birth places of the candidate's
four grandparents. In 1936, 6 percent of the students were of
Jewish background. At other "Seven Sisters" schools Jewish
enrollment varied from 2 percent of the student body at Mt.
Holyoke to 12 percent at Wellesley. While other factors were
involved (including the greater willingness of non-well-to-
do parents to send their sons, rather than their daughters,
to expensive schools), the figures clearly reflect a desire on
the part of the schools for homogeneity and the increasingly
important role of the women's colleges in providing suitable
wives for the upper class.[27]

For women's colleges, and the women's movement, in the
thirties were pulled in two directions, toward apparently
irreconcilable goals: the old goal of providing an education
equal to and modeled on the best men's colleges, and the
newer goal of perpetuating a unique women's culture based
on women's traditions. In addition, women students confronted a society in which feminism seemed out of sync.

Women lost ground in the thirties because they were confronted by a society in economic collapse. The belief that
women's place was in the home grew, strengthened by government discrimination against working women, especially
married women. Professional women suffered in many ways.
Already confined to a few traditionally female occupations,
like nursing and teaching, they lost ground even in those
areas, and in many cases married schoolteachers were fired.
At the same time the percentage of women on college faculties decreased, from 32.5 percent to 26.5 percent (a decline
that was to continue for the next two decades).[28] Faced with
an intractable economy and social norms hostile to career

women, many college women looked in another direction and rejected some of their predecessors' goals.

At some institutions this freed students to occupy themselves with political affairs. At Bryn Mawr, for example, a student editor urged the importance of being politically informed, "assuming that the members [of ASU] will be active to varying degrees in committee and club work after graduation."[29] The Bryn Mawr students also drew upon a feminist legacy. Although their own activities rarely related to specifically women's issues, many students did look to the past and to contemporary politically active women. This was true of other women's colleges as well. In many ways, the peace movement was the child of the earlier women's movement.

Deploring apathy at Bryn Mawr, a student editor in 1935 noted the role that previous alumnae had played in the suffrage movement and their disappointment at their successors' failure to take an interest in politics. In an editorial on war a student noted that "there is naturally no one more opposed to war than an intelligent and far seeing woman must be." Bryn Mawr and the other colleges often had women speakers for their peace programs, including Emily Green Balch of the WILPF, Dr. Alice Hamilton, then on the Health Committee of the League of Nations, and Vera Brittain, the British pacifist and feminist and author of *Testament of Youth*.[30]

The students at women's colleges did inherit a legacy of activism and of fears of sexual subversion. In the twenties, Calvin Coolidge had written that women's colleges were hotbeds of radicalism. This was echoed in the thirties, along with warnings of Communist seduction and racial extinction. Veterans of the women's movement on the faculties continued to influence a new generation, but their relationship to the young women was ambiguous. On the one hand, their conscious feminism sometimes seemed strident and out of date. On the other, their socialism seemed to lack the urgency of the thirties radicalism. Describing a new generation at Wellesley, Vida Scudder wrote in 1937: "Alack and alas, I share the common lot. For the younger generation views me and my contemporaries as back numbers. It turns away, this ardent youth, from the old time socialist movement; it presses into the communist ranks. . . . They feel . . . towards the whole radicalism of the last century, either contemptuous pity or angry distaste. I am chagrined, I am amused, I am sad."[31]

For the most part their radicalism did not deal with feminist issues. Vassar students protested loyalty oaths, supported the Republicans in Spain, and opposed war and fascism. Some students at Smith "supported the labor movement, marched to protest the Spanish Civil War, Fascism, and Mussolini's invasion of Ethiopia and flirted with Socialism and Communism." As one alumna of the class of 1937 recalled thirty-five years later, "We were concerned about the big problems, about peace and poverty, but changing our lives just didn't occur to us."[32] Politics was taken personally, but personal lives were not yet seen as political.

Students, however, did have some consciousness of feminist issues. This seems to have been most true at coeducational institutions, where women were exposed to hostility and discrimination. Responding to comments in the men's paper at the University of Pennsylvania, a female student suggested that "some of you boys might learn a great deal on the subject of women . . . if you read Virginia Woolfe, *A Room of One's Own,* . . . and Mary R. Beard, *On Understanding Women.*"[33]

Student Left groups, like the Left in general, did maintain at least theoretical interest in the woman question and made some efforts at sexual equality; for example, two women were among the four officers of the ASU. One of these was Molly Yard. The daughter of Methodist missionaries and a graduate of Swarthmore, she looked to Eleanor Roosevelt and Mary Fox of the SLID as examples of politically active women. Although there was not much consciousness of feminism as an issue in the student movement at that time, she was aware of discrimination against women. Her mother had desperately wanted to go to college and had been denied the opportunity by her father, who had said that college "was no place for a girl." Some leftist students were conscious of the effect of fascism on women's position in society. An editorial in the *Spectator* in April 1934 noted the abolition of coeducation in Germany and the elimination of women's rights. Women's role was to raise soldiers for the state. "The women of Germany are to devote themselves exclusively to raising Nazi cannon fodder. They are to be the mothers of a new generation of soldiers who must die for the mad schemes of fascist militarism."[34]

New Deal liberalism and Popular Front leftism had less interest in feminism. An article in *School and Society* in 1936 noted approvingly the segregation of women's CCC camps from men's and sexual division of labor within those camps. "The regimen of these sister CCC camps will in no way resemble male CCC camps, since girls cannot very well be sent into the woods to chop down trees." Perhaps reflecting the effort to popularize the ASU, the *Student Advocate* included an article in 1936 entitled "The Zest to Nest: Man-Hunt at Vassar."[35]

Although the arguments on behalf of women's role in the peace movement were sometimes based on a kind of biological determinism, students were sometimes presented with a more insidious view of women's relationship to war. In 1934, Dr. C. P. Obendorf stood in front of an audience of Barnard College women and informed them that women's "instinctive desire for security and protection" was behind the present-day drive toward war. "You may talk about women's desire for world peace, but it is true, nevertheless, that every woman wants security, and if there is to be a war she wants her husband or sweetheart to enlist, so that she may be assured of that security."[36]

In fact, many women students had a strong drive for peace and devoted to the antiwar movement the passion that a previous generation had given to suffrage. Some of this is explained in the influence of an Englishwoman who represented both feminism and pacifism. Vera Brittain was a reminder of the catastrophe of the Great War and of its personal impact on women. In her autobiography, *Testament of Youth,* and her lectures on campus, she carried the message of war as the primary evil and of human responsibility for avoiding that evil. Speaking at Bryn Mawr on the writer's obligation, she described the function of the writer "to tell the truth about war; to act as an interpreter between groups: nation and nation, capital and labor, old and young; and to present a constructive picture of a new civilization."[37]

In her memoirs of World War I, Brittain described not only the losses of lovers and brothers but the increasing burden placed upon women by their parents as "the middle aged generation, having irrevocably yielded up its sons, began to lean with increasing weight upon its daughters. Thus the desperate choice between incompatible claims—by which women of my generation, with their carefully trained consciences, have always been tormented"—increased. The war brought women suffrage but at a price. With a bitter irony, "the spectacular pageant of the woman's movement, vital and colorful with adventure, with initiative, with sacrificial emotion, crept to its quiet, unadvertised triumph in the deepest night of war time depression."[38] She wrote of England, but surely the timing was inauspicious for American women as well.

Students responded to the poignancy of a generation's lost hopes. Writing of her prewar hopes of May, Brittain declared, "The question is answered now—not only for me but for all my generation. We never have recaptured that mood, and we never shall." Perhaps the new youth could do better:

> But slowly towards the verge the dim sky clears
> For nobler men may yet redeem our clay
> When we and war together, one wise day,
> Have passed away.[39]

Chapter 7

Religion and the

Student Peace Movement

Religion joined with Marxism and progressive education as a major force in influencing and organizing student opinion on war and peace. Ultimately, the religious objection to war conflicted with more pragmatic opposition, and religious (and other) conflicts drove antiwar Catholic students into a separate movement. Still, the role of the churches and of individual ministers and members of the laity added to the breadth of opposition to war. On campuses across the country religious groups played a significant part in the ASU and in antiwar activities.

Deeply intertwined with American culture and institutions, American religion, and Protestantism in particular, had abandoned its prophetic voice in the period of the Great War and the twenties. The businessman Jesus of Bruce Barton's popular *The Man Nobody Knows* represented the domestication of Christianity. As a historian of Methodism has noted, a segment of the religious community reacted against that view. "The 1930's gave the promise that the church might break free from the fetters of American culture, for the righteousness and attractiveness of that culture no longer seemed self evident."[1]

Confronted with economic and social collapse Catholics, Jews, and Protestants all produced voices and forces for social reform. In some cases official denominational organizations, more often individual clergy or lay persons, spoke out and acted upon specific social issues, often from a leftward vantage point. Father John Ryan of the National Catholic Welfare Conference, Rabbi Stephen Wise, and John Haynes Holmes, head of the Community Church in New York, added a non-Marxist element to social activism in the thirties and represented an indeterminate but substantial segment of their religious cohorts. This was perhaps less true of the Catholics, but in each of the major religions both activists and theologians were turning away from an abstract "Kingdom of Heaven" to the concrete and turbulent "City of Man."

This was especially true of an influential segment of the ministry. Through their leadership many of the institutional churches committed themselves to social reform and to specific programs. Throughout the thirties, "in nearly all the churches one could note how periodicals, special policy committees, and general deliberative bodies showed an increased willingness to speak out on social issues in a distinctly critical manner."[2] Independent religious publications took the lead, including *Christian Century, The World Tomorrow, Unity,* and, for the Catholics, *Commonweal* and the *Catholic Worker,* but church organs and diocesan publications often joined in criticizing capitalism and the evils of the economic system.

The 1932 Northern General Conference of Methodists declared that "the present industrial order is unchristian, unethical and anti-social because it is largely based on the profit motive which is a direct appeal to selfishness." In 1935 the New York Eastern Conference reported that "the conviction grows, therefore, that capitalism must be discarded and a planned Christian economy established."[3] The

Methodist Federation of Social Services, under the leadership of Harry F. Ward and Bishop Francis J. McConnell, consistently took positions to the left of most other religious organizations, and these views found special favor among young Methodists. In 1934, at its first national convention, the National Council of Methodist Youth "endorsed socialism, chided the New Deal for its halfway measures, and circulated a pledge that began: 'I surrender my life to Christ. I renounce the Capitalist system.'"[4]

These positions aroused some criticism, both within and without the church. William Randolph Hearst syndicated a series on Communist infiltration of the Methodist church, and the Reverend Rembert Gilman Smith won support for his pamphlet *Methodist Reds* and book *Moscow over Methodism.*[5]

Some of the opposition to the current order did indeed see socialism as the answer. E. Stanley Jones, in *Christ's Alternative to Communism,* saw competitive capitalist society as the source of both war and poverty, and proposed a Christian revolution: "the creation of a new kind of society, spiritual in its basis, but issuing in a collective economic sharing and cooperation. . . . The only good news to the poor that would be adequate would be that there are to be no poor."[6]

It is not clear how deeply this attitude penetrated the laity. Many ministers remained firm fundamentalists, and most of these were in the local churches with direct contact with the people. However, whatever the situation on other issues, on war and peace there was substantial agreement. Polls during the period indicate a striking degree of pacifist sentiment, especially in the Protestant churches. Roots of this pacifism lay in the twenties and in a reaction against the churches' support for the Great War. Once again, a revisionist view, presented by Ray H. Abrams in his *Preachers Present Arms,* had deep impact. Just as many students and academics had condemned the actions of scholars and colleges in supporting the war, so religious people had repented their part in that hysteria. In the early twenties many swore that they would not be fooled again.[7]

The pacifism of the churches was transmitted to students in several ways. At the religious colleges students drew upon pacifist teachings, and often peace demonstrations were sponsored or approved by the administrations. This was particularly true at some of the Methodist and Quaker schools, though even at the Friends' schools pacifism sometimes slumbered. Still, at places like Swarthmore, Haverford, and even Whittier in California, the religious traditions, often represented by the faculty, provided stimulus to antiwar activities.

Exposed to both the spirit of the decade and to social gospel theologians, seminary students often were more active than established ministers, especially in the peace movement. The Interseminary Group, a Protestant ecumenical group, was cosponsor of the April peace strikes, and individual seminaries often cooperated with other local schools in antiwar demonstrations. In New York City, for example, both Union Theological Seminary and Jewish Theological Seminary participated in the rallies at Columbia. At universities with separate religious schools, as at Temple, many of the most fervent peace workers came from the divinity school.

Religious activism was also represented by groups on nonreligious campuses. These included the YMCA and YWCA, the Student Christian Association, sometimes the Episcopal Canterbury Club, the Jewish Student Association, the Menorah Society, and, to a much lesser extent, the Catholic Newman Club. These were primarily social groups where students could meet religiously compatible marriage partners. At more radical campuses Marxist groups overshadowed or took away members that might have gone to religious organizations. Even there, however, the influence of religious ideas may have been stronger than it would appear from the numbers involved in the groups. Young Marxists may have abandoned religion as an opiate, but the religious and ethical values that they received in childhood were what made some of them Marxists.

Another kind of influence was that of individuals on the campuses. One of Columbia's most consistent peace activists was Arthur J. Lelyveld, successor to Reed Harris as editor of the *Spectator* in 1932–33. His position was unchangingly pacifist and based on ethical precepts. After graduation he took up rabbinical studies and became president of the Jewish Peace Fellowship from 1941 to 1943 and secretary of the Joint Rabbinical Committee on Conscientious Objectors from 1941 to 1944.[8]

Although religious groups were strongest in the Midwest, eastern colleges were open to liberal-minded religious leaders. In November 1934 Barnard held a peace symposium on war and religion. Their speakers were Father John La Farge, Bishop McConnell, and Arthur Garfield Hays. This was one of the comparatively few instances in which Catholics participated, and La Farge cited Pope Pius XI's admonition that under modern conditions war could not be justified.[9]

College chaplains also related religion to antiwar work. At the University of Pennsylvania, for example, a minister writing the chaplain's forum column in the student paper urged attendance at the Armistice Day meeting and declared that war and religion "do not mix."[10] Of the religious organizations on campus, the student YMCAs and YWCAs were the oldest and most influential. Although their numbers declined throughout the twenties and thirties, in 1930 these organizations had student groups at 594 institutions, with a total membership of 51,350. Excluding Catholic colleges, these groups were present on half the nation's campuses. This included some schools that, instead of having both a

YMCA and a YWCA, had a single coed Student Christian Association.[11]

Like other religious groups with similarly stated ideals, including the promotion of peace, the YMCAs and YWCAs capitulated to war fever in 1917. In the early twenties the student branches and their advisers took new interest in the peace movement. Their concern with peace, as well as with racism, industrial relations, and prohibition, was encouraged by such religious leaders as Henry Van Dusen, Harry Emerson Fosdick, Kirby Page, Sherwood Eddy and Reinhold Niebuhr. After 1925 the student YMCAs and YWCAs joined the effort to get the United States to join the World Court, and they participated in activities against compulsory ROTC.[12] In the thirties this interest expanded on individual campuses and in the national councils. The national YMCA and YWCA became sponsors of the annual peace strikes. A similar pattern emerged on some campuses.

The role of religion in the student peace movement can be seen by examining the activities of some young Methodists on a midwestern campus. Religious organizations were especially strong in that region. Unlike the East, where the Episcopal and Congregational churches were prominent and where Jews and Catholics were entering campus life in increasing numbers, the heartlands remained firmly Protestant, with Methodism, Lutheranism, and Presbyterianism the major denominations. At the University of Michigan, for example, registration forms asked students to indicate religious preference. Although 1,800 failed to respond, 6,262 did indicate a preference. Of these, Methodists numbered 1,233, Presbyterians 959, and Catholics 649; Episcopalians and Jews were relatively few, with other groups even fewer.[13]

Both clergy and students were active in the Michigan peace movement. At the antiwar conference in May 1934 two of the speakers were Methodist ministers.[14] The Reverend Frederick B. Fisher discussed the results of a spring 1934 poll of ministers and seminary students (which had indicated substantial pacifist sentiment among the clergy) and pointed to Gandhi and his followers as the only people in the world practicing true pacifist principles. Dr. Harold L. Bedient described the physical horror of war and his own experiences in the training camps on the Western Front.

Methodist students were active in the Michigan League against War and Militarism and the antiwar conference. There were divisions among them, however, particularly concerning their relations with the radical campus groups. Contrasting positions were taken by John Richmond and Grace Farnsworth of the student YMCA and YWCA and Gordon B. Halstead, president of the Michigan League against War and Militarism and the antiwar conference and a self-declared Christian socialist. The position of Farnsworth and Richmond indicates the degree to which conservative religion agreed with some tenets of thirties liberalism and leftism, while rejecting its basic analysis. Halstead's role, however, indicates the interplay of religious and socialist doctrine that motivated a substantial part of the student Left and the Left in general.

Like others, Farnsworth and Richmond supported the activities of the Nye Committee and efforts to control munitions. They opposed expansion of the navy and large "defense" expenditures and favored a referendum before any declaration of war. In common with most of the supporters of the peace movement, they were concerned with the power of propaganda, and urged the study of war to combat "the psychological campaign for war preparations now carried on through the press, on the screen, and over the radio."[15]

If education could not prevent war, the only response was resistance. "We believe that we are justified, with a daily increasing number of others, in breaking the 'vicious cycle' by non-violent resistance in another war which would be caused by the apathy and indifference of the people of this nation." While disagreeing with several of the points of the recent antiwar conference, they heartily endorsed the Oxford Oath. They took it with complete seriousness not as a tactic but as a principle. "We choose imprisonment or prosecution in the event of another war in which . . . the first of the youth will be killed by materials made right in our own country."

The two emphasized petitions and letters to Congress and rejected some of the leftist declarations and rhetoric of the conference. Richmond particularly objected to support for a May Day demonstration. He declared that Communists should not try to gain support for party activities at an antiwar conference.[16]

Other religious pacifists were more sympathetic to the Left. In some cases this reflected personal experience. Halstead, for example, went to Toledo to investigate conditions there during a strike in order to see how capital and labor dealt with each other and to see the position of the government.

Supplemented by a "midnight seminar on social problems" in the local jail, where he was held for "loitering," his findings apparently convinced him of the necessity for radical social change. Capital had been able to use the violence of the state against the strikers, who were fighting "for life itself, . . . a chance to earn and to live a bit better than the beasts of the field." The state militia had actually provoked disorder. The role of the mob seemed to Halstead to be "implacably leading to fascism or to civil war." He concluded, "As a Christian Socialist and one who loves his country and believes in its ultimate worth, I must dedicate myself more fully to the task of building a more just social order."[17]

These individuals and others in the Student Christian Association added numerically to the peace movement at the

University of Michigan. The same was true on other campuses. At Temple University the head of the ASU was an active Christian Scientist. At the University of Pennsylvania the religious groups formed the basis of the moderate peace activities.

One major exception to the cooperation of religious groups with the peace movement was the Catholic church, including its youth groups. No Catholic institution was reported to have participated in any of the annual antiwar demonstrations; no Catholic organization participated in the American Youth Congress. As the dean of Fordham University reported with satisfaction in April 1934, "There is no organized pacifist group in this university. I don't care whether they are demonstrating at other colleges in the city today. They are making fools of themselves. What war are they worrying about anyway?"[18]

Three years later, however, there was a peace group on Fordham's campus, and the head of the ethics department was urging Catholic teachers to instruct their students in the Catholic doctrines on war and peace so that Catholics might be conscientious objectors in the next war.[19] In addition, some students discovered in the Catholic Worker movement a group that believed that some things—racism, war, and such—were worse than making a fool of oneself. But the chasm between Catholics and non-Catholics, even, or perhaps especially, on the left, remained wide. There were some efforts, including those of the Communists during the Popular Front period, to make Catholics part of the movement, but on the whole, the Catholic student peace movement remained separate—and unequal. The position of the students reflected the contradictory position of the church, and especially its progressive element, in American society; they wanted both to fit in and adapt and to maintain a distinctive identity.

In 1930 approximately 174,000 Catholics were attending

college, about 20 percent of the total college enrollment, and of those, about 60 percent attended Catholic schools. (By 1940 the enrollment was up to 260,000, with the percentages about the same.) The experiences of those students varied according to the kind of institution that they attended and the degree to which, if they were in a non-Catholic school, they maintained connections with the church. About 20,000 Catholic students on secular campuses belonged, at least nominally, to the Catholic Newman Club.[20] Some Catholic students joined other organizations, including the ASU, and participated in antiwar and radical activity, but these seem to have been a minority.

The lack of Catholic participation was not surprising. In the thirties the Catholic church maintained a defensive attitude toward American society and especially toward liberals and leftists. Because Catholic education was largely authoritarian and dominated by the clergy and hierarchy, students either reflected those views or were squelched. In particular, the experience of the Spanish Civil War divided many Catholics from the position and emotions of the Left.[21] The most significant overt reason for the separation of Catholic students from other students was the attitude of the Catholic church toward communism, a hostility which was active and obsessive. John Cogley, one of a group of young radical Catholics in Chicago in the thirties, notes the corrosive effect that this emphasis had on efforts to promote the positive social teachings of the church:

> When he heard about the social encyclicals, it was stressed that they offered the best answer to Communism, as if that somehow made them more valid than they would otherwise be. When we organized social clubs, lecture courses, apostolic movements or interacial meetings we underlined the fact that these were effective anti-communist measures. We sent our

graduates out into the world with denunciations of
Communism ringing in their ears. When we spoke of
the need for Catholic Action, we invoked the fabu-
lous zeal of young communists as the clinching
argument.[22]

As Cogley noted, some of the anti-Communist rhetoric
of the social actionists was adopted as a protective device
against their more conservative brethren. Some of it was
also derived from a historical style of polemics and the kind
of combativeness that was devoted to collegiate sports and
intercollegiate rivalry. The effect, however, was to divide
Catholic students, who often shared concerns about peace,
from the student peace movement as a whole.

Catholic students were very much aware of the activities
of the movement and of the ASU, and so was the hierarchy.
Evidently the bishops felt that the antiwar activities had
some appeal to Catholic students, for they made a concerted
effort to prevent Catholic participation in the antiwar strikes
and organizations.

At its national conference in 1936 the Federation of Catholic College Clubs passed a resolution condemning the ASU
because of its "communist tendencies." In the closing address, the Reverend Peter B. Duffee declared that communism was "the false front of international capitalism." The
executive board of the federation issued a warning to member clubs against "affiliating with or participation in the activities of the American Student Union" and declared that
"the American Student Union is dominated by communist
organizations, Y.M.C.A. groups and similar undesirable elements." Reprinting this message, the *Student Advocate*
seemed particularly bemused by the hostility toward the
YMCA, but the historic Protestant-Catholic antagonism that
still made it impossible for a Catholic to join the "Y" was
kept alive by both sides. In 1937 the National Catholic Alum-

ni Federation urged a federal investigation of the antiwar strike and described it as "no demonstration for peace, but in reality a demonstration for war—the worst of all wars—class war." The Catholic bishops warned against participation by Catholic students in the World Youth Conference at Vassar in 1938. They declared the conference to be "communist dominated and hostile to American ideals and traditions."[23]

The concern of the Catholic bishops indicates the real appeal of the peace issue, in particular, to Catholic students. Within the Federation of Catholic College Clubs opinion was divided, and some students favored cooperation with the ASU.[24] Other students opposed or refrained from cooperation with the ASU, but sponsored their own peace activities and participated in the Student Peace Federation, under the auspices of the Catholic Association for International Peace. Formed in 1936, within a year it had groups at seventy-two schools across the country. Its activities were moderate and kept under the guidance of adults, but it did represent student concern with war and peace. It was particularly strong at Catholic women's colleges.[25]

Catholics were, after all, exposed to the same influences that promoted antiwar feeling among their fellow students. They read the revisionist views of the Great War, saw the antiwar movies, and often shared the view of war as a racket for the satisfaction of economic greed.[26] In addition, some of them were exposed to the pacifist influence of the Catholic Worker movement and of writers like Paul Hanley Furfey, associated with the *Catholic Worker*, the liturgical movement, and the Catholic Fellowship. Like many of the Protestant exponents of the social gospel, Furfey declared "the radical incompatability between the gospel and the accepted mores of the time." The times, he said, are evil. Religion ought not to support systems that produce such evil, he continued. "The great temptation for Catholics comes from their desire to be acceptable."[27]

The form that this desire took was an effort to prove that
Catholics made good Americans, and they did this by attacking those who didn't fit the American Legion's definition of
Americanism. Consequently, clerical rhetoric combined religion and patriotism as though they were identical. This was
reflected on Catholic campuses, especially at men's colleges.
At Villanova, for example, the 1939 yearbook was based on
this theme.[28] Run by Augustine fathers, Villanova was a college for men situated in the rather alien territory of Philadelphia's "Main Line." The school emphasized "study-reli-
gion-athletics," and its location was appropriate. The yearbook annually proclaimed the college to be "a community
free from the din and clatter of industry . . . a community
of greystone Gothic buildings blended with quietness and
dignity . . . a place where intellectual achievement may
flourish . . . a place where one thousand men may live
under the same sky, the same flag," a place far from the
ghettos and ethnic enclaves of Philadelphia.

The yearbook was divided into sections: "For the Preservation of Religion and Democracy" and "For God and
Country," which declared: "Under our form of government
the American state has prospered; the Catholic Church has
flourished. And where the Church flourishes democracy
need never fear, for She is ever the guardian of equal rights
among men. . . . And from the first She has condemned
Atheistic Communism." Each section was introduced by a
picture of the Statue of Liberty on a scarlet background
faced by a page describing one facet of the horrors of communism. In between, however, was a catalog of a life that
was highly unpolitical, consisting of some classes, athletics,
and the pursuit of women. It is possible that the most significant conflict in these young men's lives was not that between religion and irreligion or communism and democracy
but their football rivalry with Temple University. Their collegiate life, modeled on that of Ivy League campuses, was
an acceptance of the status quo, not a challenge to it.

Not all Catholics were obsessed with communism or identified Americanism with support of right-wing causes. Dr. Joseph Louis Apodaca of Notre Dame warned Catholic students against neglecting the evils that cause communism: "The Catholic Action clubs have a definite objective, yet they mass their forces along an oratorical front when the battle should be fought along the advance of economic reforms." Others emphasized the failure of the church in promoting justice. Father John M. Cooper wrote in 1934 that Catholics were partly responsible themselves for antireligious, anti-Catholic currents in Socialist and Communist movements. What had Christianity, and Catholics in particular, done to raise the status of women or to oppose slavery? During the rise of economic injustice during the industrial revolution, "Catholics were silent and asleep. We talked justice; we did not practice or work for it." George Shuster, editor of *Commonweal*, reflected on the causes of distrust of Catholics by liberals—"How difficult it is for many men of good will outside the Catholic Church to view it without a measure of aversion or even dread." Change was not likely to occur "unless Catholics stopped sounding like a blend of the D.A.R., Bruce Barton, and a random devotee of Torquemada."[29]

Although not ready to cooperate with the student antiwar movement actively, some students did share the belief that some common goals were more important than differences. A student writing in the *Loyola* (Chicago) *News* noted that many of the tenets of communism were opposed to Catholic teaching, but added, "Some of the postulates upon which Communism is based are Christian in character. The Catholic graduate must select the good points of the system while at the same time he must reject the bad."[30]

While confined to a small number of students and youth, the radical pacifism of the Catholic Worker movement had long-term significance. Its immediate results were meager, as was true of the rest of the peace movement. Like the non-Catholic students who had taken the Oxford Oath, most Catholics went off to war when called. The church rallied to the flag, sent the men off with chaplains, blessed their tanks, and generally remained silent when they bombed civilians. Still, the number of recorded Catholic objectors increased from none in World War I to 149 between May 1941 and March 1947.[31] In the postwar period a pacifist voice was maintained that would be raised loudly in the sixties with the emergence of the Catholic Left in opposition to the war in Vietnam.

While the religious groups and impulse added to the peace movement, they also presented difficulties. The position of the pacifist churches was clear. Others were sometimes ambiguous in their analysis of society and their position on the individual's response to war. Although in some cases they did strike clearly to the causes of war, they stopped short of offering necessary measures for its elimination. Still, the progressive wings of the churches did offer a strong moral basis for opposition to war and one that went beyond expediency or change of party platforms.

The National Council of Methodist Youth remained steadfastly pacifist.[32] In 1939 its Commission on Christian Action in Time of War urged refusal of draft registration and the draft and urged cooperation with such groups as the FOR, the WILPF, the WRL, the Methodist Peace Fellowship, the Socialist party, and the Youth Committee to Keep America out of War. In 1940 the council endorsed the "National Day of Mourning" on October 16, the day set for national draft registration, and the executive committee of the council maintained affiliation with the youth committee against war.

It is illustrative of the changes in the student movement brought by the war that in 1942 the Communists were criticizing some religious groups for their opposition to war. In "Youth Serves the Nation," Max Weiss declared that "of all the dangerous and pernicious Fifth Column forces at work to corrupt the youth and to paralyze the war effort, we must single out the degenerate influence of pacifism." In particular he attacked "such tools of Hitler as Mr. Libby of the National Peace Conference, the leaders of the Methodist Youth Fellowship, [and] certain leaders of the Student Christian Movement."[33]

There were differences between Catholics, Jews, and Protestants and within the denominations, but in each pacifism found some voice. In the thirties the churches were less prepared than they had been in previous, or would be in later, years to launch a holy war on behalf of capitalism. For most within the churches this mood vanished with the bombing of Pearl Harbor. But a remnant persisted. When war came, most of those who refused to fight offered religious motives for their resistance.

Religion, then, was a strong element in the strength of the student antiwar movement. Many campus religious groups became allies with the radicals and other activists in forming a counterbloc on the campus, creating a community based on moral and political activism rather than on sports and proms.

Chapter 8

Students and the
Spanish Civil War

In July 1936 Spanish generals, led by Francisco Franco, re-
volted against the Republican government of Spain, precipi-
tating a civil war. The aftermath was the extinguishing of
Spanish liberty and of peace in Europe. It was the beginning
of a new world war, with fascist intervention on behalf of
the rebels ensuring an international dimension to fraternal
bloodshed. In turn, the conflict in Spain caused deep division within the peace movement in Europe and America.

Though part of the antiwar movement had already shown
an increasing tendency to support collective security, the
Spanish Civil War provided the emotional catalyst and immediate issue for the breakup of the peace forces. Among
students it directly resulted in the abandonment of the Oxford Oath as the basis of the peace program of the American
Student Union. Although a superficial unity continued for
several years on specific issues, the gunfire in Spain and the
fascist bombs signified the end of the brief moment of united
action.

In America the Left and the peace groups were bitterly
divided over the proper response of the American govern-

ment. Although almost entirely in favor of the Spanish Republican government, they split on the issue of American
neutrality.[1] In compliance with neutrality legislation, President Roosevelt established an embargo on arms to the bel-
ligerents, including the legal government of Spain. Many
who had previously fought for such legislation now saw it
being used in a way that seemed beneficial to the fascists,
since the rebels could get all the supplies they needed from
Germany and Italy.

The Communist party, most liberals, and many clergymen
facored an end to the embargo and direct aid to the Spanish
government. Though deeply sympathetic to the loyalist
forces, Socialists and pacifists supported the embargo. The
pacifists believed the war to be an evil regardless of its results. The Socialists, divided among themselves, supported
worker assistance to the Republican cause, but no intervention by the American government. Although some Socialists
remained pacifists, others joined the American volunteers in
the Abraham Lincoln Brigade.[2]

Students divided along the same lines and a battle ensued
in the ASU. From the beginning the *Student Advocate* led
the fight for active support and an end to the embargo. In
this, the magazine reflected the views of Lash and Wechsler.
Before the antiwar strike in April 1937, the editors criticized
the national strike committee's weak statement on the Spanish crisis. Supposedly the basis for the strike, the call confined itself to the statement that "fascism breeds war and
increases the danger of world war as shown by the present
Spanish Conflict." Since the strike committee had been limited to this statement because of its "broad and representative character," it was up to the ASU to show that the Spanish issue was crucial to the antiwar movement.

The future of world peace was on the line in Spain. Espousing a sort of domino theory, Lash and Wechsler declared: "Whether fascism will continue its reckless path or

whether it shall be forced to retreat is in large measure dependent upon the fate of Spain. Victory for fascism there foreshadows new uprisings in other lands. Defeat will mean at least new delays— a 'breathing spell' in which the forces of progress both within and without fascist countries can impose their opinion and strength."

Neutrality was a sham that benefited the warmakers, the editors continued. "If, while fascism throws all its resources into Spain, the allies of the Spanish government remain inert, the simple and inevitable consequence will be a World War in which the chances of American involvement are vast." Answering the objections of the pacifists (and their own earlier declarations), the editors asserted that by advocating such assistance they were not "falling prey to the aims of American profiteers. In 1916 assistance to democracy was a slogan coined by vested interests. Today, when Hearst and his cohorts denounce and defame the Spanish cause, when they cry out in behalf of sham neutrality, aid to Spain is a weapon of peace."

For students to ignore Spain in their antiwar demonstration was to ignore reality, they said. "To protest against the threat of war, while failing to recognize the center and fact of war, is perilous self-delusion." It was therefore important that at each demonstration the ASU should win support for the Republican position. The national organization of the ASU would contribute to the Spanish government its share from the proceeds of the fast on that day. The motto would be "We Fast That Spain May Eat." The ASU should urge support for Spain and continue attacks on the American administration's military budget.[3]

This position did encounter some opposition within the ASU national executive committee. Jeffrey Campbell, a member of the national committee as well as the FOR student secretary for New England, opposed the editors' position and upheld the pacifist view.[4] Although agreeing with their statement that the Spanish war was a concern for American students, Campbell challenged what he called their simplification both of the conflict and of the pacifist position toward it. His basic position was that war was itself the breeding ground of fascism. Just as in the world war good intentions had been put to a bad use, so by enlisting government powers in a war supposedly against fascism, greater evil would result. Once mobilized, the antifascists could be manipulated by the government and the ruling class into pursuing their objectives and into entering a world war. "It is this powerful minority which through its control of the puppet state, the schools and colleges, the press, the newsreels, and the pulpit shapes the mass sentiment of the people for peace into the instruments of war."

War was, as Randolph Bourne had argued, the health of the state. That was one of the lessons of the Great War that the students had taken to heart. Campbell's argument that war necessarily created a militaristic society was the same one that Wechsler and Lash had used, and still would upon occasion. His description was prophetic: "Even wars whose express goal is to fight Fascism are wars and are accompanied by all the characteristics which describe wars. If a war is to be successfully advanced, the population must be regimented to its support by crushing all opposition, by choking civil liberties, by booming propaganda and withholding facts which might limit support. These are the qualities of fascism."

And how did Wechsler and Lash propose to combat "the Fascism which creeps up from behind the ranks of the most gallant and sincere of Fascist opposition"? Campbell quoted the "pacifist ditty": "Man is a moron, goodness knows / Fighting for peace to war he goes." It was an argument that could be applied to both Spain and the United States. The repression by the Spanish Communists of the Anarchists and Trotskyists might not have been so shocking if the expacifists had remembered their earlier analysis of what happens in all wars. The pacifists had a point in warning of the dangers inherent in the kind of militarization required to win a war.

So, too, did the Socialists have a real perception of the incongruity of Marxists and radicals looking to the American government as the savior of republicanism in Spain. Campbell noted with surprise that Wechsler and Lash should expect a government that they still attacked on alternate Tuesdays as militaristic and controlled by a minority to behave as though it were the instrument of peace and the people's will.

Finally, Campbell proposed an alternative to placing Spain's fate in the hands of the United States government. He urged workers' action on behalf of Spain and cited the refusal by a group of British seamen in Boston to sail a shipment of nitrates to the Spanish rebel forces. "Briefly I say damn the isolationist position. Damn the reliance placed upon governments constructed for war as agents of peace. In face of this we can do no more than clamor for complete and mandatory neutrality so far as our government is concerned. At the same time we can unleash the forces of the people who manufacture, produce, and transport the materials by which war is made possible to stifle at its source the common stream of War and Fascism." The massive aid in material and manpower from Italy and Germany for the Franco forces made these hopes futile.

The internationalization of the conflict, plus the bitterness and fury with which it was fought, gave the war an emotional dimension that left behind rational discussion. Just as many Catholic students reacted against the attack on the church and the killing of nuns and priests, so most of the Left and leftist students saw the war as a battle between the forces of progress and the forces of reaction. Trotskyists and Anarchists had doubts based on their perception that the revolution in Spain was being sacrificed to the war and that some of their compatriots were also being sacrificed or eliminated under the pretext of the war. They were a minority, however, and seem to have had little impact on the public's or the students' perception of the conflict.

A propaganda war began at home. Although students condemned the use of propaganda in the world war, they had little reluctance to employ their own. Songs, movies, and books spread over the country on behalf of the Spanish loyalists. Student literary magazines and anthologies reveal the way that the war captured interest and feelings. Most of what was written was based on third-hand information and enthusiasm rather than experience. That could come only from those who went to war themselves. At home people did what they could. A Temple University student wrote the following poem for the campus ASU journal in October 1938:

> Generalissmo Francisco Franco
> Gentle savior of Spain,
> What do you dream o' nights
> Hearing the children's choked cry
> In the wind's refrain?
>
> Daily in violent silence,
> By the winds howl in the shattered gutter,
> Beneath the spatter of the brain upon the wall,
> The shadows wait in confidence:
>
> Generalissimo Francisco Franco
> Wipe your hands and pray:
> Hate revolves like twisting sea gulls
> Gathering strength by day.[5]

As the war went on, fears grew strong, fed by the Japanese expansion in China in 1937 and German annexation of

Austria in 1938. In February 1939 seventy-six members of Temple's faculty, administration, and staff signed a petition for the removal of the embargo as a last effort to save the Republican government. The signers included President Beury, a member of the board of trustees, the dean of the college of letters and science, the dean of the teachers college, the dean of the school of commerce, the dean of men, the librarian, and the registrar. By now the shadow of another world war was indeed on the wall. The Temple chapter of the ASU declared: "The victory of Fascism in Spain means continued aggression into Czechoslovakia—witness Ethiopia, China, Austria; because this continued aggression means eventual world war; and because it is this war into which the United States will be drawn." A defeat for fascism in Spain, however, still might check the impending world conflict.[6]

Pacifists, too, did what they could. At Bryn Mawr in the spring of 1937 the Non-Partisan Committee for the Relief of Spanish Children was formed and included the college president, a representative of the faculty, and graduate and undergraduate students, including Martha Van Hoesen of the ASU. That November the group sponsored a lecture by Professor Patrick Murphy Malin of Swarthmore College on the conditions in Spain based on his observations there on behalf of the American Friends Service Committee. On November 11, at the Armistice Day chapel, Frederick Libby, of the National Council for the Prevention of War, spoke on the need for peaceful change among nations and defended the neutrality law. The opposite view was presented by Joseph Lash in December, as he discussed events in Spain and his experiences there in the summer. He took a strong anti-embargo line and urged all possible support for the loyalists.[7]

The deepest involvement came with the fighting and death of American students in Spain, volunteers to the cause of the republic. Though their numbers were not large, they represented a degree of commitment matched only by the students who became conscientious objectors. Their experience affected not only themselves and those who knew them personally but those to whom they became antifascist heroes, and who, in retrospect, came to regard them as men and women who chose to do what others had forced upon them four years later. There was, in the emotional response to their involvement, perhaps an element of admiration for martial values and ability. In spite of all the pacifist propaganda it seemed to be in war that individuals could lay their lives on the line and prove themselves and their commitment. It was a chance to act, rather than talk. Picketing Hearst newsreels paled before life on the front. And who could remain neutral when friends were being shot at?

Sponsored primarily by the Communists, though there was the Eugene V. Debs Column of Socialists, the Abraham Lincoln Brigade enlisted approximately thirty-three hundred Americans to fight in Spain in the International Brigade. Of these more than sixteen hundred were killed in action before the foreign brigades were withdrawn shortly before the war's end. American women served as both nurses and ambulance drivers.[8]

Although most of the American volunteers were workers, a substantial number were either students or had recently been students and had dropped out to do political work or to make a living. From fifty to sixty members of the brigade were or had been members of the ASU, including a number who had been officers in the campus or area groups. At least eight of them died in Spain: Paul McEachron of Oberlin, a national committee member and New York state executive secretary of the ASU, was killed in the fighting at Belchite in March 1938, the same battlefield where Sam Levinger of Ohio University had been killed by machine-gun fire the previous year. Others were Don Henry of Kansas State, Roy McQuarrie of Wayne, Nate Schilling of the

University of Chicago, Joseph Seligman of Swarthmore, Leo Torgoff of Brooklyn College, and George Walt, a member of the national executive committee of the ASU.[9]

One of the more prominent students turned soldier was Robert Merriman, a former student at Berkeley who turned his ROTC training into preparation for his command of the Lincoln Brigade. John Kenneth Galbraith, a fellow student at Berkeley, later wrote of Merriman, "He must have been the bravest of our contemporaries."[10] In fact, he became the model in part for Robert Jordan in *For Whom the Bell Tolls*. Merriman went to Berkeley from Nevada and was caught up in campus radicalism and the waterfront strike of 1934. In 1938 he was killed on the Aragon Front. Galbraith quotes John Depper, a British volunteer who had written of the Battle of Jarema:

> Death stalked in the olive trees
> Picking his men
> His leaden finger beckoned
> Again and again.

More lucky was David Cook, a former NSL organizer at Columbia. Cook graduated from Columbia in 1935, then returned to England, where he worked temporarily for the University Labour Federation before going to Spain. His report of his experiences at the front was printed in the *Advocate* in April 1937. The editors noted that Cook had since been wounded (after his first day of actual fighting), but was returned to the front.

Cooke noted that the people he was with were primarily working class and most Scots. He described their adaptation to army life and his own reasons for joining up:

> I came here because life in England was too useless a one to be living at such a time as this. If I'm to be among those who don't get back, I'll have concentrated

so much into the last short space that it will be as
good as having lasted for a normal span. I have no military experience of course and this would have kept
me home if I had found a place in the movement back
there. But I never managed to get functioning properly,
partly through having no steady job. So much by way
of apology.[11]

Each individual had his or her own reason for going. They
came from different backgrounds and differing ideologies to
the same conclusion. English students, too, as apparently
unlike as the Marxist John Cornford and the pacifist Julian
Bell, met death in Spain. The reasons often had little to do
with Spain itself, and most of the foreign volunteers knew
little about the politics, history, religion, or social customs
of that country. It was true for the Americans, as it was for
Cornford and Bell, that "theirs was an outside view, inevitably a simplification, that filtered out the Spanishness from
the struggle and made it more manageable, in England at
least, than the reality was to prove."[12]

If the reality was sometimes disillusioning, the volunteers
could cling to the belief that they were the last defense
against fascism and world war. Sam Levinger went to Spain,
because, as he wrote: "If this was a Spanish matter I'd let
it alone. But the rebellion would not last a week if it weren't
for the Germans and the Italians. And if Hitler and Mussolini can send troops to Spain to attack the government
elected by the People, why can't they do so in France? And
after France?"[13]

He was killed at the Battle of Belchite in 1937 at age
twenty. He had written:

> Comrades, the battle is bloody, the war
>   is long;
> Still let us climb the grey hill and
>   charge the guns,

Pressing with lean bayonets towards the slopes
    beyond.

Soon those who are still living
    will see green grass,
A free bright country shining
    with a star;
And those who charged the guns
    will be remembered,
And from red blood white pinnacles
    shall tower.[14]

The effect of these deaths is hard to measure, yet they seem to have given the advocates of intervention an emotional force that the pacifist side could not match. The article about Levinger was published in the December issue of the *Advocate*, just prior to the convention at which the issue of collective security versus the Oxford Oath would be debated. Without discounting the wish to write about someone who had been a friend to many ASU members, it is clear that there was another message being conveyed.

The article noted that Levinger had been in Spain by choice and that "he went into the attack under no compulsion but his own free will." He did not want to die and had a great deal to live for. But an important issue was involved in the war. "The point at odds was human liberty. That made it his fight and he could not stand back while others took the risk." He and others like him were not martyrs, and their lives were not wasted, "for they died that liberty might not perish from the earth. The liberty we have now and the greater freedom of the future is their living monument."[15]

Some of this is the desire to find meaning in the deaths of friends. But there is also here the creation of a new myth and a reordering of values and models. Even so skeptical a viewer of the radicalism of the thirties as Murray Kempton later remembered Levinger, who had been a YPSL member, as the kind of radical whose presence he missed and who in the fifties seemed a vanished breed.[16]

In the thirties, then, the road from pacifism to war was made easier by these examples of the civilian turned soldier. The stereotypes of the early thirties of the mindless militarist clearly did not apply. The pictures of World War I began to fade before the personal view of the Spanish battles. The Marne gave way to the Manzanares, and Barcelona and Madrid became the moving symbols.

Eric Sevareid, who was beginning his own odyssey from antimilitarism to interventionism (and from "Jacobin" to CBS), described the effect of the Spanish Civil War on himself and other young people. He was a newspaper correspondent in France during the return of the American volunteers from Spain. "The preliminary, practice ambush was almost over now, in Spain, and the bleeding, scattered victims were struggling toward sanctuary. The hatred and bitterness ran like a river straight from the Pyrenees to Paris. Americans that I knew—men with hearts and minds like Vincent Sheean—were returning from Spain hollow and sick from emotional exhaustion."[17]

The returning Americans received little help from the consulate or embassy, so a group of private Americans, including Hemingway, Frederick Thompson, and Louis Bromfield, organized to help. Sevareid writes of going to the American hospital and seeing the maimed and dying: "This was it, this was what was going to happen to millions more, to your friends, and perhaps to yourself. This was what the struggle, which began with ideas, came to in the end; and that what I had known—the contest by typewriter and tongue—now seemed a faint and mocking battle of the shadows."[18]

Sevareid echoes what Muriel Rukeyser wrote as she left Spain just at the beginning of the war, having witnessed its lightning change on the people and the land:

If we had not seen fighting,
if we had not looked there
    the plane flew low
    the plaster ripped by shots
    the peasant's house
If we had stayed in our world
between the table and the desk
between the town and the suburb
slowly disintegration
male and female

If we had lived in our city
sixty years might not prove
    the power of this week
    the overthrown past
    tourist and refugee.[19]

Students and intellectuals were not the only ones who had been living in a world of tables and desks, but it was their job to come to terms with the broken peace, and they struggled in the new darkness. Some found the answer by going to war.

Sevareid writes of Jimmy Lardner, who had said of why he joined up: "'All you guys will have to meet this thing somewhere pretty soon. I just decided I'd like to meet it in Spain.' He was the last American volunteer to die in battle there, for the foreign volunteers were withdrawn from the lines the next day."[20]

Those who returned alive made it their task to win the country, and the students, to the loyalist cause, the cause of active assistance. Those who, like Rukeyser, had gone to Spain in July 1936 to see the antifascist Olympics and saw instead a fascist revolt were told by a street-meeting speaker: "[You] came for Games / you stay for victory; foreign? your job is / go tell your countries what you saw in Spain."[21]

One who took the message was Joseph Lash. He toured

the battlefront (and was given "red-carpet treatment") and went home as a strong advocate of an end to the embargo and an end to the Oxford Oath.[22] He was meanwhile moving from the Socialists to the Communists, a switch that would effectively change the balance of power in the ASU and add to the breakup of the antiwar coalition.

Bombed city, Spanish Civil War, circa 1938. Etching on note paper sold to raise funds for the Republican cause. (Courtesy Library of Congress.)

Hand grenading tanks, Spanish Civil War, circa 1938. Pro-Republican etchings like these gave students a different view of war. (Courtesy Library of Congress.)

Delegates to the World Youth Congress, held at Vassar College in August 1938, listen intently as a speech is translated. (Courtesy Vassar College Archives.)

International friendship around the punch bowl. World Youth Congress, Vassar College, August 1938. (Courtesy Vassar College Archives.)

American graphic artists support the war effort. Exhibit Panel, circa 1944, Norman Rockwell, Office of War Information. (Courtesy Library of Congress.)

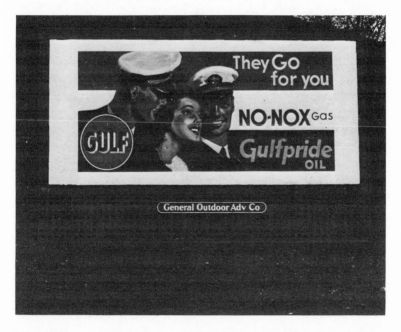

The nation moves toward war. Billboard in upstate New York, 1941, Collier, Farm Security Administration. (Courtesy Library of Congress.)

Preparing body for final disposal, Bozaches, December 2, 1918,
United States Army. Photographs like this one of World War I taken
by the United States Signal Corps helped form the pacifist mood of the
student movement. (Courtesy Library of Congress.)

Chapter 9

Collective Security
versus the Oxford Oath

The conflict in Spain increased the divisions in the peace movement. The differing views of pacifists, Marxists, and liberals could be patched over as long as they were united in fighting a theoretical "imperialist" war. Presented with a situation that met none of their perceptions of war, it was just a matter of time before gaps became chasms. The collapse did not occur overnight; the crumbling was gradual, but it was sure and steady, as the world went once again to war. Criticizing the students in the peace movement is a little like criticizing a boulder in the middle of the river for failing to hold back the torrent. The ASU could not prevent World War II. Nor could it avoid being caught up in the turmoil around it.

The division came between the Socialists and pacifists, on the one hand, and the liberals and Communists, on the other. When the ASU was formed, the Communists were well on their way to a position favoring collective security, although they refrained from pushing their view at the convention. The party itself moved more quickly, moving to support Roosevelt and the New Deal. In the student peace movement, however, there was more opposition.

The first test of the comparative strength of the collective security forces versus the defenders of the Oxford Oath came at the ASU convention in December 1936. It was preceded by debate within the organization and its leadership and in the pages of the *Student Advocate*. George Edwards, the ASU national chairman, argued for the retention of the oath as the basis of the peace program. Celeste Strack, national high school secretary and NSL officer, spoke for those who favored collective security.[1]

According to Edwards, the success of the ASU was due primarily to its antiwar program and to "its dramatic and effective summary in the Oxford Pledge." Its worth was indicated by the extent to which reactionaries had singled it out for criticism. "In the face of heightened war danger this is no time to retreat." For the convention not to reaffirm the pledge "would weaken the ASU in national prestige, enthusiasm, and activity, and in membership." It would be "a tacit compromise with the forces working for war." Edwards reiterated the classic antiwar position: (1) in any possible war the United States will fight not for justice but for trade and empire; (2) that war will in no way represent the interests of the people of this nation, and in its horrors they will learn to blame those who led them into it; (3) that war is certain to produce military dictatorship and aid in launching American fascism. These arguments had so far held the peace movement together; even the collective security advocates invoked them in their continued opposition to ROTC, munitions makers, and military spending. But now there were other arguments.

Strack urged collective security "to augment" other measures such as the Oxford Oath, anti-ROTC, and opposition to militarism in the schools. She noted that the Hearsts, DuPonts, and Morgans in the country favored militarism at home and opposed collective security abroad. The ASU, she said, should adopt a more realistic program in light of the threat of fascist aggression. "Collective action by all the peace forces—the other people of the world, the Soviet Union, and all other nations or groups desiring to maintain peace—is the most strategic way to hem in those who seek war." Some made an effort to compromise, to hold to the pledge which had built the union, while the conference as a whole moved in the opposite direction. In the process, it became clearer than ever that the Oxford Oath had always meant different things to different people. As Lash observed in his report to the convention, "The Oxford Pledge is not for the ASU, although it may be for pacifists, an ethical absolute."[2] Lash and others could attempt to obfuscate the issue by inventing their own definitions, but contradictions, as the Marxists should have known, cannot be permanently talked over or wished away.

The first round went to the pacifists. At the convention the major battle was over a YPSL-sponsored resolution attacking the concept of collective security. That lost by only thirty-seven votes, a show of strength that kept the collective security advocates from offering their own resolution. Significantly, however, Molly Yard, the ASU secretary, as well as Lash, had joined the collective security forces. This led to a bitter denunciation of both of them at the Socialist caucus.[3] In effect, the national executive committee of the ASU had become an association with its own interests rather than a coalition of leaders representing the various groups, and the future of the organization was becoming clear.

The spring and fall of 1937 were a critical period for the student peace movement. Antiwar demonstrations were characterized by battles among the peace forces, as the collective security advocates fought with the pacifists and Socialists for control of the movement. In the process, on many campuses the movement lost the support of middle-of-the-road students, perhaps put off by the sectarian battles. Victories were sometimes moot, as the triumphant group found it had won the right to dominate a rally to which no one came.

However, while the peace movement was disintegrating on the most politicized campuses, like Columbia, on others it was just reaching full growth. The movement was not, in fact, a single organism with one cycle of birth, growth, and decline. Since the movement came later to some campuses, students there were still enjoying the first exhilaration of peace activity when students at the more experienced and perhaps blasé campuses were sinking into acrimony and apathy.

In both 1936 and 1937 the numbers and schools participating in the strike increased substantially. The sponsors estimated that twice as many people were involved in 1936 as in 1935 and that the numbers doubled again the next year.[4] While the figures are somewhat dubious (the estimated one million students in 1937 would have constituted almost the entire national enrollment), it is clear that the strike did expand and had won broad acceptance.

One of the striking features of the rallies of that year was the presence of the Veterans of Future Wars and related groups, including Future Chaplains of Future Wars, Future Gold Star Mothers, and Future War Profiteers. The veterans began at Princeton as a parody of the demand for the Veterans Bonus, their idea being to get it while they were still alive. Chapters sprouted up across the country. Although the national unit at Princeton refused to endorse the strike, many chapters participated and added a somewhat ironic humor to the movement. Some of the more sober student radicals were skeptical of the approach, but it did have a wide appeal and was combined with antiwar ideology.

At Bryn Mawr the Home Fire Division joined with the Princeton chapter for a rally in late April. There was a mood of general hilarity; someone presented a live goose named "Manifest Destiny." But the representative from Haverford suggested that peace was their serious aim. While not allowing the laughter to die down, they should "laugh all the way to Washington."

The Bryn Mawr student paper endorsed the movement in an editorial "Can a Laugh Do It?"[5] There were already 415 chapters with thirty-five thousand members, including half of the Bryn Mawr student body, the editorial stated. With that popularity the Veterans of Future Wars and auxiliaries could be a unifying force in the student movement. It would be necessary, though, to broaden the issues of the organization and not get drowned in nonsense. The object should be "to continue the present freshness and to secure political effectiveness." There was something to be said for making warmakers look ridiculous, and humor could be an effective, if by itself inadequate, weapon against reaction.

Another editorial noted the demand of the Future Gold Star Mothers that they be given expense-paid trips to Europe to visit the unexcavated graves of their unborn sons. In the spirit of the times the editorial proposed an oath: "Why should teachers, after all, have the sole opportunity of swearing allegiance to the Constitution? All Americans, but most particularly future mothers of future veterans, should be accorded the same privilege."[6]

At Lawrence College in Appleton, Wisconsin, a demonstration sponsored by the campus group was broken up by local police and members of the American Legion. At the University of Washington in Seattle twelve hundred students attended the funeral of an "unknown soldier of tomorrow"; the pall bearers were Hitler, Mussolini, Araki, and J. P. Morgan; William Randolph Hearst was chief mourner.[7] The Oxford Pledge maintained its place and its power to inspire controversy. The Detroit Board of Education and the Wayne State University administration attacked the students' support for the oath. At Temple the public pledge ceremony was greeted by eggs, tomatoes, and flour bags thrown from nearby windows by members of the school's football team.[8]

In 1937 the strike was even larger, but the divisions within the movement were becoming obvious. Pacifists and collective security advocates competed for control of campus demonstrations. Nationally the strike was watered down to get wider participation. However, individual colleges reflected their own composition and that of the controlling group.

The national United Student Strike Committee was composed of most of the major student organizations including the ASU, the youth section of the American League against War and Fascism, the American Youth Congress, the CME, the youth section of the Emergency Peace Campaign, the FOR, the student department of the Foreign Policy Association, the National Council of Methodist Youth, the National Collegiate Christian Council, the Joint Committee on United Christian Youth Movement, the League of Nations Association (consultants on educational materials), the National Student Federation of America, and the WRL.[9] The national call, directed to students, faculty, and administrators, presented a program with such standard planks as "demilitarization" of colleges and universities, passage of the Nye-Kvale Bill, and courses in the economic and psychological causes of war; opposition to military spending, urging that the government define what it meant by "adequate national defense"; reaffirmation of the Oxford Pledge; and an ambiguous position regarding neutrality, which stated: "While we advocate stringent neutrality legislation we recognize that it may be inadequate. War anywhere in the world is a threat to the peace of the United States. Only by the cooperation of the people of the world can permanent peace be established." Nationally the pacifists were still winning the debate. On the local level, however, different responses were offered to the issues of Spain and collective security.

The *Advocate* report on the strike noted with satisfaction the increased participation and described it as an impressive show of unity.[10] There were difficulties, however, in both style and content. At some schools the demonstrations had become "routine," "more of a traditional holiday and less of an inspiring spectacle." To an extent, the paper suggested, this could be dealt with by more imaginative planning. More serious were the difficulties which "were primarily a reflection of the divisions throughout the peace movement," specifically, the issue of Spain.

Apparently, on some campuses ASU members had decided not to push their position in order to preserve harmony. According to the editors of the *Advocate*, this was an error. "No unity demands of a constituent group that they abandon their own program. Neither does it prevent the discussion of conflicting views." Rather than back away, advocates of aid for Spain should have fought for their position. Lash and Wechsler proposed a national antiwar congress to "explore these disagreements, evaluate their meaning and chart a meaningful program. Such a Congress should attract students of every faith and affiliation. It should open the door for as bitter a debate as events may demand." And the result should be a coherent and strong peace program for the next strike.

The editors hoped, of course, that this program would be the one they favored, and, indeed, proposing a national convention was to their advantage in this. At conventions decisions went to the best-organized group, and the meetings usually had the advantage of excluding nonaffiliated students or those who would participate in campus decision making. Those students were often the ones who supported the maintenance of the traditional peace plans and who had not yet been won over to "collective security" (increasingly a euphemism for intervention).

The divisions and their effects varied from campus to campus. At Columbia the 1937 demonstration was the smallest in three years. The *Spectator* looked for reasons for the disinterest and apathy that had overtaken the progressive forces, and it found them in the split between the proponents of collective security and the advocates of neutrality, a split that made a united front "virtually impossible, and certainly ineffectual."[11] (Another reason may have been simply that the old leadership had finally graduated, and the new student body had different interests.)

At other schools activism was growing. Even Whittier College, a small Quaker school in California with five hundred students, saw some activity. In April 1936 congressional candidate Jerry Voorhis spoke at an all-college peace observance. The student body was not much stirred, but the town and trustees were agitated. The following year, Bill Schmitt, "a dynamic student liberal," organized a student strike against war. A respected Whittier pastor and a member of the American Legion were "prudently chosen to introduce the speakers."[12] In the fall the Student Christian Association applied for a permit in the town Armistice Day parade sponsored by the American Legion. After the students had begun building a float with a scene from the antiwar play *Bury the Dead*, their entry was canceled.

In Milwaukee, too, interest in peace increased. An ASU chapter was not formed at Milwaukee State Teachers College until the fall of 1936. In late September the organizers announced that it would organize around four points: peace—opposition to militarism in education and government; freedom—to defend the right of teachers and students to speak and act on major social and political issues; security—to promote legislation for student relief; and education—to work for a "sweeping extension of educational facilities."[13] It was a program particularly well suited to the school, which had had antiwar sentiment throughout the decade. Since it was a teacher-training school dominated by progressive educators, academic freedom and educational opportunity were obvious issues to rally around. William Biddle, an education instructor, was the faculty adviser.

Although the chapter did not become very large (there seems to have been a core of about 15 members between 1936 and 1939, out of an enrollment of 1,250), it did attract a diverse group, including many students active in campus life. Organized by radicals, it attracted individuals not connected with the NSL or the SLID. In April 1937, when the first efforts were made to form a chapter, the campus paper advised liberals to join the ASU. "Those students who have radical leanings will naturally waste little time in affiliating themselves with the college branch and rightly so." If the group failed to represent student opinion, it would be the fault of the "disinterested majority rather than of the zealous minority."[14] Although some of the ASU members at Milwaukee were Marxists, the general tone seems to have been a mixture of progressivism and populism: John Dewey and Bob La Follette.

Eugene Schwartz, of the class of 1939, was the first president. Describing the rise of the American student movement, he struck a grim note: "The stark realities and conditions revealed by the depression smashed the naive sophistication of a jazz-drunk youth. Youth began to feel its own power and groups sprang up throughout the country, prompted more by objective conditions than by idealistic aims." Socialist groups and religious groups became active; antiwar strikes occurred. Youth was awake. "The materialism and sophistication of the major portion of the 8,000,000 youth, potential field for the inroads of fascism, was giving way."[15]

But the ASU's first objective at Milwaukee was the improvement of study facilities and an Armistice Day program. The keynote speaker was the pastor of Kenwood Methodist Church and a member of the Emergency Peace Campaign. The program included a dramatic production and violin selections to represent "the universality of anti-war sentiment as reflected in music and literature as well as in political activity."[16] In April 1936, four hundred students attended a meeting sponsored by the art club, *Echo*, the Representative Speakers Bureau, the philosophy club, and the YWCA and addressed by the pastor of the Congregational church. One hundred and fifty people paraded to Lake Park as a "dress rehearsal of what they would do if war began."[17] The students passed seven resolutions, including a reaffirmation of the Oxford Pledge, opposition to ROTC, support for the Nye-Kvale Bill, support for the embargo of war materials, protection of academic freedom, and alignment with other groups working for peace. The motto of the assembly was "Live, not die; build, not destroy; love, not hate."

Students at Milwaukee joined in the National Emergency Peace Campaign of 1936–37 (described by one historian as the greatest unified effort made by peace advocates until at least the Vietnamese War).[18] The Representative Speakers Bureau voted a requirement that students prepare talks on various peace topics to be presented "mostly to rural groups to arouse an active intelligent peace movement."[19] The student newspaper gave considerable attention to international issues and publicized and encouraged the April peace strikes and Peace Tag Day as the opening of Peace Week in 1937.

The 1937 demonstration at Milwaukee State Teachers College was organized by a joint committee of the Emergency Peace Campaign and the ASU. The speakers were Homer Chaney, an economics professor and California organizer of the Emergency Peace Campaign, and William Biddle, the ASU faculty adviser, as well as several students. About 250 students attended and 100 participated in a parade after the assembly. Both Chaney and Biddle indicated their skepticism that neutrality would be adequate to prevent war and emphasized the need to eliminate war's economic and social causes.[20]

In his column in the student paper, President Frank Baker reported on his speech at the University of Minnesota at the student strike there. He had shared the platform with the state's governor, Elmer Benson, who, contrary to the wishes of the school's administration, had proclaimed a state Peace Day and urged the participation of all state educational institutions.[21] Baker noted that Benson's role, which made the peaceful demonstration possible, should "suggest to those who believe that democracy can be saved only by fundamental changes in the social order, that the problem confronting all liberals is to give more attention to the election of officials friendly to the liberal movement."

The spring of 1937 saw the last unified national antiwar strike. The increasing conflict within the antiwar organizations is represented by two conferences held at Vassar in the fall and winter of 1937. The first was an "All Youth against War" meeting of pacifist young people; the other was the third annual convention of the ASU.

The pacifist gathering on November 6 and 7, 1937, was sponsored by the FOR, the WILPF, the WRL, and the American Friends Service Committee. Its purpose was to plan strategy for the campus and to try to hold the student movement to pacifism. The meeting coincided with the formation by Socialists and pacifists of a youth committee for the Oxford Pledge to fight for that position in the anticipated battle at the ASU convention.

The pacifists had disagreements among themselves over such issues as the boycott of Japanese goods, alternative service during wartime, and the provision of nonmilitary relief to one side in a war (obviously a reflection of the difficulty in providing a pacifist alternative in Spain). However, they did produce a set of common principles. Christian socialism mixed with Marxism to create a voice against the acceptance of war and the status quo.

Their statement began with a definition of a pacifist as "one who refuses to work or participate in any war, international and civil, and who works to remove the causes of war."[22] This position could be based on an "absolute ethic of love," a belief that "brotherhood transcends all other loyalties and therefore must never be violated." The pacifist repudiated war and turned to noncooperation and nonviolent resistance as alternatives.

The statement observed that in recent months the youth peace movement had become "split to the point of an open break." In opposition to the advocates of collective security, the pacifists believed "that the basic economic divisions and dislocations of world economy cannot be solved by collective security but only by a basic readjustment of natural resources, markets, and freer world trade—the method of peaceful change." They then listed points on which all agreed and then those on which most agreed. The group favored disarmament and opposed militarism, and therefore opposed ROTC, compulsory military service, the Industrial Mobilization Plan, military control of the Civilian Conservation Corps, and the large military budget; demanded the withdrawal of American troops from the Far East, since their presence there was a constant provocation to Japan; favored repeal of the Japanese Exclusion Act; opposed imperialism and favored freedom for all colonial peoples; recognized the need for "racial reconciliation."

Most of those present at the meeting also believed that neutrality should be invoked and strengthened and that the Oxford Pledge, though not pacifist, should be retained; called upon workers to refuse to manufacture or ship arms and munitions, especially to nations at war; opposed collective security as a "cloak to preserve the status quo"; and, finally, advocated the "abolition of our present economic system and its replacement with a cooperative economy based upon production for use and not production for profit."[23]

How all this was to be achieved was, again, unclear. They knew they were in a minority and did not expect a revolution or an immediate end to killing. Therefore, they adopted tactics appropriate to a minority position. In order that their "convictions and energies [might] be sharpened and not dissipated," they formed pacifist teams to be "the center to loyalty, conviction and study, as well as planning for action."[24] Cooperation with other groups was important, but the maintenance of the pacifists' distinctive position was essential. Efforts would be made to win others over, but as the movement split and they became more isolated, it became more and more a matter of pacifist fellowship and unity in a hostile world.

About 160 young people attended the pacifists' meeting; the ASU convention at the end of December had almost 500. Hal Draper, a YPSL member and peace organizer at Brooklyn College, described what happened. Roosevelt's "Quarantine Speech" in October had capped a year of increased prowar feeling. "By the end of 1937 the Communists, in bloc with Lash, were in a position to dump the last vestiges of the student movement's militant politics and antiwar activity. At the convention, a well organized Socialist bloc of delegates carried on a last ditch fight to save the Oxford Pledge, but lost 282–108."[25]

The battle over the peace program dominated the convention. As another observer related: "From the start it was known that the most heated debates, the highest feeling and a large part of the time of the convention would be spent on the peace program. . . . One could hear it debated in the halls, at the dinner table or among groups of people walking across the campus."[26]

Debate was precipitated by Lash's report to the convention. Speaking both as a national officer and as a representative for part, though not all, of the national staff, he supported collective security, declaring that "isolation is retreat before aggression and leads inevitably to world war." Lash noted that in April 1936 the ASU had condemned aggression and the embargo on Spain. In somewhat contradictory fashion, he both urged the boycott of Japanese goods and pushed the continued fight against ROTC and militarism at home. Acknowledging that the ASU national staff disagreed on peace policy, he said of the statement that it represented his own position. "We can no longer subscribe to the Oxford Pledge of non-support to any war which the government may undertake." The Oxford Pledge was "too fantastic. . . . The United States must 'snap out of a dream world.'"[27] Lash urged full support for administration foreign policy.

The battle was fought in the peace commission and then again on the convention floor. The debate was bitter, but in the end the Communists and liberals won out for collective security, and the Oxford Pledge was dropped. The convention urged the United States government to take the lead in naming aggressors and joining other nations in applying economic sanctions. At the same time, while urging material aid to Spain, it called for trade union action to prevent shipment of arms to the rebel forces. Continuing its internal contradictions, the policy reaffirmed opposition to war preparations, a large military budget, the Sheppard-Hill Industrial Mobilization Bill, and compulsory ROTC. It also urged the withdrawal of all United States military forces from foreign countries and favored passage of the Ludlow amendment.[28]

In short, although the collective security forces had carried the day, they were still attempting to reconcile their new aggressiveness with their old principles and to compromise with those who feared the trend toward involvement. The ASU was at the peak of its strength, in terms of membership, and made a desperate effort to hold itself together. The effort was to prove inadequate and was probably foredoomed. There was ultimately no middle ground between staying out and getting in. And for all the talk about economic sanctions, it was clear that many former peace workers were moving toward war.

Yet like the Roosevelt administration, the ASU members

were not ready to accept publicly the logic of their position. Their effort to paper over the differences within the group left them open to the obvious criticism of inconsistency. Pacifists, in particular, pointed this out. An editorial in the Milwaukee State Teachers College paper condemned the dropping of the Oxford Pledge. "To pacifist members of the ASU it means that one of the basic principles . . . upon which the ASU was built is gone. Now rather than a strong united group opposed to war, the anti-war group is but a one-legged peace organization which will probably be blown over under the first stiff blast from Mars."[29] The new program did not make sense, the editorial continued.

> Those who want peace so much have abandoned their
> unqualified pacifism and instead have put them-
> selves in a position of a man who attacks a mad dog and
> throws his gun away. The ASU wants the people
> of the United States to boycott Japanese goods, place an
> embargo on shipments of war material to Japan,
> and yet not to prepare for the war to which they are
> pushing Uncle Sam by this stand.

The pacifists even then perceived what latter-day hawks and critics of thirties "isolationism" would think they invented: that the moderates and liberal advocates of collective security were in fact taking steps toward war without adequately preparing for it or admitting the consequences of their actions to themselves or to the public. A gap thus continued between those favoring American intervention in one way or another and the public whom they kept trying to reassure that war could be avoided.

Indeed, after the dropping of the Oxford Pledge the ASU became virtually an arm of the New Deal. Draper later wrote that by the 1938 convention, with the Socialist left wing gone, "the complete Popular Frontization of the organization bore fruit. The Roosevelt administration gave official blessing to the ASU, in a letter of greetings to the convention from the President. . . . The student movement was now completely respectable, completely pro-administration and completely emasculated."[30] A reading of the *Advocate* for 1938 indicates the degree to which it had become a voice of support for Roosevelt's foreign policy. Indeed, at the end of the year, ostensibly because of financial difficulties, the *Advocate* was allowed to die. Wechsler had already left both the *Advocate* and the Communist party.

By 1938 the young Communists had won control of the organization, partly through their alliance with liberals who agreed with the collective security position that the party was then advocating. In turn, the Communists had become devout New Dealers. Both the Communist party and its youth branch adopted Abraham Lincoln as their hero and "Communism Is Twentieth Century Americanism" as their new slogan. In their efforts to become acceptable the young Communists turned to sports as a means of showing that they were all-American boys and girls. A bulletin of the Young Communists League at Wisconsin indicates the new attitude (as well as the male-oriented recruiting rhetoric).

> Some people have the idea that a YCL'er is politically minded, that nothing outside of politics means anything. Gosh, no. They have a few simple problems. There is the problem of getting good men on the baseball team this Spring, of opposition from other ping-pong teams, of dating girls, etc. We go to shows, parties, dances and all that. In short, the YCL and its members are no different from other people except that we believe in dialectical materialism as the solution to all problems.[31]

This was a long way from the radical attacks on the commercialization of athletics and the priorities of university expenditures. Sports was still political, but now the Communists used it to attempt to improve their own public image and to minimize their militance.

The ASU also revised its image. This process began at the 1937 convention and became pronounced the next year. These efforts are indicated in the song that became popular in some circles that year: "ASU Swings the Nation."

> From CO_2 to Pi R Square,
> From the Great Garbo to Fred Astaire,
> From Kalamazoo to anywhere;
> Everybody's doin' it
> A*S*U'in it.

> From the Lamda Pi to the D.A.R.,
> From Junior High to old Vassar,
> From the loop in Chi to Union Square,
> Everybody's doin' it—
> A*S*U'in it.

> Alma Mater's goin' modern,
> Lash's dream is coming true.
> It's an academic epidemic
> Gonna join the A*S*U.

The only concession to politics was a stanza excluding Hearst, Walter Lippmann, Ford, Morgan, and the "Du Pont Brothers."[32]

This trend was also evident on some campuses. A promotional ad for the ASU at Temple, for example, urged students to join the organization in order to "meet the people who do things around Temple."[33] The campus group's accomplishments included a book co-op, the publication of *Tempo*, "intelligent action for peace," "a stiff fight against fascism," "an even break for labor," and "Saturday night music parties." The ad noted that on weekends "Progressives relax" and listen to Brahms Fourth Symphony or "One Big Union for Two." It was a logical, if excessive, extension of Lash's idea that the ASU should create a real community. However, at least in its publicity, camaraderie sometimes appears to be the end rather than the means of radical action. Likewise, the interest in campus issues sometimes took odd turns. In December 1938 an article in *Tempo*, the chapter magazine, urged that the university offer band scholarships. Football was itself a great sport, the writer noted, but "it would not hold its present place in the American heart were it not for the color and amusement supplied by the band."[34]

There were still limits to the degree to which some students were willing to accept uncritically the virtues of the American sports world. Perhaps taking his theme from the Odets play, an ASU member wrote an article entitled "The Golden Boys," which described boxing as an exploitative racket. "Who is Joe Bananas? He is any boxer who comes up from the slums with marked ability and no brains, to dance awhile in the hot, white glare. Then to pass on crushed. He is a rising champ; he is just a fallen star."[35] He was an obvious victim of a capitalist society, the article concluded, where poverty can be profitable for promoters.

The ASU statement of purpose could have been found in a Democratic (or Republican) party platform. An ad in the *Advocate* in March 1938 urged students to join the ASU to keep them "going places," "doing things for peace and progress," for "throughout the country the American Student Union leads the student crusade for a peaceful and prosperous social order, spotlights international crisis and domestic emergency with reason and understanding, [and] chronicles the modern undergraduate temper in cogent, applicable terms through the *Student Advocate*."[36]

Although nationally the ASU was rather a tamed tiger, it remained active and sometimes militant on individual campuses. However, it tended to change its focus from international events to campus concerns: the promotion of student co-ops, problems related to dorm life and student affairs, and, still on some campuses, ROTC. Indeed, its membership continued high throughout 1938 and 1939; substantial decline came only with the Stalin-Hitler pact, which, in fact, spelled the death of the ASU. Even then, some chapters managed to continue, often downplaying the latest twists in foreign policy. At Temple, for example, the chapter directed its attention toward Asia or toward student issues like National Youth Administration programs and financial aid.[37]

But if international events could be downplayed, they could not be made to disappear. Through 1938–39 the world condition worsened. Although the changing position of the Communist party and its youthful allies was a force in changing the current of the ASU, other developments were equally significant. Events abroad altered the perceptions and opinions of both the young Communists themselves and many of the non-Communist members. The Spanish Civil War in particular was a major, emotional force in moving former pacifists into the collective security camp.

Still, the resistance within the ASU and the student movement was remarkable. A strong corps of pacifists continued active, and on campus there continued to be a general reluctance among students to join the calls for American intervention or preparation for war. But the flood of events was sweeping closer, and the campus could not remain untouched.

Chapter 10

Movement to War

In September 1939 German armies invaded Poland, giving final impetus to a new world war. It was to be another two years before the United States formally joined the conflict. During that time an internal struggle took place over public policy and public opinion. Both interventionists and those opposed to American involvement attempted to win popular support for their positions. Government officials also attempted to swing public opinion in the direction of policies that they favored.

One group whose opinions aroused particular concern was youth, and specifically college students. Partly because they were more organized and accessible than other young people, students were the targets of both internal and external efforts to shape their views on foreign policy. Discussion in the country at large was echoed on the college campus and in the student movement. As the United States approached involvement, the increasing intolerance for dissenting views in the nation was reflected and sometimes preceded by limits on dissent on campus. These limits added to the serious internal divisions of the student movement and the antiwar forces in general. Throughout the period, however, students remained reluctant to support American involvement.

In August 1939 Germany and the Soviet Union signed a

nonaggression pact. It was a stunning blow to the American Left and to the student movement. The ASU, like the Communist party, abandoned the collective security line and became once again anti-interventionist.

Their move back into the antiwar camp created difficulties for the peace movement and the student movement. The overt identification of the ASU with the Communist party and the identification of the Communists with the interests of the Soviet Union made them an awkward ally. At the same time, those opposed to any views to the left of the American Legion were given an excuse for increasing suppression of dissenting organizations or unpopular ideas.

That fall the young Communists and the ASU chapters that they dominated made an abrupt about-face; their motto was now "The Yanks Are Not Coming." In December the ASU and the American Youth Committee were the focus of hearings of the Dies Committee (the Special Committee on Un-American Activities of the House of Representatives). Supposedly investigating the political behavior of both fascist and Communist propaganda activities in the United States, the committee spent most of its time looking into the political activity of the Left in general and students in particular. Joe Lash was called to testify regarding the ASU, of which he was still an officer in spite of his split with the Communists over the pact. Eleanor Roosevelt attended the hearings to take note of any unnecessary browbeating of her young friends. The committee proceeded to list the ASU as a Communist front.[1]

Much of this hostility preceded the Nazi-Soviet pact, and its increase was related to increasing pressures for United States entry into the war and general opposition to dissent. This was true on the state and local levels as well as the national. Even without the Left's own errors, many of its opponents were quick to take advantage of the opportunity to move against "radicals and subversives."

Throughout the decades there had been investigations of alleged radicalism on campus, and private organizations had sometimes made accusations. The Daughters of the American Revolution, for example, had drawn up a list of schools and organizations said to be "contaminated" by "subversives." The list included, among others, the Berkeley Divinity School, Smith College, the Barnard College Social Science Club, the Vassar College Political Association, the Bryn Mawr Summer School, and the Bryn Mawr Liberal Club.[2]

State legislatures also conducted inquiries into conditions at both public and private schools. The New York City Colleges were the targets of especially bitter attack. Although in many ways the student movement there had died down by 1939, its image and the continuing activity of radical teachers still frightened people. In March 1940 the New York state legislature created a joint legislative committee for the alleged purpose of studying educational administration, policies, and costs, but much of its effort was applied toward discovering the level of "subversive activity" in the schools and colleges of New York. This inquiry closely resembled the post–World War I activity of the Lusk Committee. In the course of the new hearings, which concentrated on the faculty, 503 witnesses appeared before the committee and 13,340 pages of testimony were taken.[3]

Two witnesses named faculty members who, they claimed, had belonged to a Communist party cell on the City College campus. The Red Hunt was supported by the college administration, and many of the faculty went to great lengths to disassociate themselves from the radicals. In statements to the press, President Harry Wright (who had succeeded Robinson) and the alumni association emphasized that those suspected amounted to only a small minority of the college staff. The Board of Higher Education established its own investigation and instituted charges against teachers and staff members named as subversives by the Senate report. As a result seventeen teachers were fired; eighteen others were suspended; six others were "not reappointed"; and seven signed "under charges."

Academic freedom, never very secure, was foundering. It was not always a matter of political views. During this time a state supreme court justice voided the appointment of Bertrand Russell to the City College philosophy department. This followed considerable pressure, particularly from church groups, and the judge's own determination that the college had no right to appoint Russell, because he was an alien, had not taken a civil service exam, and his teaching would adversely affect public morals, since it would tend to "aid, abet, or encourage any course of conduct tending toward a violation of the penal code."[4] It appears to have been the philosopher's views on sex, rather than his politics, which concerned the judge, but the two questions were related.

In both cases—the action of the state legislature and of the judge—opposition to interference by external organizations was minimal on the part of the college administration and most of the faculty and students. What is most striking is not the actions of the reactionaries but the silence of the liberals. Increasingly convinced of the necessity of intervention in the European war, they were increasingly caught up in and indeed helped foster the mood of repression that they had previously predicted. Reinhold Niebuhr provided the philosophical-theological rationale. In an article in the *Nation* in January 1939, Niebuhr, who had become an advocate of collective security, criticized liberalism for its self-destructive tolerance. It did not understand "the necessity of coercion for the sake of securing social cooperation" (or, he added, "the necessity of resistance to power for the sake of securing justice"). Force was sometimes necessary. "Some of the best medicines are poisons taken in moderation."[5]

Legislation defeated in 1935 and 1939 now passed with some liberal support. The Alien Registration Act was passed by the House of Representatives in July 1939. It was declared unlawful for any person to teach or advocate the overthrow of the government, to print or distribute materials urging such an overthrow, to organize a group for such purposes, or knowingly to belong to such an organization. In July 1940 Roosevelt signed it into law as the Smith Act. By 1940 the FBI was running name checks, opening files, and making reports on people sending telegrams to the president that were "more or less in opposition to national defense."[6]

In the fall of 1940 oaths of allegiance were required for the first time by the National Youth Administration for all students receiving assistance. Loyalty oaths received new impetus in state legislatures. The governor of Pennsylvania decided that all state employees should take loyalty oaths. Compared to battles waged in previous years, resistance was slight. The student editor of the Temple *News* thought the oath a good idea: "No longer may we, as students, wrap ourselves in a cloak of theory and leave the practises of the world to those who hold the reins. . . . These are exciting times we live in. They will make great stuff for tales to tell our grandchildren."[7] As one increasingly lonesome civil libertarian observed, "A nation which had successfully passed through six wars unprotected by teachers' oaths and the compulsory flag salutes of children found them sweeping state after state like an epidemic."[8]

On individual campuses the ASU was attacked by both administrators and students. In June 1940 twelve members of the ASU at the University of Michigan were expelled, apparently as the result of chapter activities including the formation of a CIO union of campus employees, antiwar activities, and the participation of two black students in a sit-in in an Ann Arbor restaurant. The following December the managing editor and editorial director of the student paper were suspended for a week for having published a letter from the head of the campus ASU.[9]

At the University of Pennsylvania both student newspapers supported the university's demand that ASU submit a membership list. This was required of all organizations, but the ASU members believed that it posed a particular threat to their organization, since students might be reluctant to join, fearing that the list might be used against them. In the spring of 1941 a large group of undergraduates disrupted an ASU meeting. Student efforts to have the group's charter revoked finally succeeded the following fall. At about the same time, at Temple, by a unanimous vote of the student senate, the ASU chapter there was revoked, following a petition to that effect signed by five hundred students. The reason given for the revocation was that "the American Student Union conduct has been the cause of unfavorable outside opinion which is unjust to the entire student body and a detriment to our University." It should perhaps be noted that previously the ASU had urged that a Trotskyist group be denied a charter, ostensibly because of the undemocratic way in which the club was run.[10]

Hostility, however, was extended to all antiwar groups. The attitude of many administrators was expressed by the president of the University of California. Attacking a movement against conscription in 1940, Robert Sproul declared that students in the peace movement had no place on campus. "For those who prefer to fiddle while Rome burns or to accelerate the pace of destruction by building bonfires, I shall have little sympathy. Indeed, I may find it necessary to ask some of them to defer the enjoyment of an education at the state's expense until the life and prosperity of the state have been made secure again by their more patriotic fellows."[11]

Some student newspapers continued to defend the right

to express, and to hear, dissident views. At Columbia, President Butler refused to allow Earl Browder to speak at a civil liberties symposium at the university. The *Spectator* defended the Communist party leader's right to speak and declared that the passport evasion charges against him, which were the alleged reason for the prohibition, did not invalidate his constitutional rights.[12]

In Milwaukee, too, the student newspaper remained a defender of free expression. The *Echo Weekly* noted attempts at suppression of free speech at Columbia and the University of Michigan and the suggestion in the Marquette University paper that books by authors like John Dewey and Harold Rugg be burned. Such efforts, the editor declared, "would make the university and college a factory which merely processes raw, ignorant, and uninformed freshmen into properly uniform and indoctrinated professional men." Advocates of censorship were "petty dictators" who "would circumvent truth and deny the existence of the free personality and the objective and inquisitive mind." The editor of the *Echo* defended the values of a society at peace in the midst of a world at war. In the spring of 1941 the paper opposed a resolution in the Milwaukee Common Council urging that the state require teachers to take a loyalty oath.[13]

Attacks on the ASU and other groups were probably less significant in the decline of the student movement than were divisions within the movement itself. These divisions, always present, were exacerbated by the nonaggression pact, and by subsequent events. Specifically, the Soviet invasion of Finland in November 1939 created considerable acrimony both nationally and on individual campuses. Student opinion resembled the divisions in the nation at large: young Communists supported the invasion and others opposed it as an act of aggression upon a smaller nation.

The debate within the ASU also reflected the failure of the advocates of collective security to win over the masses of students. Although students were sympathetic to Finland, they were, on the whole, still far from supporting any United States intervention abroad and fearful of taking any position that might lead to that involvement. Although the positions taken by the ASU and the American Youth Congress received the most notoriety, more significant voices were heard on individual campuses.

At the ASU convention in December 1940, Lash led a move to condemn the invasion. By a vote of 322 to 49 the motion was defeated. The margin apparently surprised both Lash and the Communists. Explaining the vote to Eleanor Roosevelt, Lash noted that the Soviet sympathizers had been joined by a large number of liberals who feared that such a condemnation would add to war hysteria and recreate the conditions that led to American intervention in World War I. Others feared that the resolution would force a break-up of the ASU and felt that only resolutions on which there was a general agreement should be passed.

Indeed it is clear from Lash's own description of the fight that it was his intention to divide the ASU on pro-Communist and anti-Soviet lines, and to win over the non-Communist bloc to collective security as well as condemnation of Soviet aggression.[14] A manifesto was drawn up by Molly Yard, Agnes Reynolds, and Lash, after consultation with Wechsler, which described the division within the ASU as one "between those who desire to base ASU policy on the needs and traditions of the American people, and those who identify the interests of mankind with the Soviet Government." The ASU vote provoked a torrent of criticism and gave the House Un-American Activities Committee an excuse to place the ASU on the subversive list as a "front" for the Communist party.

A similar dispute, with a similar result, took place at the American Youth Congress. Its meeting in Washington in February 1940 was distinguished by the fervor of antiwar speeches and the booing of Franklin Roosevelt when he gave a hard-line speech attacking the congress for failing to condemn the Soviet invasion.[15] That the president appeared before the group at all indicates Eleanor Roosevelt's influence, and the administration's belief that the two groups did represent a significant segment of youth and one which needed to be won over. Lash's memoirs may perhaps naturally exaggerate the government's concern with youth's antiwar activities, but they do testify to some unease among those in power about the persistence of anti-interventionist feeling. It was not merely the existence of antiwar sentiment that was of concern but the potential of national organizations to mobilize that sentiment.

This concern was probably unwarranted. The lopsided nature of the votes at the national meetings contrasts with developments on individual campuses. There, sympathy for Finland was stronger and opposition to the Soviet Union broader. Although the ASU and the American Youth Congress did represent a segment of youth, they increasingly lacked the broad support to be effective antiwar organizations.

Developments at Temple University were similar to those on several other campuses. Debate was kicked off by an editorial in the Temple *News* deploring the failure of the ASU convention to condemn the Soviet Union. The Temple delegates responded by stating that although many delegates felt the invasion to be unjustified, they feared that the issue was being used by those who wanted to drag the United States into war. Prior to the national convention the Temple chapter had passed a resolution condemning Finland as a "tool of British imperial interests" and declaring that the Finnish people did not wish to resist Russia but had been forced into it by the British. (This is not as strange a position as it may sound. Even Harold Ickes had his doubts about Finland. He described Marshal Mannerheim as a man who had repressed the peasantry and who was tied to "the aristocratic and monied interests of England and France.")[16]

The Temple *News* described as inconsistent the Temple chapter's failure to condemn Soviet aggression when it had recently passed a resolution condemning Japan. The editorial criticized the ASU inaction as a blunder that would endanger "every liberal movement in America."[17]

The editor, who was supporter of the antiwar movement, was not alone in his opinion. In March the issue caused a split in the Peace Council when a motion to condemn Soviet aggression was defeated thirty-one to thirty-two. Significantly, however, even the resolution that was voted down did not call for American intervention or even financial or military assistance to Finland. It had merely condemned "this useless method of solving problems" and expressed sympathy" for both the Russian and Finnish people."[18]

If the antiwar movement was divided, it was nevertheless alive. Although the April 1940 demonstrations were far smaller than those of previous years, they do indicate the continued presence of antiwar feeling on the campus. National groups competed for students' support, including the FOR, the WRL, the Student Peace Service of the AFSC, the WILPF, the Youth Committee against War, the United States Peace Committee, the American Committee for Democracy and Intellectual Freedom, the Commission to Study the Organization of Peace, the United Peace Chest, and the World Student Association for Peace, Freedom, and Culture.[19] College administrations for reason of prudence or principle found it appropriate to sponsor peace convocations that April, and an estimated five hundred campuses had meetings of some sort.

At Temple a new peace federation was formed, including the ASU, the University League for Liberal Action, the Jewish Student Association, and the Student Christian Association. On April 19 classes were dismissed and attendance taken at a "peace convocation." The speakers were all students, and the main address was by Jack McMichael, chairman of the American Youth Committee and a Union Theological Seminary student. Roy Nichols from Lincoln University spoke of the need for activity by people of all races and warned of a repetition of the World War I experience. Another antiwar meeting was held in May, sponsored by the All University Peace Movement and organized by thirty-five student leaders. The dominant note was pro-Ally but anti-intervention, and the meeting was attended by five hundred people.[20]

At the University of Pennsylvania both student newspapers supported the April rally, at which Jack McMichael was also the principal speaker. The papers noted that though the effort seemed futile, antiwar activity deserved the attention of all students to "let the country know what its coming generation feels about its own future."[21] The meeting was based upon the platform of the United Student Peace Committee, the provisions of which show the stripping of antiwar activity to the bare bones of resistance and the relinquishing of ideology and analysis to achieve broad agreement:

> Oppose all steps to war—Doughboys follow dough.
> Don't follow the headlines into the front lines.
> Fight for democracy at home.
> Strengthen civil liberty, war's first victim.
> Make our campus a fortress for democracy, not a fortress.
> Extend international fellowship.

Ironically, the conservatives of the peace movement at Penn were now rallying around the program of what was basically the Communist peace organization (though the editors seem not to have noticed this). This testifies not only to the agility of the left wing but also to a common stream of antiwar emotions and concepts that cut across ideological and political boundaries.

Meanwhile, in Milwaukee, Frank Baker, president of Milwaukee State Teachers College, continued to encourage students in resistance to American involvement. He was not an isolationist, and had no sympathy or tolerance for fascism. Yet, while many of his fellow progressive educators were becoming avid interventionists, he remained a pacifist. Baker was sixty-three in 1940, and for him the last war was no distant event. War no longer seemed a crusade or an adventure. There were enough enemies at home, enough fascists at home who could only benefit from a militarized society. (Since in Wisconsin the war was preceded by the Age of La Follette and followed by the Age of McCarthy, this was somewhat prophetic.)

In his commencement address in June 1940, Baker urged the graduates to beware of war hysteria and to work to keep America out of war.[22] He warned: "Our defense against this same technique [Hitler's appeal to hate] of perversion of the human spirit will vanish with our entry into the second world war. If we would preserve our culture, our liberty, our sanity, we must stay out. By entering the second world war we shall not save Europe and we shall destroy the America we love."

With Baker's encouragement and example, the peace movement did continue at Milwaukee State Teachers College. In April 1940 the students joined in the national strike sponsored by a committee that included the FOR, the National Council of Methodist Youth, the Student Peace Service (AFSC), the WRL, the WILPF, the YPSL, and the Youth Committee against War. The peace platform included support for the Ludlow Amendment, which would require a popular referendum for any declaration of war, and the Oxford Oath. The Student Teachers Union led the strike on campus, and speakers included a local pastor, the director of the Wisconsin extension division, William Biddle, an art instructor, two teachers from the economics department, and representatives of the United Electrical Workers, the

Radio and Machine Workers local, and American Federation of Teachers Local 79.[23]

Baker's support for the movement was an exception. On the whole, administrators and faculty members were much more interventionist than were students. In their 1940 study of war propaganda, Wechsler and Harold Lavine observed that "as in the last war American faculties were predominantly interventionist. But undergraduate resistance was far more widespread."[24] This brought students into "frequent and bitter" conflict with hawkish faculty members.

As Harvard, for example, when a group of undergraduates petitioned Roosevelt to maintain American neutrality, Professor Roger B. Merriman, a senior professor of history, accused them of being blind to the moral issues involved. On the other hand, in December 1940 some students picketed a rally by the Militant Aid to Britain Committee. One placard read, "Let's Send 50 Overage Professors to Britain."[25]

Some of the anti-interventionist sentiment at Harvard was isolationist rather than pacifist. In January 1941, at Harvard Law School, Joseph P. Kennedy, Jr., wrote to John T. Flynn, a leading America First Committee representative, to invite him to speak on behalf of the Harvard Committee against Martial Intervention. Kennedy himself spoke a few weeks later as a member of College Men for Defense First in Washington at a meeting at which Senator Robert Taft was the main speaker.[26]

Wechsler and Lavine described students as one of the groups most opposed to intervention in the spring of 1940. They saw this as a result of the peace movement of the previous years. In particular the Veterans of Future Wars had been effective in reducing war to an absurdity. Noble appeals and reports of Axis horrors were met with a skepticism that was alarming to those who hoped to win youth to the cause. Reinhold Niebuhr warned in an article in the *Nation* in January 1940 that "the attitude of cynicism prompted by disappointed idealism is morally intolerable." He described college students as "pretty generally engaged in proving that since all war news is propaganda they are absolved from the responsibility of seeking for the truth amid conflicting claims."[27]

Although this was not true of all students, according to Lavine and Wechsler, "Nowhere did the distrust of Allied proclamations seem more pronounced than on the campus." In this, students reflected both national opinion and that of their age group. "Allied spokesmen professed to encounter the deepest hostility among undergraduates and youth groups in general; among those who were most clearly of draft age."[28] This vulnerability obviously had something to do with the reaction of a West Coast group which called itself "We Who Would Die." This is not a total explanation; other generations in the same position have not been so reluctant.

The ghost of the Great War kept reappearing. As Wechsler and Lavine wrote, "Most students had grown up in the era of 'revisionism' and the last war overshadowed the new one."[29] Summarizing their analysis of student opinion, the authors wrote, "None of these manifestations was final proof that the interventionist cause was lost on the campus or among young people generally. What it did show was that idealistic proclamations were viewed with unease and continuing suspicion." Responding to criticism like that of Niebuhr and others, they noted that youth could not be convinced to fight for a lesser of two evils. "A 'lesser evil' is not a fighting faith. Men are mobilized to die 'for' ideals; negative slogans are not enough." The differences between the sides involved, between Germany and Britain, would have to be drawn more clearly before young people could be convinced of the need to go to war.

Events of the summer of 1940, however, did tend to erode the anti-interventionist position. In May the German armies struck into the Lowlands and into France. In July Paris fell, and on 17 July, Petain surrendered the country to the Germans. Their bombers were then free to turn their full attention on England, and that summer the Battle of Britain began. The rapid success of the Axis destroyed the argument that the Allies could hold their own without American involvement. The only questions remaining were whether the United States could afford to allow a German victory in Europe and, if not, what form American action should take.

Some of the strongest support for some degree of involvement came from former members of the peace movement. Among these were Walter Millis, whose *Road to War* had presented a revisionist view of the world war; Charles P. Taft, a former leader of the Emergency Peace Campaign; and Rabbi Judah L. Magnes, an opponent of World War I who believed that war was against God's will but who had come to believe that there was no alternative.[30]

Perhaps the most prominent and effective convert to interventionism was Niebuhr. He had come full circle. Niebuhr had supported World War I, but in the postwar disillusionment he had become a pacifist. In the thirties Marxism led him to renounce complete pacifism and to accept the use of violence as a revolutionary measure. In 1934 he had resigned from the FOR (of which he had been a national chairman), as he saw no possibility of reconciliation in a class war. But this acceptance of revolutionary violence opened the way to his final position: belief in war as a necessary evil. By early 1940, Niebuhr had become a vocal and influential advocate of collective security and intervention.[31]

The hostility with which he then began attacking the pacifists bespeaks the emotional nature of the break. He joined other clergymen, including Henry Sloane Coffin of Union Theological Seminary, in founding *Christianity and Crisis* in early 1941 to combat pacifism in the churches and to support intervention. That they felt this was necessary indicates that even at that late date there was still antiwar feeling in the major Protestant denominations.

Other liberals and former leftists rallied to the cause of the Allies, forsaking and attacking their former comrades in the peace movement. Archibald MacLeish set off a bitter argument over the role of intellectuals and pacifists in encouraging fascist aggression. In an article titled "The Irresponsibles" in the *Nation* in May 1940, the poet and librarian of Congress condemned the idea of "disinterested scholarship" and decried the failure of academics and artists to defend democracy and attack its enemies. Expanding on the theme, he addressed himself to the role of the peace movement in delaying American involvement. MacLeish specifically attacked antiwar novels such as Dos Passos's *Three Soldiers* and Hemingway's *Farewell to Arms* for their "demoralizing" effect upon youth and their encouragement of skepticism toward government propaganda and flag waving. "If the young generation in America is distrustful of all words, distrustful of moral judgments of better and worse, then it is incapable of using the only weapon with which fascism is fought—the conviction that fascism is evil and that a free society of free men is good and worth fighting for."[32]

Responses came from Max Lerner, Harold Laski, and Edmund Wilson, all antifascist and pro-Allies, but reluctant to turn their backs entirely upon the recent past and their loathing of war. Ironically, Rexford G. Tugwell, the New Dealer and nemesis of Columbia radicals, offered a strong opposition to turning campuses into war factories, and defended the provoking of doubt and skepticism toward government propaganda. What, after all, he asked, was the point of a "free society" if free inquiry was to be discouraged or renounced?[33]

Students also responded to MacLeish, in particular to his assertion that their views had been shaped by novels. One young woman at Wilson College noted that he implied that youth were incapable of thinking for themselves. She added, "We have learned from history, not fiction, that the last war was fought because of the desires and ambitions of a few selfish statesmen." It was true that novels like *Men in War* and *Three Soldiers* did destroy "a certain degree of youthful romanticism. . . . We became sceptical, even a bit cynical, about the glory of democratic freedom." Movies, too, had played a part. When the writer was eleven, her father had taken her to see *Journey's End*. She described its effect:

> Uniforms and guns excited me, but I can never
> quite erase from my mind the final scene. It
> flashed before my eyes just a second, yet I can still
> see it as plainly as I did nine years ago. The
> hero, a soldier who bore no hatred toward anyone,
> reached out over the top of the trench to
> capture a little yellow butterfly. He was shot just as
> his finger touched a wing. This morning's
> paper said 500,000 such boys had been killed in one
> battle.[34]

She concluded that young people were not cynics or cowards. They wanted to know that the same mistakes would not be made again.

Time had run out for the peace movement in Europe, but in America the debate went on. The period between September 1939 and December 1941 was one of great tension. For the perennial hawks and right-wing isolationists the answers were easy, but for many leftists and pacifists it was a time of moral and intellectual anguish. There seemed to be no way to combat fascism short of war, and no way the war could be won without American participation. At the same time, the defense of the British and French (and American) empires was not a cause to inspire great devotion on the left. Nor was it clear what the results of the new world war would be—or whether the price paid would be worth the victory. Modern war could not be made (except with effort) to look like a choice between virtue and wickedness; at best, the choice was between the lesser of two great evils.

Students underwent the same conflicts and changes that affected the peace movement in general. By 1940 there was a new "generation" of students who had not, by and large, participated in the mass demonstrations of 1935, 1936, and 1937 and who did not engage in political activity as a matter of course. The former leaders of the student movement had gone their way: Wechsler, Lash, and Molly Yard had joined the interventionists. Other former student activists had reached similar conclusions.

One of these was Eric Sevareid. His experiences in Europe as a newspaper correspondent convinced him of the urgent need for American assistance. Although the Spanish Civil War had made an initial impact on him, the bombing of London seems to have been the event that changed his mind. It convinced him of "the impossibility of living with fascism. . . . It was something to come to," he would write later, "to desire your own people to take up arms and join the killing. But there it was; nothing could be done about it. There was no other way." Sevareid and others now devoted to the cause of intervention the same energy they had given to their antiwar activities. Now there was, if anything, more intensity, fueled by the sight of war and, perhaps, by their own sense of guilt. Describing the satisfaction with which he greeted the Japanese attack on Pearl Harbor and the declaration of war that followed, Sevareid wrote: "The stunned and anxious nation slept badly that night, I have no doubt. For me there was a feeling of enormous relief; the feeling that we had won, even before the fight began; had survived even before the onslaught. I slept like a baby."[35]

This feeling derived not merely from the journalist's experience with fascism but from his own sense that he was in part responsible. In his view, and that of some other former student activists, the antiwar movement had lulled people, prevented a full and early recognition of what needed to be done, and allowed the fascists to strike the first blow. Pearl Harbor would resolve all that and settle any remaining doubts. "The new war, when it came, was for us not merely a crisis in our physical lives but an intellectual and moral purgatory."[36]

The period from 1939 to the summer of 1940 was one of change and conflict. Like the peace movement in general, the student antiwar movement was divided and its organizations under attack. Many of its leaders had moved into the interventionist camp. Still, antiwar feeling persisted among students in general, even more than in the general population. Events of the next year would gradually work to lessen resistance and to prepare the campuses and the nation for war.

Although events of the summer of 1940 made inroads into the prevailing anti-interventionist sentiment, most Americans still insisted that assistance must stop short of American entry into the war.[37] Polls indicate the strength of this position—and its ambiguity. Perhaps more revealing was the way that public opinion was perceived by Roosevelt and how it affected his campaign strategy, if not his foreign policy. Following his reelection, however, Roosevelt would take actions to prepare the country and the campus for war. Opposition would be left to a handful of pacifists and some ill-matched allies.

Debate over foreign policy became increasingly bitter in the summer of 1940. William Allen White's Committee to Defend America by Aiding the Allies was formed in May. In July a mixed group of right-wing isolationists and progressive anti-interventionists formed the America First Committee. Both groups immediately began a campaign to win over public opinion.[38] A smaller group, the Keep America out of War Congress, consisted primarily of pacifists and Socialists, with the latter increasingly dominating.[39]

Roosevelt's description of America's role in the war varied according to his audience. The president's classic tribute to the strength of anti-interventionist feeling and to his own willingness to say whatever was needed to win the election came in a speech in Boston. Echoing a similar statement in the 1936 campaign in which he had declared that no one hated war more than he, Roosevelt now declared: "While I am talking to you mothers and fathers, I give you one more assurance. I have said this before, but I will say it again and again and again; your boys are not going to be sent into any foreign wars." On November 2 in Buffalo, he informed the people that "your President says this country is not going to war."[40]

Safely back in office, Roosevelt gave another speech on December 29. Identifying American interests with the survival of Great Britain, the president proclaimed that the United States would be "the great arsenal of democracy."[41] Although the United States was still a year away from formal military involvement, the decision had been made and the first steps taken.

One action taken before the election had immediate impact upon students and upon college campuses. On September 16, 1940, the president signed into law the Selective Training and Service Act. On October 16, registration of all males between the ages of twenty-one and thirty-five took place across the country. At many colleges registration was conducted on campus for students from out of town. The process was carried out peacefully and with little resistance. The absence of large-scale protest indicates how far the country and the students had progressed toward war. However, the fact that it applied only to students twenty-one or over probably limited the response, and the absence of large-scale protest may also indicate how far away actual involvement still seemed.

There was, however, some resistance. In New York City the Youth Committee against War sponsored demonstrations at City College, Columbia, and other metropolitan colleges. Attendance at these rallies was small. The *Spectator* noted a gathering of eight to twelve people at 115th Street and Broadway. Throughout the city one thousand to two thousand students participated in the protests.[42]

The FOR sponsored a morning service for conscientious objectors at Broadway Tabernacle Church. About 450 men heard John Haynes Holmes urge opposition to the draft. Those attending took a pledge describing conscription as "an overt step in the direction of war and dictatorship" and declaring that they would oppose it "by methods of non-violence and direct action."

That day four members of the FOR and WRL, two Socialists, the executive secretary of the New York district of the YPSL, and eight divinity students at Union Theological Seminary publicly refused to register. Another twelve seminary students registered as conscientious objectors, three of them stating that they would leave school so as not to take advantage of that exemption. At the same time, A. J. Muste, the Trotskyist turned pacifist, and Evan Thomas, who had been an objector in World War I, issued a declaration stating that if they had been of draft age, they would have refused to register. On the other hand, Henry Sloane Coffin, head of Union, condemned the refusal. He declared that since as ministerial students they were exempted from the draft, they should have complied with the law in respect to registration.[43]

All those who refused to register immediately were subpoenaed by a federal grand jury. They were subject to up to five years in prison and five-thousand-dollar fines. Efforts were made to convince the resisters to recant, and they were offered leniency if they would agree to late registration. Acting as a group, the eight seminary students refused all such offers, and on November 14 they were sentenced to a year and a day in federal prison. In September 1941 the eight were released on parole from Danbury.[44] One of them, David Dellinger, would figure in another antiwar trial thirty years later.

Others refused to cooperate on pacifist grounds. Among the three hundred or so who refused to register were nonpacifist Black Muslims and Black Jews, as well as Quakers and Christian pacifists. Smaller numbers were Socialists or members of the WRL.[45] In Philadelphia two Temple students publicly refused to register. Their refusal was received with considerable hostility by other students, as well as by the authorities. The Temple student paper refused to print a letter from them explaining the basis of their action. According to a Temple *News* editorial, the letter was not printed "because it sanctioned breaking the law by those not in accord with it. . . . The *News* simply does not condone law breaking, and it will not permit others to use its columns for that purpose." The editors had earlier written that "refusal to register was nothing more than a violation of the law. To have the courage of one's convictions may be an admirable quality, but even so there is a time and a place."[46]

Much of the criticism of the resisters centered on their violation of the law and noted its provisions for conscientious objection. The actions of the ministerial students were particularly attacked, since they were automatically entitled to exemption once they registered. But the critics missed the point. The eight Union students explained their position in a statement entitled "Why We Refuse to Register."[47] In it the students described their opposition to registration and to conscription as an integral part of their opposition to the entire "war system": "To us, the war system is an evil part of our social order, and we declare that we cannot cooperate with it in any way. War is an evil because it is a violation of the Way of Love as seen in God through Christ." War was, they noted, "a concentration and accentuation of all the evils of our society." They pointed to the previous world war as evidence of the impossibility of overcoming evil with evil. Furthermore, conscription was an evil in itself, a form of tyranny. "By opposing the selective service law we will be striking at the heart of totalitarianism as well as war." They replied to those who urged them to register as conscientious objectors by stating that they felt "a deep bond of unity" with those who had made that choice, but they had rejected that alternative. "If we register under that act, even as conscientious objectors, we become part of that act." By registering and carrying the government's card, they would be complying with the act and cooperating with the militarization of society. They would not accept using a bad means to a good end.

Their arguments were a combination of religious fundamentalism and the Social Gospel. Grounded firmly in religion, they also reflected secular views of war and history, especially the revisionist view of World War I. They carried the antiwar themes of the thirties to their logical conclusion.

Few students had such a well-defined position. The mood on campus changed somewhat in the fall of 1940. Along with (and probably stimulated by) the draft came an increase in interest and enrollment in ROTC. This reflected both practical and emotional arguments. According to its advocates, participation was in the interest of both the students and the nation. Urging Temple to acquire a unit, the Temple *News* could see "nothing but advantages. . . . If college men who have devoted four years to higher education are to be called to arms, wouldn't officers commissions be the most satisfactory assignment for them?"[48] This echoed the elitist argument that claimed that college students had so much to contribute to the nation (presumably more than working youth) that if they had to fight at all it should certainly not be in the ranks. Academic hierarchy should prevail in war, the ultimate sifting and winnowing.

The mystique of the battlefield also reappeared, apparently still potent despite years of antiwar propaganda. One student invoked a pep rally approach to war. "Come on fellows! Rise up and declare your willingness to cooperate to our fullest extent to establish a ROTC course at Temple. Our founder, Dr. Conwell, was an officer. Let us all follow the leadership of our great founder 'to a deathless fame.'"[49] That prospect, however, seems not to have had much appeal, and the writer's enthusiasm went unechoed.

Ambivalence seems to have been more characteristic. The collegiate polls, which continued a popular pastime, reflect this. Though the degree to which they reflect the opinions of most students may be challenged, they do indicate the contradictions to be found in the thinking of individual students. One such poll was taken at Columbia University.[50] That school continued to be distinctive, more liberal than other Ivy League schools, more conservative than other colleges in New York City. It was one of the few elite universities to support Roosevelt in the 1940 election in the collegiate straw poll. The major impression from the results of the "peace poll" in October 1940 is the inconsistency of people's positions; they were inclined to support national policy in the abstract, including aid to the Allies, but opposed to specific measures of assistance, and indicated in general a still strong, though eroded, opposition to American involvement.

If students were still, by and large, antiwar, the same was not true of college administrators. In addition to offering their facilities for draft registration, colleges and universities became advocates for and agents of intervention. In November 1940, Thomas Gates (who was later to become secretary of defense under Dwight D. Eisenhower) offered the services of the University of Pennsylvania to the government "for the development of national defense."[51] Parts of the university, at least, were quite ready to repeat the experience of World War I, when the schools became, in effect, another war agency. As the peace movement had predicted, as the push for intervention increased, the schools not only gave in to developments but helped to accelerate them.

In the curriculum training for defense replaced courses on peace. College educators and administrators discussed the role of higher education during war.[52] Students began to play their part. In March the student newspaper at one school sponsored a "Bundles for Britain" ball, with proceeds from the dance going to the local Aid to the Allies Committee. The organizers did not expect to raise much money. The point was to involve students in supporting the Allies. Sometimes the effort was promoted as simply refugee relief. At Wilson College the peace council sponsored the activity.[53] The effect, in any case, was further to prepare the campus for wartime activities and attitudes. It should perhaps be said that there is no evidence that most students leaped to participate in these activities.

Other forces were at work to dissipate antiwar feeling and to create, if not a positive desire for intervention, at least an acceptance of its inevitability. Commercial advertising both reflected the nation's mood and that of the campus and helped to shape them. A study of the advertising in a nationally syndicated collegiate digest indicates not only what was being sold students but how—and what appeals were thought most successful. Throughout the decade most of the ads were for cigarettes. The usual approach was a testimonial from a famous person or a figure engaged in some glamorous enterprise. Before 1940 these tended to be actors or actresses and sports figures of both sexes. The only political figure was, interestingly, Senator Nye.

During 1940 a conspicuous change began. While the athletes and movie stars were still there, the figures were increasingly in uniform. One ad, for example, showed Eileen Drew dressed as Miss Veterans of Foreign Wars. By 1941 the dominant figures were test pilots and military personnel. In the spring of that year an ad appeared with a picture of a young man in a uniform offering a cigarette to an older man:

> "Dad ought to know. Look at that wall behind him—
> his personal military history. Photo of the
> troop. Dad, by himself, very proud of his old style
> choker-collar blouse. And his decorations—
> the order of the Purple Heart, Victory Medal, Croix
> de Guerre with palm.
> "You savvy quick, soldier," he says to his son as that
> chip off the old block in the new uniform proffers
> Camels. "These were practically 'regulation' cigarettes
> with the army men I knew. Lots of other things
> have changed, but not a soldiers 'smokins'".
> RIGHT! Today, and for more than twenty years
> reports from Army Post Exchanges show that
> Camels are the favorite. And in Navy Canteens too.
> Camels are preferred.[54]

War was beginning to seem inevitable. How students were to respond to the great moment was another question. The resisters offered one model; the volunteers, another. Most students were not enthusiastic about either alternative. The potential role for women during the war was also a subject for debate. The discussion around this reveals conflicting attitudes toward women's role in society as well as in the military.

There were certain limitations to the discussion. Despite the presence of some women in the armed services, it was not suggested that women be subject to the military draft or have an expanded role in conflict. Nor was it suggested that they be given a share of power commensurate with the responsibilities they were about to assume. Controversy centered on the proposal by Eleanor Roosevelt that women be registered for nonmilitary national service; she believed that a year of such service would be as valuable to young women as to men, as well as to the nation.[55]

Among female students the idea attracted interest and some support. As young men registered for the draft, the women's paper at the University of Pennsylvania took a survey of women students' views on their role in national defense. "What about the women?" the editor asked. "Is there a possibility that perhaps in the not too distant future we may be 'drafted' into special women's activities as carried out by British women . . . or is there a possibility that we shall be 'dodgers' of sorts and try to ignore the problem before us?" In response to the question whether women between twenty-one and thirty-five should register for nonmilitary service, 40 percent were in favor and 60 percent opposed.[56]

The idea provoked an outraged response from some male students. In an editorial titled "Don't Draft Our Girls," the *Daily Pennsylvanian* warned that such a proposal would destroy the American family, "which is, in the last analysis," the editorial claimed, "the whole basis of American life. . . . Let the girls stay in the home, where they belong so that the American system will be preserved for us when we are through fighting for it."[57]

In the end, women as a group were neither drafted into service nor left at home to knit. Economics was a force stronger than law or hallowed slogans; women went into defense plants to support themselves and their families. In addition, over 250,000 women enlisted in the military services during the war. Women college students took advantage of new opportunities. In the fall of 1941, as colleges adopted a new curriculum, women as well as men signed up for such courses as map reading, statistics, economic geography, and modern languages which would help qualify them for jobs opening up in the government.[58]

A combination of forces—the government, the university itself, daily news and propaganda, and the real brutalities and successes of fascism—was pushing students toward support of American entry into the war. On the whole, however, the discussion of the role of students was conspicuous in its calmness. Compared to the pre–World War I period, there was a distinct lack of enthusiasm for the prospect of battle. Most college students were not yet ready to trade their books for bayonets. This held true through the fall of 1941.

The mood on campus that autumn was mixed. At Columbia editorials urging support for the Allies mixed with others on the joy of football and homecoming weekend. At Temple, President Robert Johnson urged immediate United States entry into the war in order to dishearten the Germans and to "unify the country." Student life seemed to have returned to "normal," undisturbed by the demonstrations of previous years. The *Collegiate Digest* mixed pictures of dances and pep rallies with others of ROTC corps and one of a "girl guard at Moscow University" with the caption "The entire population of the Soviet Union, male and female alike, is taking an active part in the struggle against Germany's aggression." The same issue showed Henry Wallace as the principal speaker at a banquet celebrating the centennial of Fordham University.[59]

Debate, however, did continue, and antiwar forces, on the campus as in the nation, made a last effort to forestall American military involvement. The sides, however, had changed again. The summer had brought a new voice, or, rather, restored an old one, for intervention. In June the

German army invaded the Soviet Union, and American Communists quickly became interventionists. At the same time, the final twist was turned in the ASU's history. "The Yanks Are Not Coming" poster was put aside; the call was now for "All Out Aid to the Allies." It was a new war.

Some, however, still held to the antiwar position. The Keep America Out of War Congress, a Socialist-pacifist coalition, and its youth groups continued antiwar agitation. But they were weakened by their association with the America First Committee and that organization's association with Charles Lindberg. In September 1941, Lindberg made a speech attacking American Jews for allegedly pushing the country toward war. More than anything else, that speech identified the anti-interventionist cause with isolationism, reaction, and anti-Semitism. Efforts of the Keep America Out of War Congress and Norman Thomas to dissociate themselves were unsuccessful.[60]

Still, the coalition of the left-wing Socialists and religious pacifists continued to have some support on campuses. Thomas made his annual speech at Columbia, although he was now described in the news columns of the *Spectator* as "the isolationist leader of the Socialist Party." Arguing once again against war, Thomas emphasized the internal effects of American participation. As the peace movement had argued for years, he insisted that entering the war would turn the nation into an armed camp, with restrictions on civil liberties and no possibility of pursuing social justice at home. It would damage democracy, encouraging right-wing elements in the country, and make the existing social inequalities permanent. The editor of the *Spectator* agreed with Thomas's comments on the state of American democracy. "He's right; he's been right for years." But, the editorial continued, even if America were to stay out, it could not avoid the effects of Hitler's domination of Europe. War would bring a diminution of civil liberties, but staying out would result in "complete transformation of the nation into a permanent armed camp with a permanent military machine."[61] (In the end, of course, the United States both defeated the Axis *and* adopted a permanent military machine; so everybody was right and everybody was wrong.)

Antiwar sentiment, and what was left of the student movement, was effectively ended by the Japanese attack on Pearl Harbor. Students joined the rest of the country in nearly unanimous support for the declaration of war against all the Axis nations. On the day following the attack both student newspapers that had favored intervention and those opposed expressed similar sentiments in noting the coming of war and calling for unity. The main themes were the need for full support for the national administration and the role of students in the coming days. Many editors echoed the college administrators in formal statements urging students to continue their studies.

Much of the comment assumed that the war would be a short one. In Milwaukee, the *Echo Weekly*, noting that life must go on, declared: "The army does need men, but it also needs educated leaders to keep up the civilian morale and to get the country back on a normal basis after the emergency." Likewise, the president of the University of Pennsylvania advised students to wait until they were called up and, in the meantime, to continue normal activity. Women were urged to continue their studies and to work for organizations like the Red Cross. But like the rest of the country, students had to expect some changes in their lives. With perhaps a more realistic assessment, the *Spectator* warned: "While some of us can be of most help to the war effort by keeping at our situations, it is likely that many will find their education disrupted. Much as we hate to say it, temporary sacrifices will be necessary in some cases, and there is no use trying to hedge about it."[62]

There was a remarkable absence of jingoism or hostility

toward the Japanese. The Milwaukee paper warned against "hysteria" and "nationalist fervour." The general tone was one of calm acceptance, with neither enthusiasm nor resistance. The women's paper at Penn, for example, expressed the hope that war would not extinguish the values of peace. Noting the coincidence of the entry into war with the approach of Christmas, the editors urged students not to succumb to anger and tension. War was only temporary, but "the Christmas spirit—of love, of generosity, of kindness—has prevailed for centuries." Like other papers, the *Bennett News* accepted the view that the war had been forced on the United States. As the peace movement had predicted, war brought with it its own justification. With less rhetoric than during the previous war, but with the same mythology, the editors saw a broader purpose than mere response to attack: "to protect our own liberty and to secure a peace more lasting than any former agreements have established. The true spirit of Christmas—love and mercy and good will among men—will help to bring peace upon earth."[63]

There was, then, a calm consensus. After a decade of peace demonstrations and vows of resistance, the Oxford Oath was defunct. The Yanks *were* coming. The nation settled into war.

Chapter 11

Fire and Ice:

Students in the

Postwar World

Fostered by the antifascist rhetoric of the war effort and by the presence on campus of veterans of the war, some political activity appeared on college campuses after the war. The contradiction between the antiracist ideology of the American government and the continuing presence of racism and anti-Semitism in American society—and on the campus and in the military during the war—led some students to political activism. Pictures of the extermination camps and of the devastation visited upon Hiroshima and Nagasaki made it clear that there was no ivory tower and no place to hide.

Individuals and groups of students supported Henry Wallace and the Progressive party in 1948 and opposed universal military training and the restoration of compulsory ROTC.[1] Students at City College of New York and Brooklyn College demonstrated against anti-Semitism on campus and specifically among the faculty. Activism reached down into the high schools. In 1946 seniors at a high school in Waterbury, Connecticut, voted 150 to 60 to reject the Daughters of the American Revolution Good Citizenship Award. A student explained that they did not want to select someone for an award given by an organization that had refused to allow Marian Anderson to sing in Constitution Hall in Washington.[2]

Many of the most active students on college campuses were veterans, especially those in the American Veterans Committee (AVC). The GI Bill sent onto campus a new kind of student; older than most, often more serious or in more of a hurry to catch up, they were tired of being subjected to orders and waiting in lines. A study of four hundred Harvard students enrolled in one class indicated that the veterans in the class were "more critical of existing institutions" and "less orthodox, less conventional at every point." (Of the veterans at Harvard, three-fourths had either been enrolled or accepted for admission before entering the military.)[3]

Some of the veterans had been political to begin with; others had had personal experiences during the war that pushed them to the left or stung them into commitment. They had also acquired some experience with organization and protest. In Europe and the Pacific servicemen and servicewomen had demonstrated against delays in demobilization, which some officials found disconcerting. One high-ranking officer in Berlin insisted that recent demonstrations by United States troops "clamoring" to go home had "done more than anything else to lower the prestige of the United States in the eyes of the German population." The veterans may well have found it hard to understand why the officials should care about American prestige among the Germans, in the rapid change of friends and enemies that marked the start of the Cold War. According to the War Department's chief psychiatrist, the troops needed "neuropsychiatric treatment" to get them to accept occupation duty and to understand its justification.[4]

Back home, the veterans flooded the campuses. While many concentrated on getting degrees and jobs, others on campuses across the country organized around campus and national issues. At the University of Wisconsin at Madison, for example, the AVC was the key organization in student protest between 1946 and 1949. Issues included demands for an increase in the veterans' allowance, the elimination of discrimination in campus housing, attempts to get the football coach fired, defense of civil liberties, and opposition to compulsory ROTC. Veterans on the Milwaukee State Teachers College campus engaged in similar activities, and some of them supported Henry Wallace and the Progressive party in 1948.[5]

By 1950, however, such activity had largely been squelched. The veterans had left the campus, the Korean War had begun, and the Cold War had settled upon the nation. A remnant of student dissent remained, but on the whole the triumph of conservatism in the nation was matched in the colleges. The revolt on the campus had failed. The following decade would be one of adaptation and adjustment, on campus and off.[6] But beneath the surface of the "Silent Generation," underneath the Cold War consensus, class conflict and rebellion lay dormant but alive. Analysis of events on campus in the years following World War II and in the lives of the former student activists reveals both the strength of expansionist capitalism and the institutions and culture that supported it and the persistence of the challenge. Finally, the antiwar sentiment and activity of the thirties would emerge thirty years later and bring a new uprising on campus, with roots in the old.

The students of the fifties reflected broader currents of the time and responded to specific developments within higher education. The thirties had been a time of internal turmoil. In the fifties, political conflict was externalized: class war cloaked by Cold War. Within the United States

the activists of the House Un-American Activities Committee, the loyalty programs of the Truman and Eisenhower
administrations, the persecutions of the Smith Act, and a
general anti-Communist hysteria crushed what was left of
American radicalism and made social activism and political
activity dangerous and unappealing. On campus, the firing
of activist teachers and the intimidation of the faculty in
general left students with little encouragement or support
for political activity or concern.

This mood was reflected in a series of campus reports in
the *Nation,* including an article in the March 9, 1957, issue
entitled "The Careful Young Men," which tells more about
the teachers than about the students.[7] (The title was quite
literal—no women's colleges were reported on and none
of the reporting professors was a woman.) In general, the
teachers seemed surprised and disheartened that the students were passive and seemed to have no ideals, that they
were critical, not creative, and that they lacked "the emotions of 1936."

Yet students were finding little support for critical thinking in the classroom. Literature classes pursued the New
Criticism, which was outside of history, literature divorced
from politics. History offered consensus; political science offered pluralism; and social science offered a value-free education. Business promised a job. Who wouldn't keep quiet?
What was there to say?

Student radicalism in the thirties had represented a break-
down in the functioning of higher education as a means of
social control. In that decade the universities, like capitalism
itself, had not kept up with changes in the larger society.
In the postwar period adjustments were made, in part by
some of the former rebels. American higher education responded to the needs of the economic system. Sophisticated
technology and an expanded bureaucracy required technical,
clerical, and other white-collar skills and demanded more

college-educated workers. The increased reliance of the economy on military expenditures encouraged research in those programs and government support for that research. Higher education prospered, with unprecedented growth in enrollments, development of new programs, and increases in faculty salaries.

Between 1946 and 1960 student enrollment increased from 2,078,000 to 7,920,000; the percentage of those eighteen to twenty-four enrolled in degree programs increased from 10 to 20.5 percent (and continued to increase in the sixties). Faculty expanded in the same period from 165,324 to 380,554. Most of the growth was in public universities, and the form it took was the creation of "multiversities." Yet the university did not abandon its class function as a result of this influx of students. Instead it developed a more complex system of stratification. In this (and in the later student rebellion against it) California led the way, developing a three-tiered system: universities, four-year regional liberal arts colleges, and two-year community colleges. At the same time, Clark Kerr, a former student peace activist, expounded his theory of higher education in *The Uses of the University*. Kerr described a "multi-versity" which would serve as a "knowledge factory" for business and government and which would be run by modern techniques of management. Indeed, by 1963, when his book was published, this was a realistic portrayal of many large universities.[8]

The expansion of the faculties was controlled by a broadened policy that sociologist E. Digby Baltzell describes as "aristocratic assimilation" to allow onto the faculty some of the more talented of the former outsiders. Lionel Trilling, who had pioneered in that role, testified to the function of the university in social mobility and the potential problems it posed. During the student uprising at Columbia in 1968 he acknowledged that the role of the university in creating an elite had become quite overt, and had led to its being regarded with hostility by students and people in the community. At the same time, the university had raised its own status in society, which "can be interpreted as an increase in power." Therefore, it could be regarded "with suspicion and hostility" as "privileged, vested interests." In fact, as another observer has written, the university had moved "from its traditional ivory tower to the very center of American political, intellectual, and economic life."[9]

The economic rewards for conformity were great. Punishment was also effective. In the late forties and early fifties professionalism joined with patriotism to justify a purge of the classroom. Although much of the pressure was external, internal politics played a considerable part in the elimination of teachers who were radical or simply nonconformist. The role of such exradicals and current liberals as Sidney Hook and Arthur Schlesinger, Jr., had implications for the next student revolt.[10] Their definition of academic freedom, excluding the right of Communists to teach, eventually led students to question not only their honesty and intent, and the value of liberalism, but the idea of academic freedom itself.

Not everyone agreed that Communists should be denied the right to teach. Initially, there was considerable resistance. For example, the battle against the loyalty oath at the University of California won substantial support both within the institution and at other campuses.[11] Christopher Lasch has noted that much of the criticism of the loyalty oaths and congressional investigations focused on their interference with the normal channels of authority within the university. The defense was of academic freedom in the sense of university autonomy, rather than of freedom of thought or association for the individual teacher. It was the abrogation of tenure rather than the imposition of political qualifications that aroused most opposition. The question was who would try the witches, not whether they should be burned.[12] This is pertinent, but not entirely true. In some cases, as in the University of California dispute, such arguments were the result of a tactical decision that an appeal to university autonomy would be the most effective argument and the best way of protecting individual rights.

The effect of the purge was substantial on the individuals involved, on specific institutions, and on education in general. Some of these losses were temporary, but there was a more long-term effect on the tenor of university life and on campus values. A survey of social science faculty in 1955 indicated a substantial legacy of fear on campus. This apprehension affected behavior, creating patterns of caution in the classroom and outside it. This was reinforced by other developments. As some academics were admitted into the power structure, so were government agencies admitted onto the campus. A policy of cooperation with the FBI by administrators and some faculty members was supplemented by the presence of FBI informers in the classroom. Teachers and students spied on each other.

In the fifties and early sixties two major organizations of intellectuals and students (and miscellaneous minor ones), the Congress for Cultural Freedom and the National Student Association, were covertly financed by the CIA. The mood and the reality of campus life were not conducive to a student antiwar movement or any other student political activity that smacked of the subversive.[13] Further, the experience of the earlier student activists could hardly have been encouraging.

The period of McCarthyism played an important part not only in the pacification of the campus but in dividing the former student activists into antagonistic camps. Some would emerge as Cold War liberals and part of the intellectual elite. Others would become internal exiles, surviving in a hostile culture. Some became apolitical and some were killed. How each individual responded during this period shaped that person's life for the next twenty years, and the life of the American Left.

Many former student radicals came under attack as members of labor unions, teachers, government workers, or journalists. Julius Rosenberg and Morton Sobel, ASU members at City College, were convicted of conspiracy to steal the secret of the atom bomb. Sobel was imprisoned, and Rosenberg and his wife, Ethel, were executed.

This phenomenon was not restricted to the early fifties. McCarthyism had a long arm. George Edwards, the first chairman of the ASU, had a successful career in Detroit following his activity as an organizer for the United Auto Workers in the late thirties. In the forties he was active in Detroit politics and served as president of the City Council from 1946 to 1950. After getting his law degree, he served as local and state judge. His radical past caused him little trouble in Detroit. In 1963, however, his past caught up with him. During hearings on Edwards's nomination to the Sixth United States Circuit Court, Senator Sam Ervin challenged him on his role in the ASU. Edwards was eventually confirmed. He also later served a controversial term as police commissioner in Detroit, and then served on the Michigan Supreme Court and the United States Court of Appeals.[14]

Edwards was not alone in using his experience in the ASU as training for other kinds of organizing and political work. As Hal Draper has noted, "Wherever anything was stirring in the labor movement or in liberal campaigns, wherever there was action for progressive causes or voices were raised in dissent from the establishment" there were to be found the alumni of the student movement.[15]

But the student movement had never been monolithic, and divisions had deepened over entry into World War II and relations with the Soviet Union and the Communist party. James Wechsler had broken with the Communists in

1937, after three years in the Young Communist League, while a friend, Joseph Starobin, had stayed in the party. The two did not speak for twenty years, until Starobin, after serving as foreign editor of the *Daily Worker*, left the Communist party in 1954.[16]

Conflict among the leftists and former leftists heightened with the pressures of the Cold War. Some former student activists found themselves under fire for their youthful and sometimes continuing radicalism. This was especially true of teachers, government employees, journalists, and some ministers, as well as of leaders of the Communist party. Several of the teachers investigated by the Un-American Activities Committee in Philadelphia, for example, had been active in the student movement at Temple. One of them, Francis Jennings, was a particular target as head of the Teachers Union.[17]

One of the factors that contributed to the conservatism of the fifties was the decline of the Social Gospel. Religion retreated from social concerns and especially from matters of economic justice. This was partly the result of concern with Communism and partly the result of a purge of left-wingers from the churches. In 1953 the House Committee for Un-American Activities attacked Jack McMichael, the former head of the American Youth Congress. McMichael had become executive secretary of the Methodist Federation of Social Services in 1944 and served a stormy tenure in the postwar period. He, Harry Ward, and the federation were singled out by the committee, and the federation was finally forced to drop the word Methodist from its title as a result of opposition from conservative members of that church. The Methodists were not unique. J. B. Matthews, a radical turned informer, emphasized to Senator Joseph McCarthy that the infiltration of the clergy was a key part of the Communist conspiracy.[18]

Reed Harris, the outspoken editor of the Columbia *Spec-*

tator, had in a sense precipitated the student movement with his expulsion from Columbia in the spring of 1932. In the spring of 1953 he was called before McCarthy's committee during its investigation of the Voice of America, with which Harris was associated as an official of the State Department's International Information Agency. (In the interim years he had been a newspaperman, assistant to the director of the Federal Writers Project, and chief of emergency planning in the Office of War Information.)

McCarthy's research staff dug up evidence of Harris's youthful activities, including his editorials and an endorsement by Harris of a dinner of the ASU. Particular attention was paid to *King Football*. Harris was called first before an executive session and then put on the public stand "to explain by way of radio and television that he was sorry he had written a book 21 years before, that he disavowed most of the callow opinion he had then expressed, . . . and that he did not now think that Communists and Socialists should be allowed to teach."[19]

Despite his disavowals, Harris was forced to resign on April 10, 1953. He had a second coming, however, eight years later. Edward R. Murrow, himself a student activist in the National Student Federation in the early thirties and an old adversary of McCarthy, became director of the United States Information Agency in 1961. One of his first acts was to appoint Harris special assistant. In 1974, after retiring from the USIA, Harris became president of the conservative Freedom's Foundation at Valley Forge. His rehabilitation was complete.[20]

McCarthy had particular interest in "Communist" infiltration of the press, and this interest was not entirely misplaced, especially since the press included some vocal opponents of McCarthy's methods. A number of these critics had been connected with the Communist party, although all those with jobs in the establishment press had long since broken their ties with the party.

College editors had been among the leaders of the student peace movement in the thirties. Many of them had found jobs on newspapers receptive to liberal views, especially on the leftist *PM* in the forties and later on the *New York Post*. It could be argued that the origins of the "liberal media" lay in the student movement. Wechsler, Lash, and Murray Kempton (who, like Wechsler, had been a member of the Young Communist League) all worked for the *Post* in the early fifties. Murrow and, later, Sevareid made the transition from radio newscasting to television, and both, but especially Murrow, played key roles at CBS. Of course, those two, like most of these writers, had little power over the corporations that they worked for.

An exception to this was Katharine Meyer Graham, who as publisher of the *Washington Post* during the height of the Vietnam War and Watergate helped to bring on Richard Nixon's downfall by allowing reporters to do their jobs. Though her politics had moderated (and she found herself in an adversary relationship with the newspaper unions), in the thirties Kay Meyer had been a member of the ASU at the University of Chicago and had stood vigil at the gates of Republic Steel after the "Memorial Day Massacre" of striking workers there. Her father had withdrawn her from Vassar to go to the University of Chicago to receive a "classical education." No doubt she did.[21]

Journalists who had been young Marxists included Max Lerner, Irving Howe, and John P. Roche. All of these had abandoned or adapted their Marxism and had traveled quite far on what has been described as "the strange journey into the ranks of the Liberal establishment."[22] Their political journies, and those of other exradicals, were imprinted in the pages of *Dissent*, the *New Leader*, and *Commentary*. Not all ended in the same place, of course, but (except for Howe) all broke with the past.

Others maintained their Marxist beliefs and wrote for, and sometimes founded, radical journals. Paul Sweezy, a graduate student at Harvard and an instructor there until his firing, was co-founder of the independent Marxist *Monthly Review*. Starobin wrote for the *Daily Worker* until the height of the McCarthy period was over and he left the Communist party. Draper had written for a series of socialist journals and was founder and board member of the quarterly *New Politics*. Words remained weapons even when activism diminished. Old battles as well as new would be fought on the pages of the press and sometimes on radio and television.

Wechsler testified before the Senate Committee on Government Operations, Subcommittee on Investigations, in the spring of 1953.[23] The rationale for the inquiry was the inclusion of several of Wechsler's books in United States libraries abroad. McCarthy's questioning, however, was primarily concerned with Wechsler's youthful radicalism and associates, and the possibility that Communists or former Communists were employed by the *Post*. The reason for the request for Wechsler to testify was probably, as he assumed, that he had written a series of anti-McCarthy editorials.

Although subsequently Wechsler was praised for "standing up to McCarthy," he was, in effect, a cooperative witness. By answering McCarthy's questions, he accepted the right of a congressional committee to investigate people's political beliefs and associations, although he was certainly concerned about intimidation of the liberal press. Wechsler was quick to indicate that he shared McCarthy's view of communism and Communists. Indeed, many of his statements were aimed at showing that he was more anti-Communist than McCarthy. In particular, he cited praise by Congressman Richard Nixon for an editorial on Alger Hiss. Finally, he provided, with some reluctance, a list of the people that he recalled as having been members of the Young Communist League during the time he was in that organization (1934–37).

Regarding the rights of Communists, Wechsler's position

was similar to that of Hook. Asked whether Communists should be allowed to teach in the schools, the *Post* editor replied, "If I were a dean of a college, I would not hire a Communist teacher. As the editor of the paper, I would not hire a Communist journalist. . . . I could not trust their devotion to truth above their adherence to a party line." He later added that "my basic position is that the leaders of the Communist Party are agents of a foreign power."[24]

Contrary to McCarthy's insinuations, Wechsler did have a consistent record of anticommunism since his bitter break with the party in 1937. He had given a statement regarding his past associations to the FBI. In 1948, Wechsler's wife, Nancy, who had been active in the student movement at Hunter in the thirties, had come under attack while serving as an attorney for the President's Commission on Civil Rights. Typically, the husband's associations were considered relevant to the woman's continued employment.

Wechsler subsequently continued his attacks on both McCarthy and the Communists. In the fifties and early sixties his political positions and editorials were those of an uncomfortable Cold War liberal. His views, and accommodation, would be challenged by the rise of a new student movement in the sixties, and of a new war. How he responded to that development and how other former student radicals responded would reflect the degree to which they had become part of the Cold War elite and their own view of the student rebellion.

As Irving Howe and Lewis Coser have noted in their history of the Communist party, the ASU "quite unintentionally became a training ground for the post war political and intellectual elite."[25] This was especially true of academics (especially sociologists) and literary figures, critics in particular. Alfred Kazin has noted that this, rather than creative work, was their forte. "Boundless faith in criticism . . . became their passport to the post war world" in which they became cultural arbiters.[26] Besides those mentioned earlier, Richard

Rovere, who had contributed to the *Student Advocate*, and Pauline Kael, who had been active at Berkeley, wrote for the *New Yorker*.[27]

But their success was mixed, and some of them knew it. John Kenneth Galbraith, an economist who became a mainstay of the liberal wing of the Democratic party (and quicker than others to notice the end of the Cold War), wrote of what happened to some of his classmates at Berkeley in the thirties. The graduate students with whom he associated "were uniformly radical and the most distinguished were Communists." Galbraith never joined the leftist groups, but he was sympathetic to their goals. "In the ensuing twenty years many of those I most envied were accorded the auto-de-fé by HUAC, James Eastland, or the late Joseph R. McCarthy. Their lives were ruined."[28]

This was a lesson that many young people took to heart. While for some the fifties were the age of rock and roll, for others they were a time for more subterranean activities. Jonah Raskin, son of thirties radicals, describes the period in his autobiography, *Out of the Whale*. "Growing up in the 1950's felt like living in a New Ice Age. . . . Like the mastadon, Reds were becoming extinct." Some adapted, others went underground, one way or another. The Rosenbergs were burned. "When ice couldn't freeze them, when floods wouldn't wash them away, fire destroyed them." That execution was a crucial event in the development of fear among the survivors of the Left, especially among Jewish radicals. If the Rosenbergs could be destroyed, whose family was safe? Some responded by abandoning the Left; others, like the Raskins, lived a double life. At home and with others they shared a continuing radical culture. At school social studies teachers ascribed the Cold War to the desire of the Russians for warm-water ports. Jonah became the captain of the football team.[29]

For others the fear was different. Ron Kovic (who also

ended up in the antiwar movement) also grew up on Long Island in the fifties but in a different America (and in a working-class neighborhood that had its own differences with the dominant culture). Kovic was born on the Fourth of July, worshiped John Wayne, and feared the Communists. His public symbol was not the Rosenbergs, but John Kennedy. He made the track team and joined the Marines.[30] In the fifties they had very different fears. In the sixties, however, the war transcended those fears.

Both worlds put a premium on "masculine" values. The Marines built men who did not want to be "ladies." In the Ice Age young Raskin believed in the need for a patriarchal family. "My mother's warmth would only dwindle and eventually freeze. A match couldn't defeat a glacier. Only ice could break ice."[31] Emotions were for women, and a woman's place was in the home. An iron curtain divided the public sphere from the private and assigned each to the appropriate sex.

One element of the conservatism of the period that contributed to the silence on campus was the virtual extinguishing of feminism and of the tradition of activism among college women. Surveys of women's colleges in the fifties provide ample evidence for the assertion by Florence Howe (who graduated from Hunter and attended graduate school at Smith in the early fifties) that "from suffrage onward, higher education has been an instrument used to keep women in an educated place."[32] Their place in the fifties was to be educated homemakers with no interest in politics or public issues. Although the women's colleges did provide havens for some women of achievement, they managed to emphasize feminine passivity and to abandon the ideal of women as moral actors in society. Even in the sixties most women's colleges were characterized by a lack of institutional and individual involvement in civil rights and women's liberation. The loss of a tradition of women's activism was a loss to the student movement—and to the women who would join the new movement in the sixties and who would lack a feminist or female connection with past movements.[33]

Although increasing numbers of women went to college in the fifties, their percentage of the student body leveled off and in fact decreased slightly between 1954 and 1956, increasing to about 37 percent in 1960. At the same time, the percentage of women attending women's colleges dropped sharply, from 17.7 percent of total women enrolled in college in 1939–40 to 9.6 percent in 1956–57, and continued downward. The only exception to this was the continued enrollment in Catholic women's colleges, which by 1956–57 had 42.9 percent of the women enrolled in women's colleges. Unlike the secular women's colleges, they also tended to maintain women faculty and administrators, although in most cases their relationship to the male church hierarchy limited their potential as places for women to exercise control over their own lives.

Related to the declining percentage of women in women's colleges was a declining percentage of women on faculties. If the universities and colleges were practicing a policy of aristocratic assimilation, one group they did not choose to assimilate was women. Between 1946 and 1960 the percentage of women on college and university faculties declined from 29.8 percent to 23.3 percent, and in the peak years of faculty expansion between 1960 and 1970 the percentage dropped further, to 22.2 percent. During the Korean War, between 1950 and 1952, the number of women on faculties actually declined (by over three thousand), while the number of men increased slightly. Thus, while coeducation among students was increasing, among the faculty sexual homogeneity was the order of the day. Moreover, women faculty members were not taken seriously enough even to be harassed by Red-baiters. A study of academic women in the fifties found them less likely to be attacked during the years of McCarthyism than were men because they were taken less seriously by the inquisitors. There was a dubious advantage in marginality.[34] The silencing of women contributed to the division between the emotional and the rational, the objective and the subjective, the moral world of private life and the amoral world of government and academia. The world of the fifties was black and white, male and female, public and private— split like the atom.

It would take a combination of supposed opposites to break through the ice and create a new revolt on the campus and a new Left. C. Wright Mills, in 1954, described the basis of the decade's passivity. "The psychological heart of this mood is a feeling of powerlessness—but with the old edge taken off, for it is a mood of acceptance and of a relaxation of public will."[35] He argued against determinism: "I am contending that 'men are free to make history' and that some men are much freer than others to do so." Intellectuals and students had responsibility because they had access to information and to power. As a kind of outsider himself, Mills was free from nostalgia for the earlier radicalism. Writing in 1958, he criticized "the political default of the cultural workman," and pointed to the need "to specify private troubles out of the vague uneasiness of individuals; to make public issues out of indifference and malaise; and to turn uneasiness and indifference themselves into troubles, issues and problems open to inquiry." The personal was political. Mills offered not value-free social science but a call to responsibility (and freedom). "The radical (and even the liberal) is the man who does not abdicate."[36]

For some young people the election of John Kennedy in 1960 represented a new era. Within his Cold War rhetoric (and subsequent behavior) was an appeal to public life and a sense of possibility. His election as the first Catholic president helped to break down remaining separatist impulses and to encourage Catholics into public life. Even Abbie

Hoffman has noted this inadvertent inspiration. Kennedy
represented victory for the underdog. "Coming after Eisenhower he was spring following winter. . . . Kennedy often
lied to our generation, but nevertheless he made us believe
we could change the course of history."[37]

That year also saw the founding of two major organizations
of the student movement of the sixties. The Student Non-
violent Coordinating Committee (SNCC) was founded in
April, and Students for a Democratic Society (SDS) emerged
from the remnants of the SLID in June. Two crucial events
in breaking barriers of fear and apathy were the sit-ins
at Woolworth lunch counters in the South, beginning in
Greensboro, North Carolina, in February, and the anti-
HUAC demonstration in San Francisco in May. It was time
for action.

Black colleges had not succeeded in accommodating their
students to American society. Aristocratic assimilation did
not apply to race. Beginning in the fifties, and increasing
dramatically in the early sixties, the civil rights movement
revived the American Left and the struggle against racism.
The brutality of the system of segregation combined with a
legacy of revolt and a revival of religious concern for social
justice to give impetus to the movement. Despite opposition
from many administrators, black colleges in the South became centers of resistance and revolt. The sit-ins, the Freedom Rides, and Freedom Summer, the SNCC campaign in
Mississippi in 1964, brought organization, passion, and experience to black students and their white allies. The civil
rights movement saw a brief unity between old and new
Left. Former students activists of the thirties and early
forties—James Farmer, Bayard Rustin, and others in the
Congress of Racial Equality (CORE)—contributed to the
education and activism of the young civil rights workers. In
the end, the young people came into conflict with them,
especially Rustin, over tactics and militancy and over the

war. But for a time there was continuity and cooperation among different parts of the Left. Louis Burnham graduated from City College and became a southern organizer for the ASU in 1936. In the forties he was leader of the Southern Negro Youth Conference and was the Progressive party's organizer in the South in 1948. Burnham was editor of *Freedom* in the early fifties and then joined the *National Guardian*. He died in 1960 at a meeting for Negro History Week.[38] He and other student radicals of the thirties and the postwar period (and nonstudent radicals) helped keep the movement for black liberation alive during the Cold War.

Students became increasingly active in the South and on their own campuses. As it did in the thirties, the issue of war and peace brought the largest number of students into the movement and into activism. As the war in Vietnam began to escalate, especially with the intensive bombing by the United States of North Vietnam in early 1965, students increasingly associated oppression at home with their country's violence abroad. The deaths of students in Mississippi in the summer of 1964 and at Kent State and Jackson State universities in 1970 gave emotional impetus to the movement. Television and battles in the streets, like those in Chicago in the summer of 1968 at the Democratic Convention, finally brought the war home. The new student movement expanded from the original protests over campus issues and the war to a general critique of American foreign policy and racism and a rejection of capitalist institutions and culture. From the campus activity (and other sources) rose a "New Left," which self-consciously distinguished itself from the old Left, both Marxist and liberal.

But there were also ties between the old Left and the new, and between the new student movement and its predecessor in the thirties. Perhaps the most immediate tie was that of family. Although it was hardly true that all or even most sixties activists were children of old leftists, a significant number of them were. Most of the parents who had been Communists or Socialists had left those parties, but some of the earlier values and the rejection of the dominant culture had been passed on to their children. The inheritance was not so much a set of dogma as a world view, and, for some, a sense of alienation. As a historian of the New Left has observed of the second- (and sometimes third-) generation leftists, "What they brought was a set of attitudes favorable to peace, civil liberties, and racial tolerance, as well as a willingness to act in support of these goals. In most cases, perhaps reflecting the trauma that radicals and their families went through in the 1950's, they also brought a sense of estrangement from American society which made them feel most at home in the dissenting subculture on campus."[39]

Even in the fifties there had existed a kind of counter-culture from which to draw and parts of the old Left which could contribute to the new. Michael and Robert Meeropol, the sons of Ethel and Julius Rosenberg, describe this process and their political development in *We Are Your Sons*.[40] A radical community and culture had been preserved with leftist schools and summer camps and music. A recent collection of memoirs of the alumni of Camp Kinderland describes the eclectic activities devoted to the preservation of Yiddish and progressive Jewish culture. The young people learned to sing labor songs, met Paul Robeson, saw *Salt of the Earth*, and went roller skating. They also experienced camp as a political institution and as part of the rest of their lives, not as an isolated experience.[41]

This does not mean that all these children became leftists or that they and their parents would agree politically. Kenneth Kenniston reports a study which indicates greater difference between children of leftists and their parents than occurred in conservative families. Some old leftists were disturbed by the tactics and cultural activities of the New Left.

The Yippies seemed to owe more to Groucho Marx than to Karl. But there was continuity. The Veterans of Future Wars had been a kind of guerrilla theater. Some children brought their parents back into public protest, tying together the old Left and the new in an American radical tradition.[42]

Some of their predecessors were happy to see the new student uprising and appreciated its differences. Joseph Clark wrote an introduction to a collected edition of the *Student Advocate,* with which he had been associated in the thirties. He noted similarities between the new Left and the old: both of them considered the liberal the enemy along with the capitalist-imperialist. But Clark welcomed the fact that the new movement had not yet "the deadening, all-embracing ideology which made a secular religion of what had been Marxism."[43]

Some faculty and staff members were also sympathetic to the students and their causes. Hal Draper at Berkeley was an unobtrusive supporter of the Free Speech Movement there. But if there was some faculty support, there was also bitter hostility. The campus rebellion of the sixties brought a violent response from some who had been involved with its predecessor. As Draper noted of the Free Speech Movement at Berkeley in 1964–65, "The bitterest and most virulent enemies of the FSM among the faculty were not the conservatives or rightists and not Kerr's admirers, but rather a hard core of ex-radicals who had made their own peace with the system." These included sociologists Nathan Glazer and Seymour Lipsett and psychologist Lewis Feuer.[44]

Feuer in particular was the major opponent on the campus of both the Free Speech Movement and its specific demands for freedom of political activity on campus. He described the movement as "a melange of narcotics, sexual perversion, collegiate Castroism, and campus Maoism" and termed it a "Soviet style Coalition."[45]

In more scholarly moments, Feuer offered a generational

explanation of student activism, describing it as a rebellion of sons against their fathers. (This of course says nothing about women activists, but that is quite typical of the "world of our fathers" approach to history and sociology.) Feuer's theory and his anger reflect both the perceived threat to the established order and his interpretation of his own past. Describing his participation at a rally at City College of New York protesting the suspension of two radical students in 1927, Feuer writes: "I recall the excitement and enthusiasm which burgeoned with each speech of defiance toward the elder authorities." His anger, however, seems directed more at the Communist party, and perhaps himself for having been associated with it. In the thirties, he writes, the student movement, though "never large or politically consequential [soon] became the academic auxiliary of the adult leftist parties, especially the Communist Party." The "moral ambiguities of generational protest were corrupted by a self-destructive subservience to Communist discipline."

At Berkeley this domination was hardly the case. However, Feuer saw in both movement "traits of elitism, suicidalism, populism, filiarity, and juvenocracy." He detected in the Free Speech Movement "a demonic quality in the students' emotions and actions" and did what he could "to combat the drive to irrationality" that was exhibiting itself "with growing intensity."[46]

The attack on "emotionalism" was also made by Sidney Hook in discussing student uprisings in general and in particular that at Columbia in 1968. He and other exradicals consistently equated "emotionalism" with "irrationality" and seemed to find that element of the student revolt particularly disturbing.[47] "Emotionalism" was, of course, the charge leveled against the student movement in the thirties.

The anger of the academic exradicals was quite logical. For the new student revolt and antiwar movement were aimed directly at the universities themselves. The challenge

was not just to aspects of higher education but to the whole
structure, one in which some of the former student rebels
had found shelter and success. Although some students in
the earlier movement had connected education to the military and economic system, they had not gone about their
attack so bitterly. Indeed, often the students had argued for
the university and saw education as a victim rather than as
part of the problem. There was indeed ambiguity in their
rejection of traditional collegiate culture.

This was no longer the case (at least at the large universities like Berkeley, Columbia, and Wisconsin). Both the
university, as part of the "military-industrial complex," and
the values that were directly associated with it were directly
challenged. Objectivity, "value-less" social science, detach-
ment, and neutrality, on the one hand, and ties to business
and government through contracts, grants, and interchange
of personnel, on the other, were objects of student attack.[48]
Academia was no longer a safe haven for dispassionate exradicals.

The reactions of Hook, Lipsett, Glazer, Feuer, and others
were based on many factors: fear of the destruction of the
university, misunderstanding of the students and the antiwar
movement, philosophical disagreement, concern for their
own careers, a defensive reaction against the tactics of a
segment of the movement, a rejection of their own youthful
radicalism, and, perhaps, some envy. Kazin, no great ad-
mirer of the students himself, wrote of one group of exradicals with whom he was associated that, for them, "critical
intelligence had replaced passionate conviction." He wrote:
"They were intellectuals, and the new age of American power . . . was to be more indulgent to intellectuals. But though
they went on to make brilliant careers in the elitist society
that was coming, they would not be happy. The elan of
their lives, revolutionary faith in the future, was missing."[49]

A classic example of this confrontation occurred at Columbia University, again a center of activity, in the spring of 1968 (which also saw uprisings in Europe), a sign of things to come in a year of escalating conflict. Student demonstrations and the occupation of buildings focused attention on the university's involvement with the war and defense research and its racism. The assault on the university brought out deep divisions on views of the war, education, and responsibility: students charged that the university was part of a system of racism and war; the faculty condemned the threat to liberal values and institutions. The conflict was irrepressible.

Lionel Trilling became for many of the young Left the embodiment of the evils of liberalism and the establishment. This was, in a way, ironic. In his writing and literature courses he did maintain a connection between literature and life and politics that had been rejected by the New Critics of the fifties. But his belief in the importance of adversary culture and the inadequacy of liberalism had become muted. Now he was the voice of Reason and Culture. He denied that the university was a microcosm of society, and while acknowledging some legitimate grievances of the students, he insisted that the issues involved in the student strike were "largely factitious." In an interview concerning the causes of the strike he managed to avoid any mention of the war in Vietnam. Yet he had not been untouched by the turmoil on campus. Asked about his feelings about Columbia since the uprising, Trilling responded that it was "amazing" how difficult it was for him to answer that question. "If we speak of feelings, I scarcely know what mine now are, or even if I have any at all. And I find it increasingly hard to recollect what they were at the beginning of the troubles or at any point in between."[50]

This gap between intellect and feelings was one thing that students were increasingly rejecting. What then were they to make of Trilling's comments concerning his youth in the thirties (described in May 1966)? He noted that the anti-

Semitism that he (and others he worked with) saw "did not arouse our indignation," because they took it "to be a kind of advantage" against which they could define themselves. For others, indignation had apparently died with the discovery of Stalin's "betrayal." Asked why he and his colleagues were alienated by the antiwar movement's violent reaction to the war in Vietnam when they agreed that it was wrong, a sociologist at New York University responded that "we don't feel that rage. Is this the ultimate crime after Stalin and Hitler? I find the reaction excessive. Vietnam isn't important. It's just a nasty little war."[51]

These men and their universities were remnants of Raskin's Ice Age. They perpetuated an environment hostile to emotions, and, not coincidentally, to women. In *Reinventing Womanhood*, Carolyn Heilbrun, a student and then colleague of Trilling's at Columbia, acknowledges a debt to him as a teacher, but notes that women had no real place in his discussion of self and culture (or among his disciples).[52] Ironically, it was this paternalism, the patriarchal values of the university, that would be hardest for the male New Left to reject. The counterculture would not be counter enough.

The role of the exradicals angered some students and depressed others. Some of them worried about what they would be like in twenty years. As one student asked Draper, "How do I know that won't happen to me?" Draper answered cheerfully, "You don't."[53] This view of exstudent radicals also added to student disillusionment with liberalism. The mockery of the Yippies was a logical response to the "rationality" of Trilling, Hook, and Robert McNamara.

Student activists of the sixties also came into conflict with exrebel administrators. Grayson Kirk, president of Columbia during this period, had been a political science instructor at the University of Wisconsin in the thirties and had been a member of SLID and peace activist. According to Feuer, Clark Kerr in the fifties and sixties still seemed to be "almost a Marxist in his conception of the university," and his basic theory, of the university as a knowledge factory, "converges strikingly with dialectical materialism."[54] J. Martin Klotsche, once a popular history instructor and sponsor of the student peace group at Milwaukee State Teachers College in the thirties, played another role for a later generation of students. In 1970, during the student strike after the United States invasion of Cambodia, Klotsche had the city police called on campus to expel students from the student union.

All this seemed to make prophecy out of a poem in the *Student Advocate* in 1936 entitled "Remembrance of Things Past." The poem was dedicated to "that gallant company of college officials who, if all had been radicals once would long ago have destroyed, by sheer force of numbers, the existing order." It began:

> When I was young and immatuah
> I was very, very radical just as you are.
> I went to demonstrations and upheld free speech;
> On the slightest provocation I'd sedition preach
> But expressed this grave sedition so judiciously
> That I now administrate this university.[55]

There was a generation conflict, but it seems often to have been a reaction of the old against the young. The response of some adults to the police violence in Chicago in 1968 and the killings at Kent State—that the students had gotten what they deserved—exacerbated the conflict inherent in a situation in which it was, as Phil Ochs put it, "always the old who send us to the wars, Always the young who fall." In "Love Me, I'm a Liberal," Ochs echoed the thirties verse, singing:

> Sure once I was young and impulsive
> I wore every conceivable pin

Even went to a socialist meeting
   and learned all the old union hymns
      oh
But now I am older and wiser
and that's why I'm turning you in.[56]

The songs of Ochs, Bob Dylan, Joan Baez, and Pete Seeger and the pictures—of children burning with napalm, of American planes bombing the countryside into mud—released emotions and action, breaking through barriers and setting up barricades. Academic culture and the system it represented were left behind.

But while many old leftists were skeptical or hostile toward the new student movement and supported the war in Vietnam, others found themselves bound to the students in a common cause. For it was, finally, the issue of war and peace that gave new life to the student movement and reactivated parts of the old. The war in Southeast Asia, its nature and persistence, revived something in even the apolitical.

Some of the thirties students had never left the peace movement or had rejoined it after World War II.[57] They worked with the WILPF, the FOR, the WRL, the National Committee for a Sane Nuclear Policy, or with groups like CORE in the civil rights movement. Others had been active in the Left in a variety of causes. Pete Seeger, who had been a member of the ASU during his year and a half at Harvard, had remained the minstrel of the Left and inspired a new generation of folksingers and political activists.

But for some, the new antiwar movement brought back to life something that had lain dormant. Murray Kempton of the *New York Post,* whose writings in the fifties and sixties had been like the ghost of radicalism past, rejoined the antiwar movement and went to jail in Chicago in 1968 during the demonstrations at the Democratic convention. Wechsler, who was confronted by Jerry Rubin, Abbie Hoffman, and Rennie Davis on an interview program, nevertheless found himself in some agreement with the movement's critique of American society and foreign policy, and in particular with its view of the American conduct of the war. Arnold Beichman, Wechsler's predecessor on the *Spectator* in the thirties, wrote an article in 1971 attacking what he termed the "six 'big lies' and half truths" about America by the New Left. The second alleged "big lie" was that the United States was committing genocide in Vietnam. Wechsler noted that Beichman was setting up a straw man and avoiding the question of what problems there really were in American society and its conduct of the war. Although the word *genocide* had been loosely used, Wechsler continued, there was evidence that "a cheap appraisal of Asian life had swayed many of our military decisions, and that the Vietnamization policy is in fact calculated not to bring peace to that battered country but to 'change the color of the bodies.'" In 1977 the *New York Times* conducted an investigation of CIA involvement with journalists and revealed that Beichman had accepted material from the CIA for a story about a Russian defection which, Beichman admitted, might never had occurred.[58]

Just as religious pacifists had stayed most consistent during World War II, so they now took leadership within the new antiwar movement. Arthur Lelyveld once again opposed war as the chairman of the Justice and Peace Commission of the Conference of American Rabbis. Catholics, in particular, had shed some of their separatism and hostility toward radicalism. Thomas Merton, who had joined the Young Communist League at Columbia in the thirties and later become a Trappist monk, helped develop a theology of peace that influenced Catholic activists.[59] Daniel Berrigan, on trial for the destruction of draft files, explained: "Our apologies good friends for our fracture of good order, the burning of paper instead of children." John Cogley, the editor of *Commonweal*, was active in the Catholic Worker movement in Chicago in the thirties and opposed blacklisting in the fifties.[60] Eugene McCarthy, too, had been influenced by the Catholic Worker philosophy as a student in the late thirties. Though not a pacifist, McCarthy became a catalyst for the moderates in the antiwar movement, and his challenge to Lyndon Johnson in the presidential primaries of 1968 revealed the growth of antiwar sentiment.

David Dellinger was another link between the earlier peace movement and a new antiwar generation. In 1940 he had gone to prison for refusing to register for the draft. In the sixties and seventies he was a defendant in the Chicago Seven trial rising out of the demonstrations in Chicago and remained a strong voice for nonviolence and a restructuring of American society. Barbara Deming, a graduate of Bennington in the thirties, a pacifist and an editor of *Liberation*, and an antiwar activist, joined with other women in the movement in seeking their own liberation from sexism in American society and in the Left.[61]

Separations—of the intellect from the emotions, religion from politics, scholarship from morality, the public from the private—carried over from the fifties and defined American culture. Berrigan wrote that "the great sinfulness of modern war is that it renders concrete things abstract."[62] Language was used to cloak reality—"protective reaction strikes," "strategic hamlets," "Operation Sunrise." Rejecting this meant rejecting the values and structures of the university, the system they served, and, finally, the patriarchy behind it. Women from the old Left and the new sought to create a truly new culture with new institutions, but with ties to the past. Molly Yard, a veteran of the ASU who had remained active in support of labor and then in opposition to the war, joined the National Organization of Women and the women's movement to work for the Equal Rights Amendment. Writing in the winter of 1980–81, she remembered that one of "the great emotional issues of the late '30's was the Spanish Civil War. . . . At Oberlin College—should you go there—you will find a memorial to Paul MacEachron, an Oberlin student who died in Spain. As I write this I could weep—it is an issue of democracy and justice that will be with us always."[63]

Muriel Rukeyser was asked by a friend, "Why do you care about Spain so much? It was so long ago." In the thirties, Rukeyser had gone to Harlan County and to the Scottsboro Boys' trial and been arrested and released on condition that she leave town. She crossed the border into Spain on the first day of the Civil War and stayed to see the first fighting. In the sixties she went to Hanoi.[64]

During all those years she wrote poetry, and her writing reflects her travel to "storm centers of revolt." There is an interesting contrast between Rukeyser and another graduate of the student movement of the thirties. Ad Reinhardt, editor of the *Jester* at Columbia and cartoonist for the *Student Advocate*, also remained politically engaged on the Left and before his death in 1967 participated in opposition to the war. But he divided his artistic life from his politics and, becoming "the black monk of abstract impressionism," finally painted totally black imageless art, declaring that "art comes from art only, always, everywhere, never from life, reality, nature, earth or heaven." The artist as a person was responsible to society, but art was only responsible to itself. He infuriated the art establishment—Hilton Kramer, the art critic for the *New York Times*, accused him of "nihilism"— and a new generation of artists for quite different reasons. In a symposium on "black" one artist criticised Reinhardt for "ruling out the human element in his art" and encouraging that kind of Western dichotomy which had resulted in "paranoia."[65]

Yet in his life he combined the personal, artistic, and

political and was a radical, in dissent from his culture and from capitalism and opposed to the role of the artist as "a professional schnook or as a company man." His humor might well have been instructive to the Yippies. In his "Chronology" for an exhibition of his work in 1967, he mixed personal, political, and significant events. But he declared, regarding art, that "content is nothing, nothing at all."[66]

Rukeyser, however, saw no hope in such dichotomy. She was opposed to such divisions, determined that "our lives would not be shredded, not as athletes nor as women nor as poets, not as travelers, tourists, refugees."[67] In the sixties and early seventies she joined the antiwar movement in demonstrations, poetry readings, and acts of resistance. She had not adjusted; she stood with one foot in the dominant culture and one out. She became, especially in her volume of poems *Breaking Open,* a bridge between the past and the future. As though in response to those who accused students of being "emotional," she wrote in her poem "Rational Man" a catalog of horrors: "Anything you can imagine . . . Rational Man has done." But she continued,

> I do and I do,
> Life and this under-war,
> Deep, under protest, make
> For we are makers more.

> but touching teaching going
> the young and the old
> they reach they break they are moving
> to make the world.[68]

Notes

Introduction

1. Philip Altbach, *Student Politics in America* (New York: McGraw-Hill, 1974,), p. 57. Altbach estimates that proportionately more students engaged in left-wing activity in the thirties than did during the New Left period of the sixties.

2. "Presidential Platitudes," Columbia *Spectator*, September 26, 1935.

3. According to Paul Sweezy, colleges have also served as "recruiters for the ruling class, sucking upward the ablest elements of the lower class and thus . . . infusing new brains into the ruling class and weakening the potential leadership of the working class" ("Power Elite or Ruling Class," in *Modern Capitalism and Other Essays* [New York: Monthly Review Press, 1972], p. 105). See also William Domhoff, *Who Rules America?* (Englewood Cliffs, N. J.: Prentice-Hall, 1967), p. 77; Merle Curti and Roderick Nash, *Philanthropy in the Shaping of American Higher Education* (New Brunswick: Rutgers University Press, 1965). For a critique written in the sixties see James Ridgeway, *The Closed Corporation—American Universities in Crisis* (New York: Random House, 1968).

4. Irwin Wylie, *The Self Made Man in America: The Myth of Rags to Riches* (New Brunswick: Rutgers University Press, 1954), pp. 168, 101; E. Digby Baltzell, *The Protestant Establishment: Aristocracy and Caste in America* (New York: Random House, 1964), pp. 209, 212. See also Mary and Oscar Handlin, *The Ameri-*

can *College and American Culture: Socialization as a Function of Higher Education* (New York: McGraw-Hill, 1970).

5. Quoted in Harold Wechsler, *The Qualified Student: A History of Selective College Admissions in America* (New York: John Wiley and Sons, 1977), p. 183. On both administrative selection and student discrimination see Marcia Graham Synott, *The Half-Opened Door: Discrimination and Admissions at Harvard, Yale, and Princeton, 1900–1970* (Westport, Conn.: Greenwood Press, 1979).

6. Abbott Lawrence Lowell, *At War with Academic Tradition* (Cambridge: Harvard University Press, 1934), p. 183.

7. Handlin and Handlin, *American College and American Culture*, p. 56.

8. Edward Cole, "Athletes Aren't So Dumb," *Student Advocate*, February 1936, p. 9.

9. Handlin and Handlin, *American College and American Culture*, p. 57.

10. Earnest Earnest, *Academic Procession* (New York: Bobbs-Merrill, 1953), p. 204.

11. Similar developments were occurring in the legal profession. See Jerold Auerbach, *Unequal Justice—Lawyers and Social Change in America* (New York: Oxford University Press, 1976).

12. Wechsler, *Qualified Student*, p. 162; William Chafe, *The American Woman: Her Changing Social, Economic, and Political Roles, 1920–1970* (New York: Oxford University Press, 1972), p. 60.

13. Sister Mary Marietta Bowler, *A History of the Catholic College for Women in the United States of America* (Washington, D.C.: Catholic University of America, 1933), p. 122.

14. Altbach, *Student Politics*, p. 6.

15. Paul Fussell, *The Great War and Modern Memory* (New York: Oxford University Press, 1975).

16. Carol S. Gruber, *Mars and Minerva* (Baton Rouge: Louisiana State University Press, 1975), p. 123.

17. Quoted in Aileen S. Kraditor, *Means and Ends in Abolitionism* (New York: Random House, 1969), p. 95.

18. For a thorough treatment of the peace movement in this period see Charles Chatfield, *For Peace and Justice: Pacifism in*

America, 1914–1941 (Knoxville: University of Tennessee Press, 1971).

19. Murray Kemptom, *Part of Our Times* (New York: Simon and Schuster, 1955), p. 303.

20. Hal Draper, "The Student Movement of the Thirties," in Rita Simon, ed., *As We Saw the Thirties* (Urbana: University of Illinois Press, 1967), pp. 183–84.

21. See the *Literary Digest* poll in "Pacifists in the Colleges," *Literary Digest* 115 (May 27, 1933): 17, cited elsewhere as well as various student polls.

22. Lillian Hellman, *Scoundrel Time* (Boston: Little, Brown, 1976).

Chapter 1

1. Robert Morss Lovett, introduction to *Revolt on the Campus*, by James Wechsler (New York: Covici-Friede, 1935), pp. viii, ix.

2. George R. Leighton and Richard Hellman, "Half Slave, Half Free: Unemployment, the Depression, and American Young People," *Harper's*, August 1935, pp. 342, 349.

3. Ruth Douglas Keener, "The Vagrant Generation," *Scribner's*, February 1935, p. 90.

4. Leighton and Hellman, "Half Slave, Half Free," p. 346; one school indicated the low point of placing its education graduates in 1933, when only 51.3 percent of those graduating got jobs. Frank Baker, "History and Prophecy: A Statement to the Alumni of Milwaukee State Teachers College," July 1, 1940, p. 4, unpublished manuscript, Baker Papers, University of Wisconsin—Milwaukee.

5. Cited in Hal Draper, "The Student Movement of the Thirties: A Political History," in Rita Simon, ed., *As We Saw the Thirties* (Urbana: University of Illinois Press, 1967), p. 156.

6. Temple University *News*, October 10, 1932: *Michigan Daily News*, February 24, 1934.

7. Among magazines that had frequent articles were *American Scholar, Christian Century, Forum, Harper's, Nation, New Republic, Scribner's, School and Society,* and *World Tomorrow.*

8. American Association of University Professors, Committee Y, *Depression, Recovery, and Higher Education* (New York: McGraw-Hill, 1937), p. 315; Christian Gauss, "Youth Moves toward Higher Standards," *Scribner's*, February 1935, p. 1.

9. Reported in AAUP, *Depression, Recovery, and Higher Education*, p. 322.

10. See George P. Rawick, "The New Deal and Youth" (Ph.D. dissertation, University of Wisconsin, 1957), for treatment of the government's youth programs, especially the National Youth Act, as well as the student movement, especially the American Youth Congress; Walsh bill cited in Leighton and Hellman, "Half Slave, Half Free," p. 342.

11. Dorothy Hopkins Yates, "How the Depression and Its Consequences Have Affected Teachers College Students," *Schools and Society* 39 (May 1934): 571–74; Hilding B. Carlson, "Attitudes of Undergraduate Students," *Journal of Social Psychology* 64 (May 1934): 211.

12. Harold Laski, "Why Don't Your Young Men Care?" *Harper's*, July 1931, pp. 129–36.

13. Paul Fussell, *The Great War and Modern Memory* (New York: Oxford University Press, 1975), p. 8.

14. Charles Chatfield, *For Peace and Justice: Pacifism in America, 1914–1941* (Knoxville: University of Tennessee Press, 1971), pp. 121–22. For a complete discussion of the revisionists and their differences see Warren I. Cohen, *The American Revisionists: The Lessons of Intervention in World War I* (Chicago: University of Chicago Press, 1967).

15. Chatfield, *For Peace and Justice*, p. 135.

16. Carol S. Gruber, *Mars and Minerva* (Baton Rouge: Louisiana State University Press, 1975), p. 135. See also George T. Blakey, *Historians on the Home Front: American Propagandists for the Great War* (Lexington: University of Kentucky Press, 1970).

17. Gruber, *Mars and Minerva*, p. 5.

18. For further discussion of students' view of the relationship between higher education, society, and the state see chapter 8.

19. Columbia *Spectator*, March 28, 1933. Weinstein also called for emphasis on international economic stability and expressed

confidence that moral pressure and economic boycotts would halt anti-Semitic activity in Germany.

20. "Carnage for $1.35," editorial in Columbia *Spectator*, March 31, 1932; reprinted in Columbia *Spectator*, March 31, 1933.

21. "Dulce et Decorum Est," in *The Collected Poems of Wilfred Owen*, C. Day Lewis, ed. (London: Chatto & Windus, 1964), p. 55.

22. Eric Sevareid, *Not So Wild a Dream* (New York: Knopf, 1956), pp. 62–63.

23. J. E. Kirkpatrick, *The American College and Its Rulers* (New York: New Republic, 1926), pp. 197–224.

24. Committee on Militarism in Education, "The Campaign against Militarism in Education," 1931, CME Files, Swarthmore College Peace Collection.

25. *New Student*, April 26, 1924, p. 5.

26. Ralph Ellison, *Invisible Man* (New York: Random House, 1947), p. 109.

27. For a discussion of these protests see Raymond Wolters, *The New Negro on Campus: Black College Rebellions of the 1920's* (Princeton: Princeton University Press, 1975).

28. Lester C. Lamon, "The Black Community in Nashville and the Fisk University Student Strike of 1924–1925," *Journal of Southern History* 40 (May 1974): 225–44.

29. *New Student*, April 1922 (reprint, Westport: Greenwood, 1970; introduction by George P. Rawick, April 19, 1922, p. 3).

30. *New Student*, October 7, 1922, p. 3.

31. For a history of the LID see Rodolph Leslie Schnell, *National Activist Student Organizations in American Higher Education, 1905–1944* (Ann Arbor: University of Michigan, School of Education, 1976).

32. Ibid., p. 47.

Chapter 2

1. Columbia *Spectator*, October 11, 1930, October 13, 1932. Of the class of 1936, upon entering, of about 500 students over half were from New York City, and 344 of the total were from there or the

rest of New York State. Another 64 were from New Jersey and 15 from Pennsylvania, with mere sprinklings from other states. *School and Society* gives different figures: total university enrollment of 31,978 in November 1930, with 2,396 at Columbia College and 1,006 at Barnard (*School and Society* 32 [December 1930]: 786).

2. Columbia *Spectator*, October 24, 31, 1932.

3. Ibid., October 17, November 21, 1930, January 7, 1931, September 25, 1930.

4. Ibid., February 24, 1931.

5. *New York Times*, April 3, 1932.

6. Ibid.

7. Ibid., May 13, 1932; James Wechsler, *Revolt on the Campus* (New York: Covici-Friede, 1935), pp. 108–20.

8. Earnest Earnest, *Academic Procession* (New York: Bobbs-Merrill, 1953), pp. 223–28.

9. Ibid., p. 209.

10. Doris Kearns, *Lyndon Johnson and the American Dream* (New York: Harper and Row, 1976), pp. 55–56.

11. Mary Handlin and Oscar Handlin, *The American College and American Culture: Socialization as a Function of Higher Education* (New York: McGraw-Hill, 1970).

12. Earnest, *Academic Procession*, p. 284.

13. Columbia *Spectator*, October 22, 1930.

14. Ibid., October 28, 1932.

15. Reed Harris, *King Football* (New York: Vanguard Press, 1932); Reed Harris, "College Fraternities—Obstacles to Social Change," *Revolt* (*Student Outlook*), December 1932. Harris's subsequent career will be related in chapter 11. After a brief excursion to the left, he found himself back in the anti-Communist establishment.

16. Columbia *Spectator*, October 14, 1935.

17. "Building a Militant Student Movement," Program of the National Student League (pamphlet, March 1935).

18. Harvard *Crimson*, October 1931.

19. "Won by Decision," editorial in ibid., October 1, 1931.

20. "Difference," editorial in ibid., October 5, 1931.

21. Columbia *Spectator*, December 9, 1932.

22. For general discussion of the controversy nationally and

analysis of the results of the Olympics, see Richard D. Mandell, *The Nazi Olympics* (New York: MacMillan, 1971), and Moshe Gottlieb, "The American Controversy over the Olympic Games, 1936," *American Jewish Historical Quarterly* 61 (March 1972): 181–213.

23. Harvard *Crimson*, September 26, 1935.

24. Blan W. Hale, class of '36, letter to the editor, ibid., November 4, 1935.

25. Ibid., November 5, 1935. This was the same argument that the *Crimson* and others made for signing loyalty oaths in spite of disapproval of the requirement.

26. A. D. Peterson, "Berlin Jewess to Compete for Germany," *Daily Pennsylvanian*, October 28, 1935.

27. B. F. (name withheld), letter to editor, ibid., November 4, 1935.

28. (Name withheld), letter to editor, ibid., October 10, 1935.

29. Columbia *Spectator*, September 27, October 2, 1935.

30. *New York Times*, April 7, 1932. Editing the *Spectator* could be hazardous. A few years later a group of fraternity boys who were displeased with James Wechsler's editorial positions attempted to "kidnap" him.

31. For further discussion of antipeace activity and right-wing groups see chapter 4.

32. This disparity seems primarily the result of decisions by judges and prosecutors. The city police, especially in Boston, seem to have been more than happy to get their cracks in at students on any occasion. This may testify to the policemen's own consciousness of the class base of the university.

33. "Death Stalks the Gridiron," editorial in Columbia *Spectator*, April 10, 1932.

34. Paul Fussell, *The Great War and Modern Memory* (New York: Oxford University Press, 1975), pp. 25–28.

Chapter 3

1. Hollis Christopher, *The Oxford Union* (London: Evans Brothers, 1965), chapter 10, "King and Country." The Churchill response

is taken from an article by Lord Mattisone in *Public Opinion*, date unknown, cited by Hollis, p. 191.

2. Winston Churchill, *The Gathering Storm* (Boston: Houghton-Mifflin, 1948), pp. 85, 168.

3. "War against War," editorial, Brown *Daily Herald*, March 22, 1933.

4. Columbia *Spectator*, April 3, March 24, 1933. It is difficult to say how representative this was, since several of the university units had their own polls, but the numerical turnout was considerably greater than for most polls throughout the decade, indicating at least the student interest in the subject (*Spectator*, April 7, 1933).

5. "Pacifists in the Colleges," *Literary Digest* 115 (May 27, 1933): 17.

6. *Nation* 140 (February 6, 1935): 142–43.

7. "Rally Once Again," editorial, Columbia *Spectator*, March 20, 1933.

8. George Edwards, *Pioneer-at-Law* (New York: Norton, 1974), p. 130; Columbia *Spectator*, April 6, 3, 1933.

9. Ben Fischer, "Realism in Anti-War Discussion," *Student Outlook*, February 1933, p. 13.

10. Columbia *Spectator*, March 27, 1933.

11. *New York Times*, December 29, 1933.

12. Columbia *Spectator*, May 10, 1934.

13. "Gouging eA1-eA2," editorial, ibid., March 23, 1933.

14. Ibid., December 8, 1932.

15. Ibid., April 5, 1933.

16. Ibid., January 4, 1933.

17. Ibid., January 9, 1933; "Revolt against Caesarism," editorial, ibid., February 15, 1934.

18. Harvard *Crimson*, November 2, 1933.

19. Columbia *Spectator*, December 15, 1932.

20. James Wechsler, ibid., April 24, 1933; Lawrence Wittner, *Rebels against War: The American Peace Movement, 1941–1960* (New York: Columbia University Press, 1969), p. 12.

21. Columbia *Spectator*, October 9, 1933.

22. L. L., "The Stroller," ibid., April 4, 1933.

Chapter 4

1. Columbia *Spectator*, 1934–35 school year series of editorials and "exposes"; Harvard *Crimson*, spring 1933, fall 1934; Columbia *Spectator*, Harvard *Crimson*, 1935–36.

2. Jerold Auerbach, "The Depression Decade," in Alan Reitman, ed., *The Pulse of Freedom: American Civil Liberties, 1920–1970s* (New York: Norton, 1975), pp. 66, 83, 84.

3. Quoted in ibid., p. 84, from the *New York Times*, April 11, 1933.

4. Columbia *Spectator*, May 14, 1934, February 1935.

5. Ibid., October 23, 1933.

6. James Wechsler, "Notes on Freedom 11," ibid., March 20, 1935.

7. Ibid., March 20, 1935.

8. Ibid., March 22, 1935, letter to the editor.

9. Ibid., January 17, 1935, letter to the editor by Emmanuel A. Sander.

10. Sander, letter to the editor, ibid., November 12, 1934.

11. Alfred Raizen, class of '38, letter to the editor, *Spectator*, March 22, 1935.

12. Jerold Auerbach, "Depression Decade," p. 118.

13. Columbia *Spectator*, April 13, 1935.

14. Although quota systems originated in the twenties, exclusion or limitation of Jewish students, especially from professional schools, increased dramatically between 1936 and 1946 (*Higher Education for American Democracy: A Report of the Presidential Commission on Higher Education* [New York: Harper, 1948], pp. 38, 39).

15. Harvard *Crimson*, September 1934, September 1935; *School and Society* 42 (December 1935): 788; *School and Society* 40 (December 1934): 793.

16. Harvard *Crimson*, October 20, 1933.

17. Ibid., September 1934.

18. Ibid., November 6, 1931.

19. Ibid., January 10, 1936, June 1936, October 1933.

20. For a discussion of student life at Harvard see Seymour Lipsett and David Riesman, *Education and Politics at Harvard* (New York: McGraw-Hill, 1975).

21. Mary Handlin and Oscar Handlin, *The American College and American Culture,* (New York: McGraw-Hill, 1970), p. 57.

22. Quoted in Joseph Lash, *Eleanor and Franklin* (New York: Norton, 1971), p. 173.

23. Harvard *Crimson,* November 6, 1931.

24. Ibid., November 10, 1932.

25. Ibid., March 17, 1934.

26. Ibid.

27. Ibid., October 24, 1931.

28. Ibid., March 19, 1934.

29. Ibid., February 16, 1934.

30. Ibid., January 6, 1932.

31. "Sic Semper Tyrannus," editorial, ibid., April 27, 1934.

32. Ibid., April 14, 1934, letter to the editor from J. Le B. Bayle II.

33. Ibid., November 9, 1933.

34. Ibid.

35. Ibid., November 10, 11, 13, 1933. The demonstration was attended by six cadets, two news cameramen, and sixty students.

36. Ibid., May 17, 1934.

37. Ibid., May 18, 1934.

38. "Boston's Finest," editorial, ibid.

39. Lipsett and Riesman, *Education and Politics at Harvard,* p. 159.

40. Harvard *Crimson,* June 1, 1934.

41. Ibid., May 14, 1934.

42. Ibid., May 17, 1934.

43. Ibid., May 9, 1934, letter to the editor from Howard S. Whiteside, class of '34, and Warren Richards, class of '36.

44. Ibid., October 4, 1934.

45. Ibid.

46. Ibid., June 8, 1934.

47. Columbia *Spectator,* October 5, 1934.

48. Harvard *Crimson,* October 18, 1934.

49. Ibid., April 11, 1934.

50. *New York Times,* April 13, 1934; Harvard *Crimson,* April 14, 1934.

51. *New York Herald-Tribune,* reprinted in the Harvard *Crimson,* April 18, 1934.

52. Columbia *Spectator*, April 18, 1934; *Daily Princetonian*, reprinted in the Harvard *Crimson*, May 29, 1934.

53. *Higher Education for American Democracy*, p. 29.

54. Ibid., pp. 30, 31.

55. Ibid., pp. 36, 38, 39.

56. Diana Trilling, "Lionel Trilling: A Jew at Columbia," *Commentary* 54 (March 1979): 44.

57. Lionel Trilling, "Young in the Thirties," *Commentary* 41 (May 1966): 43–51; Diana Trilling, "Lionel Trilling," pp. 44, 43.

58. James Wechsler, *Revolt on the Campus* (Seattle: University of Washington Press, 1963), originally published 1935, p. 373–96.

59. Ibid., pp. 390–92.

60. In the winter session of 1934, for example, there were 8,029 students enrolled in the day session, 2,519 in the afternoon, and 13,339 in the evening. See *City College Bulletins*, 1934–39. See also Solomon Willis Rudy, *The College of the City of New York* (New York: City College Press, 1949), pp. 396–99.

61. *City College Bulletin, 1934-35*, Jan. 1, 1935, p. 13.

62. *Report of the New York City Subcommittee of Rapp-Coudert Committee of the New York State Legislature*, 1944, cited in Rudy, *The College of the City of New York*, p. 398.

63. John Higham, "Social Discrimination against Jews in America," *Publication of the American Jewish Historical Quarterly* 47 (September 1957): 21; Benjamin Stolberg, "Degradation of American Psychology," *Nation* 131 (October 15, 1930): 395–98; Higham, *Strangers in the Land* (New York: Atheneum, 1974), pp. 275–76.

64. Wechsler devotes several chapters of *Revolt on the Campus* to "vigilantism" on campus. One chapter is titled "Goosestep at Harvard." For examples, see chapter 6 in this volume.

65. City College of New York archives, "Anti-war and anti-fascist publications and notices, 1934."

66. Harvard *Crimson*, May 10, 1934.

67. J. P. C., "America's Black Legion," *Student Advocate*, July 25, 1939, p. 914.

68. *Daily Pennsylvanian*, February 24, March 2, 1936.

69. Paul E. Queneau, letter to editor, Columbia *Spectator*, May 18, 1933.

70. Wechsler, *Revolt*, pp. 354–62. Wechsler drew much of his

information from *Christians Only* by Haywood Broun and George Britt.

71. University of Chicago *Daily Maroon,* April 13, 1934. It was not until after the World War II that Harvard, Yale, Princeton, or the University of Pennsylvania had a single Jewish tenured professor in English (Baltzell, *The Protestant Establishment,* p. 336). *Michigan Daily News,* April 4, 1934.

72. E. M. Miler, letter to editor, Harvard *Crimson,* May 17, 1934.

73. Eric Sevareid, *Not So Wild a Dream* (New York: Knopf, 1956), pp. 62, 63.

Chapter 5

1. Lawrence Wittner, *Rebels against War* (New York: Columbia University Press, 1969), p. 11.

2. "Less Profit, Less War," editorial, *Michigan Daily News,* March 11, 1934.

3. "For Whom the War?" ibid., April 28, 1934.

4. "Dealers in the Death," Columbia *Spectator,* March 4, 1934; Markets for Armaments," Harvard *Crimson,* April 23, 1934, reprint of "Arms and the Men . . . ," *Fortune,* May 1934.

5. Doris Rodin, "Opposition to the Establishment of Military Training in the Civil Schools and Colleges in the United States, 1914–1940," M.A. thesis, American University, 1949, p. 106.

6. Morris Raphael Cohen, *A Dreamer's Journey* (Boston: Beacon Press, 1949), p. 152.

7. Associated Press Dispatch, Columbia *Spectator,* January 11, 1934; *Michigan Daily,* March 22, 1934; Columbia *Spectator,* January 9, 1934; Rodin, "Opposition," p. 106.

8. *Hamilton* v. *Regents of the State of California,* 293 U.S. 245, cited in Rodin, "Opposition," p. 106.

9. *Hearings before the Subcommittee of the Senate Committee on Military Affairs,* on S. 3309, 75th Congress, 2nd session, June 2, 3, 4, 1936.

10. *Citizenship,* M.T. no. 20000-25 (Government Printing Office, Nov. 30, 1928).

11. *Daily Pennsylvanian*, October 1, 1935.

12. Robert Morss Lovett, *All Our Years* (New York: Viking, 1948), p. 253.

13. Maury Maverick, "The R.O.T.C. Builds Women," *Student Advocate*, March 1936, p. 11.

14. James Wechsler, *Revolt on the Campus* (New York: Covici-Friede, 1935), p. 108.

15. "Challenge to Defend," editorial, Columbia *Spectator*, October 27, 1933.

16. Editorial, ibid., April 13, 1934.

17. Wechsler, *Revolt*, p. 171; *New York Times*, April 14, 1934.

18. University of Chicago *Daily Maroon*, April 15, 1934.

19. *New York Times*, April 14, 1934.

20. Ibid.

21. University of Chicago *Daily Maroon*, April 12, 1934; Temple University *News*, April 16, 1934; on the expulsion of CCNY antiwar leaders and high school students, see Columbia *Spectator*, April 25, 1934.

22. *New York World Telegram* editorial, reprinted in Columbia *Spectator*, April 16, 1934.

23. Columbia *Spectator*, October 5, 1934.

24. *Bennett News*, November 11, 8, 1934.

25. Hal Draper, "The Student Movement in the Thirties: A Political History," in Rita Simon, ed., *As We Saw the Thirties* (Urbana: University of Illinois Press, 1967), p. 170.

26. Columbia *Spectator*, January 7, 14, 1935.

27. Except where otherwise indicated, the source is the post-strike survey in the *Student Outlook*, "The Great Student Strike," May 1935, pp. 3–10; see also Wechsler, *Revolt*, pp. 166–81.

28. Columbia *Spectator*, April 15, 1935.

29. In the 1934–35 school year City College had 8,286 full-time students and 22,702 total registration.

30. Wechsler, *Revolt*, p. 401.

31. *Philadelphia Bulletin*, February 16, 1935.

32. Ibid., April 12, 1935.

33. Ibid., April 13, 1935.

34. *Bennett News*, April 11, 1935.

35. Rayford W. Logan, *Howard University: The First Hundred*

Years, 1867–1967 (New York: New York University Press, 1968), p. 392.

36. *New York Times,* January 18, 1938. U.S. House, Special Committee on Un-American Affairs, "The Communistic Tenants [*sic*] of Mordecai W. Johnson, President of Howard University," 5 November 1938, 2142–61.

37. *Badger* (University of Wisconsin yearbook), 1935, pp. 133–34.

38. *Echo Weekly,* May 22, 1934.

39. Ibid., April 3, 1935.

40. *Milwaukee Journal,* April 12, 1935.

41. Ibid., April 12, 1935.

42. *Echo Weekly,* March 27, 1935.

43. Eric Sevareid, *Not So Wild a Dream* (New York: Knopf, 1956), pp. 54, 61.

44. Ibid., pp. 54, 61. Sevareid notes that Loevinger went as an officer on the first U.S. naval mission to England.

45. *Milwaukee Journal,* April 12, 1935.

46. *Daily Californian,* October 30, 31, 1934, January 31, 1935.

47. Ibid., January 25, 1935.

48. Ibid., November 6, 1934; Wechsler, *Revolt,* pp. 268–86, 280.

49. *Daily Californian,* April 15, 1935.

50. *Chicago Tribune,* April 12, 1935.

51. *Nation* 140 (June 19, 1935): 699; Columbia *Spectator,* September 26, 1935; Wechsler, *Revolt,* p. 191.

52. Wechsler, *Revolt,* p. 173.

Chapter 6

1. *New York Times,* December 29, 30, 1935; *Nation,* "American Students Unite," January 8, 1936.

2. "American Students Union—A Necessity, a Fact," *Student Review,* October 1935, p. 3.

3. Joseph Cadden, in *Student Review,* October 1935, p. 16.

4. *Student Review,* October 1935, pp. 2–4, 16, 17; *Student Outlook,* October 1935, pp. 3–5.

5. *Student Outlook*, October 1935, p. 4.

6. Joseph Lash, *Student Review*, October 1935, p. 16; Joseph R. Starobin, *American Communism in Crisis, 1943–1957* (Berkeley: University of California Press, 1975), p. 235.

7. Irving Howe, *Steady Work* (New York: Harcourt, Brace, and World, 1966), p. 350.

8. Ibid., p. 358.

9. Quoted in Peter Stansky and William Abrahams, *Journey to the Frontier: Two Roads to the Spanish Civil War* (New York: Norton, 1966), p. 348.

10. Jessica Mitford, *A Fine Old Conflict* (New York: Vintage, 1978). For discussion of the relationship of John Cornford and Julien Bell's poetry and politics to England in the thirties see Stephen Spender, *The Thirties and After* (New York: Random House, 1978), pp. 146–54.

11. Alfred Kazin, *Starting Out in the Thirties* (New York: Little, Brown, 1965), p. 4.

12. Eric Sevareid, *Not So Wild a Dream* (New York: Knopf, 1956), p. 59.

13. Muriel Rukeyser, "The Blood Is Justified," in *Theory of Flight* (New Haven: Yale University Press, 1935), p. 98.

14. Howe, *Steady Work*, p. 364.

15. Earl Browder, "Education—An Ally in the Workers Struggle," *Social Frontier*, January 1935, pp. 22–23.

16. James Wechsler, *Revolt on the Campus* (New York: Covici-Friede, 1935), pp. 66–68.

17. A. Gordon Melvin, "Education or Revolution," *School and Society*, April 21, 1934, p. 510.

18. Barry Rubin, "Marxism and Education—Radical Thought and Educational Theory in the 1930's," *Science and Society* 36 (summer 1972): 193, 200. Rubin cites Richard Frank in the Communist party theoretical journal, the *Communist*, May 1937. The *Communist* was renamed *Political Affairs* during World War II.

19. See the files of the Committee on Militarism in Education, 1925–40, Jane Addams Peace Collection, Swarthmore College.

20. Clifford McVeigh, "Academic Napoleons: No. 1—Ruthven of Michigan," *Student Advocate*, February 1936, pp. 13–15.

21. Sydney Holtzman, *New Horizons*, February 1939, p. 7;

Joseph Whitt, "Fascism vs. Education," *New Horizons*, November 1938, p. 13.

22. Juanita Bitler, "Lines to a Professor," *Cheshire* (Milwaukee State Teachers College literary magazine), November 1936, p. 11.

23. C. C. Milner, "Peace and the College Curriculum," *Catholic Education Review* 32 (February 1934): 98–103; Bob Gilka, class of '39, Marquette *Tribune*, March 18, 1937.

24. "The Will to Peace," editorial, *Christian Front*, June 1936, pp. 83–84. This was a journal at Villanova University, not connected with the Coughlinite Christian Front.

25. Richard Neuberger, letter to editor, *Social Frontier*, June 1935, p. 16.

26. Columbia *Spectator*, September 28, October 3, 1934.

27. Dan Dodson, "Religious Prejudice in College," *American Mercury* 63 (July 1946): 5–13.

28. William H. Chafe, *The American Woman: Her Changing Social, Economic, and Political Roles, 1920–1970* (New York: Oxford University Press, 1972), pp. 91–92.

29. Bryn Mawr *College News*, October 20, 1937.

30. "Politics to the Fore," editorial, Bryn Mawr *College News*, March 20, 1935; "War," editorial, January 9, 1935, June 6, 1936.

31. Vida Scudder, *On Journey* (New York: E. P. Dutton, 1937), p. 427.

32. Nadine Brazan, *New York Times*, June 24, 1972, p. 20, on reunion of Smith class of 1937; on Vassar see *New York Times*, March 3, 1935, section 2, p. 5.

33. *Daily Pennsylvanian*, letter to editor, April 15, 1936.

34. Molly Yard, correspondence with the author, February 17, 1981; Columbia *Spectator*, April 13, 1934.

35. *School and Society* 44 (July 13, 1936): 80; "The Zest to Nest," *Student Advocate*, December 1936, pp. 10–11.

36. Columbia *Spectator*, March 28, 1934.

37. Bryn Mawr *College News*, October 13, 1937.

38. Vera Brittain, *Testament of Youth* (London, 1933; reprint, New York: Wideview Books, 1980), pp. 401, 405.

39. Brittain, *Testament of Youth*, pp. 270, 662.

Chapter 7

1. Emory Stevens Burke, ed., *The History of American Methodism* (Nashville: Abingdon Press, 1964), 2:403.

2. Sydney E. Ahlstrom, *A Religious History of the American People* (New Haven: Yale University Press, 1975), 2:413.

3. Burke, *American Methodism*, 2:404.

4. Ahlstrom, *Religious History*, 2:412–13.

5. Walter G. Muelder, *Methodism and Society in the Twentieth Century* (Nashville: Abingdon Press, 1961), pp. 208–9, 164–65. See also G. Bromley Oxnam, *I Protest* (New York: Harper, 1954).

6. E. Stanley Jones, *Christ's Alternative to Communism* (New York: Abingdon Press, 1935), p. 83.

7. Ray H. Abrams, *Preachers Present Arms: A Study of the Wartime Attitudes and Activities of the Churches and the Clergy in the United States, 1914–1918* (Philadelphia: Round Table Press, 1933).

8. *Who's Who in America*, 1976–77 (Chicago: Marquis Who's Who, 1977).

9. Columbia *Spectator*. November 5, 1934.

10. *Daily Pennsylvanian*, November 7, 1935.

11. C. Howard Hopkins, *History of the YMCA in North America* (New York: Association Press, 1951), p. 646. The decline in membership coincided with a decline in membership in mainline Protestant churches to the benefit of such groups as Mormons and Christian Scientists (Paul A. Carter, *The Decline and Revival of the Social Gospel, 1920–1940* [Ithaca: Cornell University Press, 1954], p. 222).

12. Hopkins, *History of the YMCA*, p. 645.

13. *Michigan Daily*, March 15, 1934.

14. *Michigan Daily*, May 6, 1934. The poll is discussed in Charles Chatfield, *For Peace and Justice* (Knoxville: University of Tennessee Press, 1971), pp. 127–28.

15. Grace Farnsworth and John Richmond, letter to editor, *Michigan Daily*, May 23, 24, 1934.

16. John Richmond, letter to the editor, *Michigan Daily*, May 15, 1934.

17. Gordon Halstead, letter to editor, *Michigan Daily*, May 30, 1934.

18. *New York Times*, April 14, 1934, p. 10.

19. Rev. Ignatius W. Cox, S.J., cited in *New York Herald Tribune* article, pamphlet, Catholic Association for International Peace Files, Swarthmore College Peace Collection.

20. John Whitney Evans, "The Newman Movement: A Social and Intellectual History of Roman Catholics in Higher Education, 1883–1969" (Ph.D. dissertation, University of Minnesota, 1970), p. 844. These figures exclude the 13 percent of Catholic college enrollment who were non-Catholic.

21. David J. O'Brien, *American Catholics and Social Reform: The New Deal Years* (New York: Oxford University Press, 1968), p. 67. For a student view see George Fleming in *Loyola News*, March 29, 1938.

22. John Cogley, "The Failure of Anti-Communism," *Commonweal*, July 21, 1950, pp. 357–58.

23. "Statement of the Administrative Board, N.C.W.C. on the Second World Youth Congress," July 11, 1938, *Our Bishops Speak* (Milwaukee: Bruce, 1952) p. 317; *The Catholic Standard and Times* (Philadelphia), April 30, 1937; *New York Times*, July 12, 1936; *Student Advocate*, April 1936, p. 12.

24. See an exchange of letters between Margaret Ann Hogan, secretary of the Federation of Catholic College Clubs, and chapters at Vassar and Cornell, spring 1936, in archives, National Newman Apostolate, American Catholic Historical Society of Philadelphia, and discussion in Evans, *Newman Movement*, p. 491.

25. See Catholic Association for International Peace (CAIP), Student Peace Federation files, Swarthmore College Peace Collection.

26. Elizabeth Sweeney, executive secretary, CAIP, "Catholic Youth and World Peace," *The Christian Front*, Peace Leaflet No. 1, 1936, CAIP files, Swarthmore College Peace Collection; L. D., Marquette *Tribune*, April 8, 1937.

27. Charles Curran, "Paul Hanly Furfey: Theorist of American Catholic Radicalism," *American Ecclesiastical Review* 5 (December 1972): 658.

28. Villanova University *Belle Air*, 1939.

29. *Christian Front* 2 (May 1937): 80; Rev. Dr. John M. Cooper, "Christ and the Other Sheep," *American Ecclesiastical Review* 91 (May 1934); George N. Shuster, *The Ground I Walked On: Reflec-*

tions of a College President (New York: Farrar, Straus, 1961), p. 23.

30. Ted Merkle, *Loyola News*, October 31, 1935.

31. *Directory of Civilian Public Service, May 1941–March 1947*, p. xviii. The Catholic Worker movement sponsored Pax, a Catholic organization of conscientious objectors. *Commonweal*, December 25, 1936, p. 231. On the influence of the Catholic Worker movement on a generation of young Catholics see Edward Duff, "Catholic Social Action in the American Environment," *Social Order* 12 (September 1962): 306–7.

32. Muelder, *Methodism and Society*, p. 155.

33. Max Weiss, "Youth Serves the Nation," pamphlet (New York: International Publishers, 1942), p. 4.

Chapter 8

1. For the Left's reaction see Allen Guttmann, *The Wound in the Heart: America and the Spanish Civil War* (New York: Free Press, 1962); Charles Chatfield, *For Peace and Justice* (Knoxville: University of Tennessee Press, 1971), pp. 241–45.

2. For the Socialist debate see Frank Warren, *An Alternative Vision: The Socialist Party in the 1930's* (Bloomington: Indiana University Press, 1974).

3. "We Must Remember Spain," *Student Advocate*, April 1937, pp. 3, 4.

4. Jeffrey Campbell, letter to the editor, *Student Advocate*, April 1937, p. 27.

5. "Harry," "Dispatch to the General," *Tempo*, October 1938, pp. 4, 5.

6. Ibid., February 1939, pp. 4, 5.

7. Bryn Mawr *College News*, November 10, 17, December 8, 1937.

8. Arthur Landis, *The Abraham Lincoln Brigade* (New York: Citadel Press, 1967), p. xviii; John Gates, *The Story of an American Communist* (New York: Nelson, 1958), p. 46.

9. Landis, *Abraham Lincoln Brigade*, p. 249; Joseph Lash, "The Campus: A Fortress of Democracy," report to the ASU National

Convention, Vassar College, December 1937, p. 11; *Student Advocate*, December 1937, p. 22; Gates, *Story*, p. 58.

10. John Kenneth Galbraith, in Irving Stone, ed., *There Was Light: An Autobiography of a University* (Garden City, N.Y.: Doubleday, 1970), pp. 24–26.

11. David Cook, "From Columbia to Madrid," *Student Advocate*, April 1937, pp. 9, 10.

12. Abraham and Stansky, *Journey to the Frontier* (London: Constable, 1966), p. 313.

13. Quoted in Clara Distel, "Modern Odyssey," *Student Advocate*, December 1937, pp. 7, 22.

14. Samuel Levinger, "The War Is Long," *Student Advocate*, December 1937, p. 7.

15. Distel, "Modern Odyssey," p. 22.

16. Murray Kempton, *Part of Our Time* (New York: Simon and Schuster, 1955), p. 334.

17. Eric Sevareid, *Not So Wild a Dream* (New York: Knopf, 1956), pp. 94–96, 94.

18. Ibid., p. 96.

19. Muriel Rukeyser, "Mediterranean," in *U.S. 1* (New York: Covici-Friede, 1938), pp. 140–41.

20. Sevareid, *Not So Wild a Dream*, p. 94.

21. Rukeyser, "Mediterranean," p. 140. See also Muriel Rukeyser, "We Came for Games: A Memoir of the People's Olympics, Barcelona, 1936," *Esquire*, October 1974, pp. 192–94, 368–70.

22. Landis, *Abraham Lincoln Brigade*, p. 249.

Chapter 9

1. *Student Advocate*, December 1936, p. 29.

2. Joseph Lash, "Toward a 'Closed Shop' on Campus," report to the Second Annual ASU Convention, Chicago, 1936, p. 25.

3. Hal Draper, "The Student Movement of the Thirties," in Rita Simon, ed., *As We Saw the Thirties* (Urbana: University of Illinois Press, 1967), p. 179.

4. *Student Advocate*, May 1936, May 1937.

5. Bryn Mawr *College News*, editorial, April 29, 1936, p. 2.

6. Ibid., April 8, 1936, p. 2.

7. *Student Advocate*, May 1936, pp. 3–5, May 1937, p. 4.

8. Joseph Lash, "500,000 Strike for Peace: An Appraisal," *Student Advocate*, May 1936, pp. 3–5.

9. *Student Advocate*, April 1937, p. 2.

10. "The Great 1937 Strike in Review," *Student Advocate*, May 1937, p. 4.

11. Wittner and Thayer, "Another Angry Decade," *Columbia College Today*, summer 1971, p. 48.

12. Charles M. Cooper, *Whittier: Independent College in California* (Los Angeles: Ward Ritchie Press, 1967), p. 258.

13. Information from the *Echo Weekly* and *Echo Yearbook*, including *Echo Weekly*, September 30, 1936.

14. *Echo Weekly*, editorial, April 22, 1936.

15. Ibid., November 16, 1937.

16. Ibid., October 28, 1936.

17. Ibid., April 22, 1936.

18. Chatfield, *For Peace and Justice* (Knoxville: University of Tennessee Press, 1971), p. 256. Chatfield discusses the EPC's own divisions and also the role played by students. He notes that the April Student Strike in 1936 was planned for the opening week of the Emergency Peace Campaign, and the campaign appropriated one thousand dollars for the strike (p. 272).

19. *Echo Weekly*, January 13, 1937.

20. Ibid., April 28, 1937.

21. Frank Baker, "From the Executive," ibid.

22. *Fellowship*, December 1937, p. 9.

23. Ibid.

24. Ibid., p. 8.

25. Draper, "Student Movement," pp. 179–80.

26. Vivian Liebman, "The American Student Union Meets at Vassar," *Student Advocate*, March 1938, p. 6.

27. Joseph Lash, "The Campus as a Fortress of Democracy," report to the ASU National Convention, Vassar College, December 1937, p. 11.

28. Liebman, "American Student Union," p. 8.

29. "Pacifists Drop Principles as Conflict Spreads," editorial, *Echo Weekly*, January 12, 1938, p. 2.

30. Draper, "Student Movement," pp. 180–81.

31. Ibid., p. 181.

32. "ASU Swings the Nation," *Student Advocate*, March 1938, p. 18.

33. *Tempo*, October 1938, p. 23.

34. Roger Allen, "Reward the Band," *Tempo*, December 1938, p. 15.

35. Sol Leon, "The Golden Boys," *Tempo*, February 1939, p. 14.

36. *Student Advocate*, March 1938, p. 18.

37. *Tempo*, February 1939. Issues at Temple in 1938–39 included ROTC, appeasement at Munich, the Bund in Philadelphia, student government, and a suggestion that Temple should hire Freud to head the psychology department.

Chapter 10

1. Joseph P. Lash, *Eleanor Roosevelt: A Friend's Memoir* (Garden City, N.J.: Doubleday, 1964), pp. 8–15; U.S. Congress, Special Committee on Un-American Activities, *Hearings*, December 1, 1939, pp. 7061–93.

2. "Blacklisted," Bryn Mawr *College News*, November 17, 1937. The editor noted that there was no such organization as the Bryn Mawr Liberal Club.

3. Solomon Willis Rudy, *The College of the City of New York: A History, 1847–1947* (New York: City College Press, 1949), pp. 450–52; New York State Legislature, "Interim Report and Conclusions of the New York City Subcommittee Relative to Subversive Activity among Students in the Public High Schools and Colleges of the City of New York" (December 1, 1941); Legislative Document (1942) no. 49A.

4. Rudy, *College*, p. 449.

5. Reinhold Niebuhr, "Peace and the Liberal Illusion," *Nation* 143 (January 28, 1939): 119.

6. *New York Times*, December 4, 1975.

7. Temple University *News*, September 15, 1940.

8. Zechariah Chafee, Jr., *Free Speech in the United States* (1941; reprint, New York: Atheneum, 1969), p. 440.

9. Columbia *Spectator,* December 6, 1940.

10. *Daily Pennsylvanian,* March 3, May 4, 1941; *Bennett News,* March 6, 1941; Temple University *News,* April 25, May 28, 1941; *Tempo,* February 1939.

11. Quoted by Alden Whitman in Sproul's obituary, *New York Times,* September 12, 1975.

12. Columbia *Spectator,* October 1940.

13. *Echo Weekly,* November 6, 1940, March 26, 1941.

14. Lash, *Eleanor Roosevelt,* pp. 21, 22.

15. Ibid., pp. 56–68.

16. Harold Ickes, *Secret Diary* (New York: Simon and Schuster, 1954), 3:134.

17. "'The Boys' Pull a Bloomer and Turn the Sword Inward," editorial, Temple University *News,* January 5, 1940.

18. Ibid., March 8, 1940.

19. Ibid., April 12, 1940.

20. Ibid., April 24, May 22, 1940.

21. *Bennett News,* April 18, 1940.

22. Manuscript, Frank E. Baker Papers, Box 3, University of Wisconsin—Milwaukee Area Research Center.

23. *Echo Weekly,* April 19, 1940.

24. Harold Lavine and James Wechsler, *War Propaganda in the United States* (New Haven: Yale University Press, 1940), p. 152.

25. James S. Martin, *Revisionist Viewpoints* (Colorado Springs: R. Myles, 1971), p. 38.

26. Arthur M. Schlesinger, Jr., *Robert M. Kennedy and His Times* (New York: Ballantine, 1978), p. 42.

27. Reinhold Niebuhr, "Idealists or Cynics," *Nation* 150 (January 20, 1940): 74.

28. Lavine and Wechsler, *War Propaganda,* pp. 150–51, 152.

29. Ibid., p. 152.

30. Charles Chatfield, *For Peace and Justice* (Knoxville: University of Tennessee Press, 1971), p. 312.

31. Ibid., p. 312; James F. Childress, "Reinhold Niebuhr's Critique of Pacifism," *Review of Politics* 36 (October 1974): 467–91.

32. Archibald MacLeish, "The Irresponsibles," *Nation* 150 (May 1940): 618–23; *New Republic* 102 (June 1940): 784–90.

33. Rexford G. Tugwell, "The Crisis of Freedom," *Common Sense* 10 (October 1941): 291–95.

34. Beverly Hill, Wilson College *Billboard*, June 7, 1940.

35. Eric Sevareid, *Not So Wild a Dream* (New York: Knopf, 1956), p. 183.

36. Ibid., p. 51.

37. Robert Divine, *The Reluctant Belligerent* (New York: John Wiley and Son, 1968), p. 88.

38. William E. Leuchtenburg, *Franklin D. Roosevelt and the New Deal* (New York: Harper and Row, 1963), pp. 310–11.

39. Chatfield, *For Peace and Justice*, pp. 319, 322–32.

40. Franklin D. Roosevelt, *Public Papers*, 9:517.

41. U.S. State Department, *Peace and War: The United States Foreign Policy, 1931–1941* (Washington, D.C.: Government Printing Office, 1943), p. 607.

42. Columbia *Spectator*, October 17, 1940.

43. *New York Times*, October 17, 1940; Coffin quoted in Columbia *Spectator*, October 18, 1940.

44. Columbia *Spectator*, November 15, 1940, October 29, 1941.

45. Peter Brock, *Twentieth Century Pacifism* (New York: Van Nostrand Reinhold, 1970), pp. 201, 202.

46. Temple University *News*, "We Make Ourselves Clear," November 13, October 23, 1940.

47. "Excerpt from a Joint Statement by Donald Benedict, Joseph J. Bevilaqua, Meredith Dallas, David Dellinger, George M. Houser, William H. Lovell, Howard E. Spragg, and Richard Wichlei, *Why We Refused to Register*," in Straughton Lynd, ed., *Non-Violence in America* (New York: Bobbs-Merrill, 1966), pp. 296–99.

48. Temple University *News*, October 4, 1940.

49. Ed Kowalczyk, class of '44, letter to editor, ibid., October 7, 1940.

50. Columbia *Spectator*, October 1940. Nine hundred and thirty-seven undergraduates responded.

51. *Daily Pennsylvanian*, November 5, 1940.

52. For the attitudes of progressive educators toward the war and their part in it, see C. A. Bowers, *The Progressive Educator and the Depression* (New York: Random House, 1969), pp. 181–94.

See also issues of *Frontiers of Democracy*, the symbolic change in title of the *Social Frontier* as war approached.

53. *Bennett News*, March 13, 1941; Wilson College *Billboard*, October 11, 1940.

54. *Collegiate Digest* 14, no. 2, in the *Bennett News*, April 24, 1941.

55. Joseph Lash, *Eleanor Roosevelt: A Friend's Memoir* (Garden City: Doubleday, 1964), p. 156.

56. "To Draft or to Dodge," editorial, *Bennett News*, October 24, 31, 1940.

57. *Daily Pennsylvanian*, April 24, 1940.

58. *Collegiate Digest*, vol. 2, no. 1, in the *Bennett News*, September 25, 1941 (caption—"Coeds Rush to Fill War Courses"). For the role of women in World War II, see William Chafe, *The American Woman: Her Changing Social, Economic, and Political Roles, 1920–1970* (New York: Oxford University Press, 1972), pp. 135–95; Shirley J. Bach and Martin Binkin, *Women and the Military* (Washington: Brookings Institute, 1977).

59. Columbia *Spectator*, October 17, 1941; ibid., issues for fall 1941; Temple *News*, fall 1941; *Collegiate Digest*, vol. 10, no. 4, in the *Bennett News*, October 30, 1941.

60. Chatfield, *For Peace and Justice*, p. 325.

61. Columbia *Spectator*, October 28, 1941.

62. *Echo Weekly*, December 10, 1941; *Bennett News*, December 11, 1941, p. 1; editorial, Columbia *Spectator*, December 8, 1941, p. 1.

63. "No Undermining," *Bennett News*, December 11, 1941.

Chapter 11

1. Besides the sources indicated, some of the information for this chapter is based on interviews with people involved in student activism in the postwar period and my own experience in antiwar activity as a student in the late sixties and early seventies.

2. *New York Times*, January 13, 1946.

3. Marcia Graham Synnott, *The Half-Opened Door: Discrimination and Admissions at Harvard, Yale, and Princeton, 1900–1970* (Westport: Greenwood Press, 1979), p. 205.

4. *New York Times*, January 13, 1946.

5. Milwaukee State Teachers College *Echo Weekly*, 1946–49; University of Wisconsin—Madison *Cardinal*, 1946–49; Schlomo Swirsky, "Four Decades of Student Activism," in Philip Altbach, Robert S. Laufer, and Sheila McVey, eds., *Academic Supermarkets* (San Francisco: Jassey-Bass, 1971), pp. 322–42.

6. For the student movement in the fifties, see Andre Schiffrin, "The Student Movement in the 50's: A Reminiscence," *Radical America*, May-June 1968, and the SLID files, Tammiment Institute, New York City.

7. "The Careful Young Men: Tomorrow's Leaders Analyzed by Today's Teachers," *Nation* 184 (March 9, 1957). By 1961, the *Nation* could publish a report entitled "Rebels with a Hundred Causes."

8. *Historical Statistics of the United States* (Washington, D.C.: Government Printing Office, 1976), pp. 383, 382. Student figures are for degree-credit enrollment at all institutions of higher learning. Neil J. Smelser and Gabriel Almond, *Public Higher Education in California* (Berkeley: University of California Press, 1974); Clark Kerr, *The Uses of the University* (Cambridge: Harvard University Press, 1963).

9. E. Digby Baltzell, *The Protestant Establishment: Aristocracy and Caste in America* (New York: Random House, 1964), pp. 338, 339; Stephen Donadio, "Columbia: Seven Interviews," *Partisan Review* 35 (winter 1968): 387, 388; Philip Altbach, *Student Politics in America*, pp. 113–14.

10. Michael Wreszin, "Arthur Schlesinger, Jr., and the Liberal Reaffirmation of American Life," paper delivered at the American Historical Association convention, December 1981.

11. George Stewart, *The Year of the Oath* (New York: Doubleday, 1950); David Gardner, *The California Oath Controversy* (Berkeley: University of California Press, 1967).

12. Christopher Lasch, "The Cultural Cold War," in Barton Bernstein, ed., *Towards a New Past* (New York: Random House, 1968).

13. Paul F. Lazarsfeld and Wagner Thielens, Jr., *The Academic Mind* (Glencoe, Ill.: Free Press, 1958); Lasch, "Cultural Cold War," p. 349.

14. U.S. Senate Hearings before the Subcommittee of the Judiciary Committee, October 1 and November 21, 1963, "Nomination of George Edwards, Jr."; George Edwards, *Pioneer-at-Law* (New York: Norton, 1974), pp. 15–19.

15. Hal Draper, "The Student Movement of the Thirties," in Rita Simon, ed., *As We Saw the Thirties* (Urbana: University of Illinois Press, 1967), pp. 187–88.

16. Interview with Joseph Starobin, Hancock, Massachusetts, October 11, November 15, 1975.

17. *Philadelphia Inquirer,* November 11, 1953. Jennings later became a history professor at Cedar Crest College and recently published *The Invasion of America: Indians, Colonialism, and the Cant of Conquest* (Chapel Hill: University of North Carolina Press, 1975).

18. Walter G. Muelder, *Methodism and Society in the Twentieth Century* (Nashville: Abingdon Press, 1961), pp. 208–9, 226.

19. Earl Latham, *The Communist Controversy in Washington* (Cambridge: Harvard University Press, 1966), p. 331; Jerry Mangione, *The Dream and the Deal* (Boston: Little, Brown, 1972), pp. 59–61; U.S. Senate, Permanent Subcommittee on Investigations, "Voice of America," February 16, 1953. According to Mangione, Harris "stood up like a man" in the hearings.

20. David Caute, *The Great Fear* (New York: Simon and Schuster, 1978), p. 324; *Philadelphia Bulletin,* March 25, 1974.

21. Laura Bergquist, "Kay Meyer Goes to College," *Ms,* October 1974, p. 53.

22. Lawrence Wittner and Julia Thayer, "Another Angry Decade," *Columbia College Today,* summer 1971, p. 49.

23. U.S. Senate, Committee on Government Operations, Permanent Subcommittee on Investigations, Hearings pursuant to S. Res. 40, "State Information Program, Information Centers," April 24, May 5, 1953. For a defense of Wechsler, see Murray Kempton's comments on Lillian Hellman's *Scoundrel Time* in the *New York Review of Books,* June 10, 1976, p. 25. Kempton disagrees with Wechsler's decision to give names (including Kempton's) to the committee, but defends his motives and insists that Wechsler was not a "friendly witness" but a "manifestly hostile one."

24. U.S. Senate, Committee on Government Operations, Per-

manent Subcommittee on Investigations, April 24, 1953, pp. 274, 280.

25. Irving Howe and Lewis Coser, *The American Communist Party: A Critical History, 1919–1957* (Boston: Beacon Press, 1957), p. 358.

26. Alfred Kazin, *Starting Out in the Thirties* (New York: Little, Brown, 1965), pp. 158–59.

27. Pauline Kael's recollections of her student life are recorded in Studs Terkel, *Hard Times* (New York: Avon, 1970), pp. 398–99.

28. Irving Stone, *There Was Light: Autobiography of a University* (Berkeley: University of California Press, 1968), pp. 19–28.

29. Jonah Raskin, *Out of the Whale: Growing Up in the American Left* (New York: Links, 1974), pp. 12, 13, 29, 35.

30. Ron Kovic, *Born on the Fourth of July* (New York: McGraw-Hill, 1976).

31. Ibid.; Raskin, *Out of the Whale*, p. 27.

32. Florence Howe, "Introduction: The History of Women in Higher Education," *Journal of Education* 159 (August 1977): 7.

33. For women's colleges in the fifties, see Betty Friedan, *The Feminine Mystique* (New York: Norton, 1963). The Vassar class of 1958 is described (by a male commentator) in Nevitt Sanford, ed., *The American College* (New York: Wiley, 1962), pp. 509–10. For the sixties, see Liva Baker, *I'm Radcliffe! Fly Me! The Seven Sisters and the Failure of Women's Education* (New York: Macmillan, 1976). Nonelite women's colleges could stand some attention, since most comment is based on elite women's institutions. Some young left women came from a different background, and some did have ties to feminist ideology in the Old Left. See Sara Evans, *Personal Politics: The Roots of Women's Liberation in the Civil Rights Movement and the New Left* (New York: Knopf, 1979).

34. *Historical Statistics* (Washington, D.C.: Government Printing Office, 1976), pp. 383, 382; Mable Newcomer, *A Century of Higher Education for American Women* (New York: Harper and Row, 1959), p. 49; Jessie Bernard, *Academic Women* (University Park: Pennsylvania State University Press, 1964), p. 203.

35. C. Wright Mills, "The Conservative Mood," *Dissent*, December 1954, p. 291.

36. C. Wright Mills, "On Fate and the Radical Will," in Mills, *The Causes of World War Three* (New York: Simon and Schuster, 1958), pp. 171, 169.

37. Abbie Hoffman, *Soon to Be a Major Motion Picture* (New York: Perigee, 1980), p. 59.

38. For a description of the rise of the New Left see Paul Jacobs and Saul Landau, *The New Radicals: A Report with Documents* (New York: Random House, 1966); Cedric Belfrage and James Aronson, *Something to Guard: The Stormy Life of the National Guardian, 1948–1967* (New York: Columbia University Press, 1978), pp. 149–51. For generational continuity and a young leftist's report on the civil rights activity of students see Sally Belfrage, *Freedom Summer* (New York: Viking, 1965).

39. James P. O'Brien, "The Development of a New Left in the United States, 1960–1965," Ph.D dissertation, Harvard University, 1971, pp. 229, 230.

40. Robert and Michael Meeropol, *We Are Your Sons: The Legacy of Ethel and Julius Rosenberg* (New York: Ballentine, 1975).

41. *Kinderland* (New York: Faculty Press, 1979).

42. Kenneth Keniston, *Radicals and Militants* (Lexington, Mass.: Lexington Books, 1973), p. xvi. Joseph Starobin's son Robert became a New Left historian at Cornell. Following Robert Starobin's death, his father criticized his New Left associates in the introduction to his *Communist Party in Crisis*. On the other hand, Jonah Raskin emphasizes generational continuity (*Out of the Whale*, p. 215).

43. Joseph Clark, introduction to new edition of *Student Advocate* (Westport: Greenwood, 1968).

44. Hal Draper, *Berkeley: The New Student Revolt* (New York: Grove Press, 1965), p. 168.

45. Draper, *Berkeley*, p. 61.

46. Lewis Feuer, *The Conflict of Generations: The Character and Significance of Student Movements* (New York: Basic Books, 1969), preface.

47. Martin Duberman, *The Uncompleted Past* (New York: Dutton, 1971), p. 316.

48. For a classic statement of the position of some students

and New Leftists see Theodore Roszak, *The Making of a Counter Culture* (New York: Doubleday, 1969).

49. Kazin, *Starting Out in the Thirties*, p. 158.

50. Donadio, "Columbia: Seven Interviews," p. 391.

51. Lionel Trilling, "Young in the Thirties," *Commentary* 41 (May 1966): 43, 47; Dennis Wrong, quoted in Philip Nobile, *Intellectual Skywriting: Literary Politics and the New York Review of Books* (New York: Charterhouse, 1974), p. 133.

52. Carolyn G. Heilbrun, *Reinventing Womanhood* (New York: Norton, 1979), pp. 125–37.

53. Draper, *Berkeley*, p. 169.

54. Quoted in Draper, *Berkeley*, p. 61.

55. "Gilbert Sullivan," "Remembrance of Things Past," *Student Advocate*, February 1936, p. 12.

56. Phil Ochs, "I Ain't Marching Anymore," Appleseed Music, "Love Me, I'm a Liberal," Barricade Music.

57. For the peace movement in the forties and fifties see Lawrence Wittner, *Rebels against War: The American Peace Movement, 1941–1960* (New York: Columbia University Press, 1969).

58. Arnold Beichman, "Six 'Big Lies' and Half Truths about America," *New York Times Magazine*, June 6, 1971; James Wechsler, *New York Post*, June 8, 1971; *New York Times*, December 25, 26, 27, 1977, series on the CIA and the media; also cited in Carey McWilliams, *The Education of Carey McWilliams* (New York: Simon and Schuster, 1979).

59. For the Catholic Left see Patricia McNeal, "The American Peace Movement, 1928–1972," Ph.D. dissertation, Temple University, 1974; for Lelyveld, see *New York Times*, August 6, 1966.

60. Daniel Berrigan, *The Trial of the Catonsville Nine* (Boston: Beacon Press, 1970), p. 93; John Cogley, *A Canterbury Tale: Experiences and Reflections, 1916–1976* (New York: Seabury Press, 1976). Cogley became an Episcopalian in the mid seventies.

61. Barbara Deming, *We Cannot Live without Our Lives* (New York: Grossman, 1974); Robert Cooney and Helen Michalowski, ed., *The Power of the People: Active Nonviolence in the United States* (Culver City: cooperatively published, Peace Press, 1977), p. 204.

62. Berrigan, *Trial*, p. 82. On the use of social science language to legitimize the American presence in Vietnam see Frances Fitzgerald, *Fire in the Lake* (New York: Random House, 1972), p. 115.

63. Molly Yard, letter to the author, February 17, 1981.

64. Muriel Rukeyser, "We Came for Games: A Memoir of the People's Olympics, Barcelona, 1936," *Esquire*, October 1974, p. 370.

65. Barbara Rose, ed., *Art-as-Art: The Selected Writings of Ad Reinhardt* (New York: Viking, 1975), editorial note, pp. 171–72; *New York Times*, obituary, September 1, 1967; Hilton Kramer, *Nation* 196 (June 22, 1963): 534; "Black: A Simultaneous Conversation," *Artscanada*, October 1967, p. 15.

66. Ad Reinhardt, "Chronology," in Rose, ed., *Art-as-Art*, pp. 4–8, 156.

67. Rukeyser, "We Came for Games," p. 370; Theodore L. Gross, ed., *The Literature of American Jews* (New York: Free Press, 1973), pp. 364–69.

68. Muriel Rukeyser, *Breaking Open* (New York: Random House, 1973), pp. 127, 129.

Bibliographical Essay

This is not a complete list of all works used or cited. It includes those primary sources that I found most useful and secondary sources that provided valuable background information or analysis.

The student movement of the thirties has not received much scholarly study. Two useful general studies of student political activism which include sections on the thirties are Philip G. Altbach, *Student Politics in America* (New York: McGraw-Hill, 1974), and Marvin Bressler and Judith Higgins for the United States Department of Health, Education, and Welfare, *Final Report: The Political Left on Campus and in Society: The Active Decades* (Princeton University, December 1972, ERIC Microfilm).

Studies which include discussion of this period on individual campuses include Lawrence Wittner and Juliette P. Thayer, "Another Angry Decade," *Columbia College Today* (summer 1971), and Seymour Lipset and David Riesman, *Education and Politics at Harvard* (New York: McGraw-Hill, 1975). Some institutional histories also cover the period, for example, Charles M. Cooper, *Whittier: Independent College in California* (Los Angeles: Ward Ritchie Press, 1967); Thomas Evans Coulton, *A City College in Action: Struggle and Achievement at Brooklyn College, 1930–1955* (Brooklyn: Brooklyn College, 1955); and Solomon Willis Rudy, *The College of the City of New York: A History, 1847–1947* (New York: City College Press, 1949). With rare exceptions, these histories of individual colleges reflect the positions of the administrations and a conservative and anti–student activist bias (if, indeed, they mention students at all).

Two useful scholarly studies are Doris Rodin, "The Opposition to the Establishment of Military Training in the Civil Schools and Colleges in the United States, 1914–1940" (M.A. thesis, American University, 1949), and George P. Rawick, "The New Deal and Youth" (Ph.D. dissertation, University of Wisconsin, 1957) which concentrates on the American Youth Congress.

Alumni of the movement discuss it in their memoirs and semi autobiographical writings. Among such works are: George Edwards, *Pioneer-at-Law* (New York: Norton, 1974); Nathan Glazer, *Remembering the Answers: Essays on the Student Revolt* (New York: Basic Books, 1970); Irving Howe, *Steady Work: Essays in the Politics of Democratic Radicalism, 1953–1966* (New York: Harcourt, Brace, 1966); Alfred Kazin, *Starting Out in the Thirties* (Boston: Little, Brown, 1965) and *New York Jew* (New York: Knopf, 1978); Murray Kempton, *Part of Our Time* (New York: Simon and Schuster, 1955); Joseph Lash, *Eleanor Roosevelt: A Friend's Memoir* (Garden City: Doubleday, 1964); Thomas Merton, *The Seven Story Mountain* (New York: Harcourt, Brace, 1948); John P. Roche, *Shadows and Substance: Essays on the Theory and Structure of Power* (New York: Macmillan, 1964); Eric Sevareid, *Not So Wild a Dream* (New York: Knopf, 1956); Morton Sobell, *On Doing Time* (New York: Scribner, 1974); and James Wechsler, *The Age of Suspicion* (New York: Random House, 1953). Many of these are more useful for providing information about a writer's attitude toward his past than about that past itself. An article which does both is Muriel Rukeyser, "We Came for Games: A Memoir of the People's Olympics, Barcelona, 1936," *Esquire*, October 1974, pp. 192–94, 368–70.

Two alumni of the student movement have written explicitly and in sharply contrasting fashion about the student antiwar activity in the thirties. Hal Draper provides a good survey and friendly interpretation in "The Student Movement of the Thirties," in Rita Simon, ed., *As We Saw the Thirties* (Urbana: University of Illinois Press, 1967). Lewis Feuer uses his own experience as a background for a psychological interpretation of student revolt in *The Conflict of Generations: The Character and Significance of Student Movements* (New York: Basic Books, 1969).

Sources I found most useful in drawing a picture of the student peace movement in the thirties include student publications on

individual campuses and nationally, some general studies and surveys, and government reports of investigations and of hearings at
which student leaders testified.

Student newspapers provided useful information on activities
on the local level on a variety of campuses. Those which I read
most extensively include: Brown University *Daily Herald*; Bryn
Mawr *College News*; Columbia *Spectator*; Harvard *Crimson*; Loy-
ola *News*; Marquette *Tribune*; Milwaukee State Teachers College
Echo Weekly; Temple University *News*; University of California,
Berkeley, *Daily Californian*; University of Chicago *Daily Maroon*;
University of Michigan *Daily*; University of Pennsylvania *Bennett
News* (the women's paper) and the *Daily Pennsylvanian*; Villanova
Villanovan; and Wilson College *Billboard*. Other campus publica-
tions that I referred to include *Cheshire*, the literary magazine of
Milwaukee State Teachers College; the *Christian Front* at Villa-
nova; and, at Temple, *New Horizons,* the journal of the Secondary
Education Association, and *Tempo,* a publication of the ASU chapter there. The archives of the City College of New York contain
a large quantity of material from the campus organizations and activities of the period.

Student activists of the time demonstrated their inclination toward writing as well as demonstrating. Two revealing books by
leaders of the movement are Reed Harris, *King Football* (New
York: Vanguard Press, 1932) and James Wechsler, *Revolt on the
Campus* (New York: Covici-Friede, 1935; reprint, Seattle: University of Washington Press, 1973, with a new introduction by Wechsler). The journals of the national student organizations are particularly valuable: The *Student Outlook* of the SLID and the *Student Review* of the NSL merged in early 1936 to become the
journal of the ASU, the *Student Advocate,* which was published
from 1936 to 1939.

The response of part of the government to the student activity
is indicated by the federal and state investigations in the thirties
and in the postwar period. For an example of a state investigation, see New York State, Legislature, *Interim Report and Conclusions*, New York City Subcommittee Relative to Subversive
Activity among Students in the Public High Schools and Colleges
of the City of New York, legislative document number 49A (De-

cember 1, 1941), and New York State, Legislature, Strayer Committee, *Report of the New York City Subcommittee of Rapp-Coudert Committee,* 1944.

Relevant congressional hearings include: U.S. Congress, House of Representatives, Special Committee on Un-American Activities [Dies Committee], *Hearings,* 1 December 1939; U.S. Congress, House of Representatives, Committee on Un-American Activities, "Testimony of Jack R. McMichaels," July 30–31, 1953; U.S. Congress, Senate, Committee on Governmental Operations, Permanent Subcommittee on Investigations, "Hearings Persuant to S. Resulution 40, U.S. Information Program, Information Centers," April 24, May 5, 1953; and U.S. Congress, Senate, Subcommittee on the Judiciary, *Hearings on the Nomination of George Clifton Edwards, Jr.,* October 1, November 21, 1963.

Further information on the students and the background in which they operated was provided by contemporary news accounts and journal articles. The *Chicago Tribune,* the *New York Times,* and the *Philadelphia Bulletin* and *Philadelphia Inquirer* provided some information on student activity and more information on the press's own reactions to the antiwar movement. Magazines were filled with articles, factual and otherwise, on the condition and problems of young people during the Depression. Such general descriptions, as well as discussions of student antiwar activities, can be found in the *American Scholar, Christian Century, Forum, Harpers, Journal of Social Psychology, Nation, New Republic, School and Society, Scribner's,* and *World Tomorrow.*

Three studies of the peace movement in general provide excellent background for the student antiwar activity: Charles Chatfield, *For Peace and Justice: Pacifism in America, 1914–1942* (Knoxville: University of Tennessee Press, 1971); Straughton Lynd, ed., *Non-Violence in America* (New York: Bobbs-Merrill, 1966); and Lawrence S. Wittner, *Rebels against War: The American Peace Movement, 1941–1960.* Paul Fussell's *The Great War and Modern Memory* (New York: Oxford University Press, 1975) suggests the impact that that experience had on attitudes toward modern war and in the creation of a mood on which the peace movement could draw. The magazine *Fellowship* indicates the efforts of pacifists to influence the student movement and discusses the split between pacifists and Marxists. More information on the peace movement and its youth component can be found at the Peace Collection at Swarthmore College.

Most writing on the Left during this period is autobiographical or polemical, or both. Two good general studies are Joseph Starobin, *American Communism in Crisis* (Cambridge: Harvard University Press, 1972), and Frank Warren, *An Alternative Vision: The Socialist Party in the 1930's* (Bloomington: Indiana University Press, 1974). For the Spanish Civil War and American reactions, Allan Guttmann, *The Wound in the Heart: America and the Spanish Civil War* (New York: Free Press, 1962), and Arthur Landis, *The Abraham Lincoln Brigade* (New York: Citadel Press, 1967), can be supplemented by the personal description by an American participant, Alvah Bessie, *Men in Battle* (New York: 1939; reprint, New York: Pinnacle Books, 1977), and by Rukeyser's memoir, cited above. A fine description of the paths taken by two English students in the thirties is the dual biography of John Cornford and Julian Bell in Peter Stanksy and William Abraham, *Journey to the Frontier* (London: Constable, 1966).

In addition to the memoirs cited above by former students in the thirties, two recent autobiographies present thoughtful and sometimes moving accounts of the lives of two women in the Communist party during the thirties and the postwar period: Peggy Dennis, *The Autobiography of an American Communist: A Personal View of a Political Life, 1925–1975* (Westport, Conn.: Lawrence Hill & Co., 1977), and Jessica Mitford, *A Fine Old Conflict* (New York: Knopf, 1977). Both discuss well the role of the party in progressive organizations. Though neither deals explicitly with the student movement, Mitford's book describes the activities in the forties of a character who is clearly Celeste Strack, former officer of the ASU.

Religious journals during the thirties provide material on the influence of religion on the student movement. Ray Abrams, *Preachers Present Arms: A Study of the Wartime Attitudes and Activities of the Churches and the Clergy in the United States, 1914–1918* (Philadelphia: Round Table Press, 1933), presents the views of a pacifist minister who was also a university chaplain. Two useful secondary sources are Robert M. Miller, *American*

Protestants and Social Issues, 1919–1939 (Chapel Hill: University of North Carolina Press, 1958), and Ralph Lord Roy, *Communism and the Churches* (New York: Harcourt, Brace, 1960), though the latter is quite hostile to the Left.

The Catholic experience is discussed in Aaron I. Abell, *American Catholicism and Social Action: A Search for Social Justice, 1865–1950* (Garden City: Hanover, 1960), and David J. O'Brien, *American Catholics and Social Reform: The New Deal Years* (New York: Oxford University Press, 1968). John Whitney Evans describes the development of the Newman movement among Catholics in non-Catholic colleges and universities in his Ph.D. dissertation, "The Newman Movement: A Social and Intellectual History of Roman Catholics in American Higher Education, 1883–1969," University of Minnesota, 1970, and in his recently published book, *The Newman Movement: Roman Catholics in American Higher Education, 1883–1971* (Notre Dame: University of Notre Dame Press, 1980). A good memoir of growing up Catholic, and moving on another path, is John Cogley, *A Canterbury Tale: Experiences and Reflections, 1916–1976* (New York: Seabury Press, 1976). For the growth of the Catholic Left, see Patricia McNeal, "The American Peace Movement, 1928–1972," Ph.D. dissertation, Temple University, 1974. Related material can be found in issues from the thirties of such Catholic journals as *Commonweal, America,* and the *Catholic Worker.* The views of right-wing Catholics are vividly represented in the diocesan paper, the *Brooklyn Tablet.*

Contemporary responses of educators are presented in the *Social Frontier,* the journal of the Progressive Education Association, and in *Depression, Recovery, and Higher Education,* published by the American Association of University Professors, Committee Y (New York, 1937). An example of articles urging education as a means of social change is A. Gordon Melvin, "Education or Revolution," *School and Society* 39 (April 21, 1934): 510–11. The views of one progressive educator are contained in the Frank Baker Papers, University of Wisconsin—Milwaukee, Area Studies Center.

Providing useful background and analysis of the relationships between class, culture, and higher education are Samuel Bowles and Herbert Gintes, *Schooling in Capitalist America* (New York:

Basic Books, 1976); Oscar and Mary Handlin, *The American College and American Culture: Socialization as a Function of Higher Education* (New York: McGraw-Hill, 1970); Herbert Wechsler, *The Qualified Student: A History of Selective College Admission in America* (New York: John Wiley & Sons, 1977); and Marcia Graham Synnott, *The Half-Opened Door: Discrimination and Admissions at Harvard, Yale, and Princeton, 1900–1970* (Westport, Conn.: Greenwood Press, 1979). For the declining position of women in academic life see William H. Chafe, *The American Woman: Her Changing Social, Economic, and Political Roles, 1920–1970* (New York: Oxford University Press, 1972); Jessie Bernard, *Academic Women* (University Park: Penn State Press, 1964); and Florence Howe, "Introduction: The History of Women in Higher Education," *Journal of Education* 159 (August 1977): 7–11. Vida Scudder presents a moving account of her life as an academic and an activist and her relationship to a new generation of students in *On Journey* (New York: Dutton, 1937).

Education is the post–World War II period is discussed in David Caute, *The Great Fear: The Anti-Communist Purge under Truman and Eisenhower* (New York: Simon and Schuster, 1978), and David Gardner, *The California Oath Controversy* (University of California Press, 1967). For a contemporary account of one academic freedom controversy, see George Stewart, *The Year of the Oath* (New York: Doubleday, 1967). James Aronson, *The Press and the Cold War* (New York: Bobbs-Merrill, 1970), discusses James Wechsler's testimony before the McCarthy Committee, and Murray Kempton comes to Wechsler's defense in his review of Lillian Hellman's *Scoundrel Time*, in *New York Review of Books*, June 10, 1976, p. 25.

Researching the revival of conflict on the campus in the sixties, the following were useful: Hal Draper, *Berkeley: The New Student Revolt* (New York: Grove Press, 1965); Paul Jacobs and Saul Landau, *The New Radicals* (New York: Random House, 1966); Carolyn G. Heilbrun, *Reinventing Womanhood* (New York: Norton, 1979); and Sara Evans, *Personal Politics: The Roots of Women's Liberation in the Civil Rights Movement and the Left* (New York: Vintage, 1979). Personal accounts of the fifties and sixties often shed light on relations between the Old and New Left. Some of the most interesting are: Michael Harrington, *Fragments of a Century: A Personal and Social Retrospective of the 50's and 60's* (New York: Simon and Schuster, 1973); Abbie Hoffman, *Soon to Be a Major Motion Picture* (New York: Putnam, 1980); Ron Kovic, *Born on the Fourth of July* (New York: McGraw-Hill, 1976); Robin Morgan, *Going Too Far* (New York: Random House, 1977); and Jonah Raskin, *Out of the Whale: Growing Up in the American Left* (New York: Links Books, 1974).

There is one other valuable resource in writing a history of the student movement of the thirties and early forties—the people themselves. Some of the movement's survivors have been reluctant to discuss their past activism. I am therefore particularly grateful to those who chose to remember where they were and what they did. Among these are Gunther Haller, Albert and Eleanor Mattes, Ben Stahl, Joseph Norma, and Herman Starobin (interviewed in October and November 1975 in Hancock, Massachusetts), and, especially, Molly Yard, who has shared through correspondence her experiences and their connection with her present activism.

Index

Abraham Lincoln Brigade, 170, 176–80

Abrams, Ray, 155

Academic freedom, 4, 12, 13, 205; in 1950s, 238, 242, 245; and rights of fascists, 73–75; students defend, 26, 36

Addams, Jane, 141

Administrators, 35–37, 39; conflict with students, 34, 99–100, 142, 257–58; favor intervention, 214–15, 225–26; and peace, 120, 126

All Quiet on the Western Front (film), 27

All Quiet on the Western Front (Remarque), 31

All Youth against War Conference, 193–95

Alumni of student movement, 239–46; and children, 252–53; divisions among in postwar period, 240–41; and Vietnam, 18, 239–40

America First Committee, 214, 220, 230

American Civil Liberties Union (ACLU), 43, 74, 79–80

American College and Its Rulers, The (J. E. Kirkpatrick), 32

American Federation of Teachers, 214

American Friends Service Committee (AFSC), 13, 24, 175, 193, 211, 213

Americanism, 129, 165, 198

American Legion, 43, 62, 131, 132, 187

American Student Union (ASU), 13–15, 53, 149–50, 162–64; alumni of, 240, 251; attacks on, 203, 206–8; and collective security, 184–85, 188–89, 195–98, 201, 203; as community, 137, 200; and compulsory military training, 110, 196; and educational issues, 142–43; formation of, 39, 133–37; on individual campuses, 191–92; membership of, 14, 134, 201; and New Deal, 197–98; and Oxford Oath, 137, 169, 184–85, 192–97; and Spanish Civil War, 169–82; and Stalin-Hitler Pact, 202–3

American University, 124

American Veterans Committee
(AVC), 234–35
American Youth Congress, 119,
161, 188, 209, 241
Antioch, 126
Anti-Semitism, 92, 97–98, 104–5,
131, 230, 233
Antiwar conferences, 118–20, 123,
158–59; Student Congress
against War (1932), 57; Student
Congress against War (1933),
57–58, 67–68; World Youth
Congress (1938), 164. *See
also* Columbia University;
University of Michigan
Antiwar movement, 31, 57, 118–19.
See also Pacifism; Student
peace movement
Armistice Day demonstrations,
27, 118–19
Art, 262–63
Athletics, 4, 8, 48–56, 127–28,
181, 246, 247; and communism,
47, 48, 198; criticism of,
36, 44, 46–47, 200, 235; intercollegiate, 32, 35, 42, 50,
56, 90–91; Olympic Games, 49–
54, 181
Austria, 175

Baker, Frank, 127–28, 192–93,
213–14
Baker, James, 112
Balch, Emily Greene, 148
Baldwin, Roger, 74, 79, 120
Barnard College, 41, 61, 120, 150,
157, 204
Barnes, Harry Elmer, 25
Beard, Charles, 26, 41, 77
Beichman, Arnold, 68, 260
Benedict, Ruth, 66
Bennington College, 122
Berlin Olympics, 49–54

Black colleges, 34–36; and student
activism, 34–36, 125, 250–
51. *See also* Howard University
Black students: discrimination
against, 34, 46, 51, 98
Boston, 48–49, 90–91, 122
Boston College, 49
Boston University, 122
Brenon, Howard, 27
British student movement, 58–59,
120, 138, 178
Brittain, Vera, 30, 148, 151–52
Brooklyn College, 99, 117,
121, 177, 233
Brookwood Labor College, 42
Browder, Earl, 140, 208
Brown University, 60–61, 64, 122;
Daily Herald, 59–60
Brundage, Avery, 51
Bryn Mawr, 123, 142, 147, 204;
student peace activity, 37,
124, 148, 175, 186–87
Burnham Louis, 251
Butler, Nicholas Murray, 41, 43,
94, 109, 208; quoted, 4, 80

Campbell, Jeffrey, 171–73
Capitalism, 38, 65, 132; as cause
of war, 67–69, 110, 155; and
education, 5, 7, 17, 141–42, 236–
37; religion and, 154–55;
student opposition to, 68, 70. *See
also* Profits; Munitions industry
Case of Sergeant Grischa, The
(film), 27
Catholic Association for International Peace: Student Peace
Federation, 164
Catholic Colleges, 10, 17, 162; and
collegiate culture, 10, 165;
women's colleges, 10, 164, 248
Catholics: and Communism,
161–65; in 1960s, 249–50, 260–

61; and peace, 143–44, 157, 164; and social reform, 154, 164, 166; and Spanish Civil War, 162, 173

Catholic Students, 17, 46, 161–67

Catholic Worker, 154

Catholic Worker Movement, 161, 164

Catt, Carrie Chapman, 140

Censorship, 32, 35, 142, 145. *See also* Freedom; Student publications

Central Intelligence Agency (CIA), 239, 260

Chicago, 57, 126

Chicago Tribune, 132

Christian Century, 154

Christianity and Crisis, 216

Christian Socialism, 155, 159–60, 193

Christ's Alternative to Capitalism (Jones), 155

City College of New York (CCNY), 14, 53, 64, 137, 222, 240; antifascist demonstrations, 73, 99–100; antiwar demonstrations, 116, 121; *Campus*, 110, 145; composition of student body, 100–102, 275 (n. 60); and compulsory military training, 33, 110–11; conflict between students and administrators, 99–102; faculty, 99, 204–5; and origins of student activism, 38, 39; in post–World War II period, 233

City Colleges of New York, 99. *See also* Brooklyn College; City College of New York (CCNY); Hunter College

Civilian Conservation Corps, 22, 150, 194

Clark, Joseph, 253

Civil liberties, 72–73, 235–36; war as threat to, 25, 144–45, 230. *See also* Academic freedom; Freedom

Class, 5–7, 10, 16, 28, 45, 81, 140. *See also* Capitalism; Higher education; Collegiate culture

Class war, 60, 65, 131; opposed by pacifists, 68–71

Coffin, Henry Sloane, 216, 222

Cogley, John, 162–63, 261

Cohen, Felix, 110

Cohen, Morris Raphael, 110–11, 146

Cold War, 12, 16, 234–35, 241; and former student leftists, 18, 245–46

Collective security, 169, 184–85, 208–9. *See also* Neutrality legislation

Colleges and universities: British, 58–59; enrollment, 9, 20–21, 32, 45–46, 237; German, 94; land grant, 5, 8, 46; medical schools, 9–10; municipal institutions, 5, 17, 20; professional schools, 32; relationship to federal government, 17, 50, 217–18, 225–26, 257; state universities, 17, 20–21, 126–31; teacher's colleges, 6, 8, 17, 142; and World War I, 25, 26, 142; after World War II, 234–39, 254–57

Collegiate culture, 4, 7–8, 35–36, 42, 165, 255; changes in, 80–81, 137, 198–200, 257; conflict between old and new, 55–56, 106. *See also* Athletics; Fraternities and sororities; names of individual schools

Colligan, Eugene, 116–17, 121

Columbia University, 39, 67, 208,

Columbia University (*cont.*)
222; antifascist protests,
73; anti-Semitism at, 104–5;
athletics, 49–50, 53–54;
College of Physicians and Surgeons, 132; Columbia College
enrollment, 41, 269 (n. 1);
debate over pacifism, 68–69, 70;
enrollment, 41, 46, 269
(n. 1); law school, 9, 117; and
leftist organizations, 42–43,
70, 120; in 1960s, 237, 254–56,
257; peace activity at, 74,
117, 120–21, 189–90; Reed Harris
case, 40–45; and selective
admissions, 6, 10, 102; student
board, 42, 47, 53; and
World War I, 26. *See
also* Teachers College; Union
Theological Seminary
Columbia *Spectator*, 4, 16, 32, 94,
145, 150, 208, 230–31; and
athletics, 46–47, 53; debate on
freedom, 75–79; and Harris
controversy, 40, 42–47; on peace
and war, 28, 61, 109
Columbus, Ohio, 134
Committee on Militarism in
Education (CME), 24, 33, 110,
141, 188
Commonweal, 154, 166, 261
Communism, 125, 149; and right
to teach, 238, 242, 244.
See also Marxism
Communist party, 41, 137, 140,
170, 203, 240, 242, 245;
and collective security, 203, 230;
and education, 38, 140–41;
and popular front, 119; World
Congress (1935), 136
Communists: attacks on in student

movement, 125, 203–7;
and class war, 68–69, 71; and
collective security, 136,
183–84; at Columbia, 42; conflict
with Socialists, 136, 170,
183–84, 195; and sports, 47–48,
198; in student peace movement, 57, 60, 64, 135–36, 195,
198, 212
Communist youth groups,
119, 136. *See also* National
Student League; Young
Communist League
Compulsory military training, 32–
34; as focus of student
movement, 108, 110–14;
opposition to, 15, 194, 233, 235.
See also Nye-Kvale Bill;
Reserve Officer Training Corps
Conant, James, 90, 94
Congress (U.S.), 22
Congress for Cultural Freedom, 239
Congressional investigations,
25, 36, 125; in 1950s, 241–42,
244–45, 246. *See also* Dies
Committee; House Un-American
Activities Committee; Nye
Committee
Congress of Racial Equality
(CORE), 250, 259
Conscientious objection, 61–62,
157, 161, 222, 224, 283
(n. 31)
Conscription, 110–11. *See
also* Draft
Cook, David, 177–78
Cornford, John, 138, 178
Corporations and war, 109. *See
also* Capitalism; Profits
Counts, George S., 41, 146
Cripps, John Stafford, 120

Cultural revolt, 32. *See also* Collegiate culture
Curry, John Steuart, 28

Daughters of the American Revolution, 43, 204, 233–34
Dawn Patrol (film), 28
Death of a Hero (Aldington), 31
Dellinger, David, 233, 261
Deming, Barbara, 261
Democracy, 127–29
Depression, 20–21, 27, 147–48; influence on students, 20–21, 82–83
Detzer, Dorothy, 123
Dewey, John, 140, 208
Dies, Martin, 22
Dies Committee, 125, 203, 209
Disarmament, 67, 128, 194
Dos Passos, John, 31, 217–18
Draft, 167, 207, 220–24
Draper, Hal, 244, 253; quoted, 14, 119, 195, 240, 257
Duke University, 126
Du Pont family, 104, 109

Eagle and the Hawk, The (film), 28
Economic Consequences of the Peace, The (Keynes), 25
Education: and peace, 42, 128, 143–44, 188; and social change, 12, 26, 139–46. *See also* Higher education
Edwards, George, Jr., 88, 126, 240; as ASU officer, 113, 137, 184
Ellison, Ralph, 34, 35
Emergency Peace Campaign, 188, 192, 285 (n. 18)
Emerson College, 122
Emotionalism, 144; and thirties

students, 80, 89, 96, 144; and sixties students, 254, 256–57
Engelbrecht, H. O., and F. O. Hanighan: *Merchants of Death*, 25
England, 56, 62, 138, 150, 177–78; Battle of Britain, 216, 219; Oxford Pledge, 58–59
Episcopalians, 156
Ethiopia, 135
Europe, 27, 118, 202–3. *See also* Germany; Italy; Spanish Civil War; World War I; World War II
Evanston, Illinois, 32

Faculty, 36, 41, 47, 145; firing of for political views, 41, 146, 205–6, 236, 238–39; homogeneity of, 98–99, 276 (n. 71); interest in peace, 33, 37, 124, 156; in 1950s, 237–238; prointerventionist, 214; student criticism of, 143, 214; support student movement, 66, 91–92, 99, 116, 122, 132; women, 147, 248–49; and World War I, 12, 25. *See also* Teachers; Women's colleges; names of individual schools
Fascism, 27, 50, 71, 73, 106–7, 136; and academic freedom, 73–79; demonstrations against, 73, 91–95, 99–100, 118; student concern with, 58, 71, 73, 150; and student peace movement, 58, 71. *See also* Collective security; Spanish Civil War
Fay, Sidney B., 25, 31

Federal Bureau of Investigation (FBI), 206, 239
Federal government: and colleges and universities, 17, 50, 217–18, 225–26, 257; and youth, 21–22. *See also* Compulsory military training; Draft; National Youth Administration
Fellowship of Reconciliation (FOR), 13, 24, 65, 70, 171, 188, 193, 211, 213; and opposition to draft registration, 222–23
Feminism, 37, 147–51, 247, 261
Fenn College, 126
Feuer, Lewis, 91, 253–55
Fighting Youth (film), 47
Films, 27–28, 218
Finland, 208–11
Fish, Hamilton, 132
Fisk University, 35–36
Football, 8, 42–47, 55. *See also* Athletics
Ford, John, 28
Fordham University, 161, 229
Fortune, 109
Foster, William Z., 41
Fox, Mary, 150
France, 28, 118, 216
Franco, Francisco, 169, 174
Frank, Glen, 127
Fraternities and sororities, 4, 7–8, 35, 44–46, 83, 131
Freedom, 12, 13, 73–80; of conscience, 111–12; of speech and the press, 43–44, 92, 127, 142, 144–45. *See also* Academic freedom; Censorship; Student publications; Students, rights of
Free Speech Movement, 119
Furfey, Paul Hanley, 164

Fussell, Paul, 56; *The Great War and Modern Memory*, 11, 24
Future Gold Star Mothers, 186–87

Galbraith, John Kenneth, 177, 246
Gandhi, 68, 88, 159
Garfield, Harry A., 116
Garrison, William Lloyd, 13
General strike, 68
Generational conflict, 89, 148–49, 254, 258
George Washington University, 124
Germany, 22, 25, 27–28, 77, 173–74, 230; students view of, 104, 117, 150; and World War II, 202, 215–16. *See also* Berlin Olympics; Stalin-Hitler Pact
Glazer, Nathan, 253, 255
Goosestep, The (Sinclair), 140
Government, 24, 25, 111. *See also* Federal government; Colleges and universities, relation to federal government
Graham, Frank, 126
Graham, Katharine Meyer, 243
Grand Illusion, 28
Great War and Modern Memory, The (Fussell), 11, 24, 56

Hamilton, Albert, 111–12
Hamilton, Alice, 148
Hamilton v. *Regents of the University of California*, 112
Hampton Institute, 35
Hanfstaengel, Ernst Franz, 90, 93–95
Harlan County, 114, 262
Harris, Reed, 28–29, 56, 241–42; controversy over expulsion from Columbia, 32, 40, 42–47
Harvard University, 6, 16,

34, 81–97, 214, 234; and antifascist activity, 55, 73, 90–
93; anti-Semitism at, 9, 34, 106,
276 (n. 71); athletics
controversies, 48–49, 50–52, 90–
91; and collegiate culture,
83–84, 89–90; conservatism of,
83, 95–96; *Crimson*, 49–
53, 82–83, 96, 109; enrollment,
81–82; Hanfstaengel
controversy, 90, 93–95; law
school, 9; Liberal Club,
87, 90; liberalism of, 86–88; NSL
at, 87, 90–93, 97, 106;
peace demonstrations, 90–91, 95,
121; and vigilantism, 93,
95–96, 104, 122
Haverford College, 123–24,
156, 186
Hawkes, Herbert, 43
Hawks, Howard, 28
Hays, Arthur Garfield, 157
Hearst, William Randolph, 22,
116, 155
Heilbrun, Carolyn, 257
Hellman, Lillian, 18
Hemingway, Ernest, 217
Henderson, Donald, 39, 41
Higher education: and capitalism,
10, 34, 141, 147, 236–38,
255; and democracy, 7, 45, 141;
and social mobility, 5, 32;
student criticism of, 36, 141, 142–
43, 254–55. *See also*
Administrators; Colleges and
universities; Education;
Faculty; Students
Higher Learning in America, The
(Veblen), 140
High schools, 45, 124, 129; student
activism in, 14, 129, 233–34

Historians, 12, 25
Hitler, Adolph, 27, 51–53, 58,
73, 77, 89, 105
Hoffman, Abbie, 250, 260
Holmes, John Haynes, 154, 222
Holy Cross College, 49
Hook, Sidney, 116, 238, 254–55
Hoover, Herbert, 41
Horror of It, The, 28
House Un-American Activities
Committee, 65, 236, 241, 246,
250. *See also* Congressional
investigations; Dies Committee
Howard University, 34–36, 125
Howe, Irving, 137–38, 139, 243
Hunter College, 99, 116–17, 121

Ickes, Harold, 125, 210
Imperialism, 60, 67–69, 73, 194;
and war, 58, 71, 109, 122, 183
Intercollegiate Liberal League, 36
Intercollegiate Socialist Society
(ISS), 38
International Disarmament
Council, 61–62
International Student Committee
against War and Fascism, 119
International Women's Congress,
1919, 37
Internationalism, 25, 53, 59
Interseminary Group, 156
Invisible Man (Ellison), 34–35
Isolationism, 53, 214. *See also*
America First Committee
Italy, 22, 73, 135, 173
Ives Act (New York), 145–46

Japan, 73, 117, 174, 195,
197; attack on Pearl Harbor,
219–20, 231
Jennings, Francis, 241, 291 (n. 17)

Jewish Peace Fellowship, 157
Jewish Theological Seminary, 157
Jews, 154, 216; on faculties, 98–99,
    276 (n. 71); and selective
    admissions, 6, 9, 81, 98, 147,
    273 (n. 14); students, 46,
    101–3; student organizations,
    119, 156. *See also* Anti-
    Semitism; Berlin Olympics
Jingoism, 24, 110, 118
Johnson, Lyndon, 45
Johnson, Mordecai, 125
Jones, E. Stanley, 155
Journey's End (film), 27, 218

Karlsruhe Affair, 90–93
Kazin, Alfred: quoted, 138, 245, 255
Keep America out of War
    Congress, 221, 230
Kellogg-Briand Pact, 85
Kempton, Murray, 14, 179, 243,
    259, 291 (n. 23)
Kennedy, John F., 247, 249–50
Kerr, Clark, 237, 257
Keynes, John Maynard, 25
King Football (Harris), 47, 242
Kirk, Grayson, 257
Kirkpatrick, J. E., 32
Kirkpatrick, William, 140
Klotsche, J. Martin, 128, 258
Korean War, 235
Kovic, Ron, 246–47

Labor movement: influence on
    student movement, 23, 106–7,
    114–15, 131, 138, 160,
    213–14; students support, 206,
    240, 243
La Farge, John, 157
Laidler, Harry, 38
Lash, Joseph, 203, 209–10, 243;
    and collective security,

181–82, 185, 189, 195–96, 219;
    as co-editor of *Student
    Advocate*, 137, 170–72, 175
Laski, Harold, 23, 97, 217
Last Flight, The (film), 28
Lawrence College, 187
League for Industrial Democracy
    (LID), 38
League of Nations, 65
Left, the: influence on students,
    23, 131, 135; and sports,
    47–48, 54; and women, 149–50.
    See also Communism;
    Marxism; Pacifism; Radicalism;
    Socialism
Lelyveld, Arthur J., 62–63, 66, 68–
    70, 157, 260
Levinger, Sam, 176, 178–80
Libby, Frederick J., 123, 175
Liberalism, 16, 36, 86–88; and
    academic freedom, 13, 205–6,
    238–39; and civil liberties,
    73–75, 131
Liberty League, 104
Lipsett, Seymour, 253, 255
Literary Digest, 61–62
Literature, 28, 30–31, 217–18, 263
Long Island University, 117, 121
Lovett, Robert Morss, 19, 113
Lowell, Abbott Lawrence, 7, 9, 34,
    48–49
Loyalty oaths, 26, 101, 142, 145–
    46, 206, 208, 238
Loyola University (Chicago), 17,
    166
Ludlow Referendum, 144, 196, 213
Lusk Committee, 204
Luther, Hans, 73, 94

McCarthy, Eugene, 261
McCarthy, Joseph, 241–42, 244–45

McCarthyism, 12, 18, 239
McConnell, Francis J., 155, 157
McCracken, Henry, 116
MacEachron, Paul, 176, 263
MacLeish, Archibald, 28, 217
McMichael, Jack, 212, 241
Mahoney, Jeremiah, 51
Man I Killed, The (film), 27
*Man Who Reclaimed His Head,
   The* (film), 27
Marquette University, 143, 208
Marxism, 4, 64, 134–36,
   243–44; and antiwar activity, 58,
   115, 119; appeal of to student
   activists, 137–39; in England,
   58–59. *See also* Communism;
   Socialism
Massachusetts Institute of
   Technology, 121–22
Matthews, J. B., 65, 70, 241
Maverick, Maury, 112–13
Men Must Fight (film), 27
Merchants of Death (Engelbrecht
   and Hanighan), 25
Merriman, Robert, 177
Merton, Thomas, 260
Methodists, 111–12, 154–57, 241;
   youth and peace movement,
   57, 158–60, 167–68, 188, 213
Michigan State University, 126
Milestone, Lewis, 27
Militarism, 24–25, 28, 108, 110–13
Military establishment, 66, 130
Millis, Walter, 25, 216
Mills, C. Wright, 249
Milwaukee State Teachers College,
   17, 142, 235, 258; *Echo
   Weekly*, 127, 192, 197, 208, 231–
   32; peace activity at, 127–
   29, 190–93, 213–14
Milwaukee Vocational College, 129
Minneapolis, 106

Minnesota, 126, 130
Morehouse College, 3–4, 125
Morgan, J. P., 71, 117
Morrill Land Grant Act, 33
Mt. Holyoke, 147
Munitions industry, 11, 15, 25, 31,
   67; congressional inquiry,
   16, 108, 123, 159; proposed
   nationalization of, 67,
   71, 109, 128. *See also* Corpora-
   tions; Profits
Murrow, Edward R., 242–43
Muskingum College, 126
Muste, A. J., 42, 222

Nation, 62, 217, 236
National Council for Prevention of
   War, 123, 175
National Council of Methodist
   Youth, 167, 188, 213
National Student Association, 239
National Student Committee
   for the Limitation of Armaments,
   36
National Student Federation, 37,
   62, 188, 242
National Student Forum, 33, 36–37
National Student League
   (NSL), 14, 42–43, 47–48, 53, 57,
   119, 123, 127, 131; and
   American Student Union, 134–
   37; and antiwar strikes,
   121, 126–27; creation of, 39; at
   Harvard, 87, 90–93, 97,
   104, 106, 122
National Youth Act, 22
National Youth Administration
   (NYA), 83, 201
Neuberger, Richard, 145
Neutrality legislation, 170–71,
   188, 194. *See also* Spanish
   Civil War

New Left, 12, 13, 250–53, 257
Newman Clubs, 119, 156, 162–64
New Student, 33, 36–37, 44
New York (city), 40, 48; Board of
   Higher Education, 101;
   City Colleges, 40, 99, 204; police
   department, 121; student
   activism in, 16, 38, 114, 116,
   120, 138
New York state legislature, 101–2,
   204–5
New York Times, 43, 62
New York University, 8, 10,
   116, 121
New York World Telegram, 117–18
Niebuhr, Reinhold, 41, 117, 120,
   158, 205, 214–16
North Dakota Agricultural College,
   4
Norwich University, 62
Nye, Gerald P., 108, 226
Nye Committee: munitions inquiry,
   16, 108, 123, 159
Nye-Kvale Bill, 112, 188, 192

Oberlin College, 126, 176, 262
Ochs, Phil, 258–59
"Ode to Higher Education," 20
Ohio State University, 33, 126
Ohio University, 126, 176
Olson, Floyd, 130
Out of the Whale (Raskin), 246
Owen, Wilfred, 24, 29, 58
Oxford Oath, 3, 169, 182; and ASU,
   59, 184–97; focus of student
   peace movement, 59–61, 71, 108,
   120–21, 126–127, 130; pacifist
   view of, 160, 193, 197, 213
Oxford Union, 59
Oxford University, 58–59

Pacifism, 55–56, 59, 128, 150, 167–
   68, 230; All Youth against
   War Conference, 1937, 193–95;
   alternatives to war, 68–70,
   194–95; and antifascism, 72–73,
   218; in the churches, 156–
   57, 216–17
Pacifists: on collective security,
   185, 188, 193–97, 201;
   conflict with Communists,
   68–71, 160; and draft registration,
   222–24; organizations of,
   13, 211; and Oxford Oath, 59–60,
   185, 194; in student peace
   movement, 22, 58, 123. *See also*
   Conscientious objection;
   Fellowship of Reconciliation;
   War Resisters League;
   Women's International League
   for Peace and Freedom
Page, Kirby, 25, 158
Peace movement, 13, 23, 58. *See
   also* Pacifism; names of
   individual organizations
Philadelphia, 122–24, 241
Philbrick, Allen R., 92–93, 106
Pilgrimage (film), 28
Police, 91–95, 106, 121, 187, 258,
   271 (n. 32)
Polls, 41, 61–62, 83, 225
Popular front, 119, 134, 197, 198
Preachers Present Arms (Abrams),
   155
Press, 21, 23–24, 242–45; response
   to student peace activism,
   62, 117–18. See also *Chicago
   Tribune; Nation; New
   York Times; New York World
   Telegram*
Princeton, 6–7, 32, 45, 83, 97, 186
Profits, 11, 71, 108–10, 128

Progressive education, 41, 139–46, 190–91, 213

Progressivism, 4, 26, 126–27, 134

Propaganda, 31, 174, 226–27; fear of, 53, 144, 159, 217; and war, 25, 65, 144, 214–15

Protestant churches: peace sentiment in, 155–56, 217. *See also* Religion; names of individual denominations

Psychological tests, 10, 102–3

Quakers, 123, 223; colleges, 122–23, 156. *See also* American Friends Service Committee

Quotas. *See* Selective admissions

Racism, 7, 34, 36, 97, 125; student opposition to, 35–36, 206, 233, 250–51

Radicalism, 3, 5, 22–23, 67, 117, 138, 204

Rankin, Jeanette, 124

Raskin, Jonah, 246–47

Red Salute (film), 47

Reinhardt, Ad, 262–63

Religion, 4, 7; and peace movement, 111–12, 114, 134, 156, 260–62. *See also* Catholics; Jews; Protestant churches; names of individual denominations

Religious groups: on campus, 119, 156–61, 188, 211, 213; clergy, 154–55, 158–59; colleges, 6, 17, 126, 156; and interventionism, 216–17; publications, 154, 166, 216, 261

Remarque, Erich, 27

Renoir, Jean, 28

Reserve Officer Training Corps (ROTC), 103, 224–25; cadets as vigilantes, 54, 122, 126; manual, 66, 113. *See also* Compulsory military training

Revolt on the Campus (Wechsler), 19, 99–100, 114, 140

Reynolds, Aronzo, 111–12

Rhode Island state legislature, 64

Right-wing students, 103–6, 117. *See also* Vigilantism

Road to Glory (film), 28

Robinson, Frederick, 99–100, 121. *See also* City College of New York

Rockefeller, David, 84

Rockefeller family, 71

Roman Catholic church, 104. *See also* Catholics

Roosevelt, Eleanor: concern with youth, 22, 203, 210; influence of, 150

Roosevelt, Franklin D., 84; foreign policy of, 170, 195, 210, 220–21; student support for, 41, 130, 225

Rosenberg, Ethel and Julius, 240

Rukeyser, Muriel, 139, 180, 262–63

Russell, Bertrand, 205

Ruthven, Alexander, 132, 142. *See also* University of Michigan

Ryan, John, 154

San Jose Teachers College, 23

San Marcos State Teachers College, 45

Sassoon, Siegfried, 24, 56, 58

Scottsboro case, 125, 262

Scudder, Vida, 149

Seeger, Pete, 259

Segregation, 36. *See also* Racism
Selective admissions, 9, 10, 32, 81, 97–98, 147
Selective Training and Service Act, 1940, 221. *See also* Draft
Seth Low Junior College, 117, 121
Sevareid, Eric, 31, 130, 243; and interventionism, 180, 219–20; on Teamsters strike, 106–7, 138–39
Sinclair, Upton: *The Goosestep*, 140
Smith, Bernadotte E., 25
Smith Act, 1940, 79, 206, 236
Smith College, 114, 116, 149, 204
Sobel, Morton, 240
Social Frontier, 140
Socialism, 70, 127–28, 138, 149. *See also* Marxism
Socialist party, 38, 41. *See also* Norman Thomas
Socialists, 39, 49; and Spanish Civil War, 70, 170, 173, 176; in student peace movement, 57, 115, 136–37, 184–85, 193–95, 197; and war, 68, 115; and World War II, 222–23, 230. *See also* League for Industrial Democracy, Student League for Industrial Democracy, Young People's Socialist League
Sororities, 10. *See also* Fraternities and sororities
Southern Methodist University, 64, 126
Southwestern University, 126
Soviet Union, 19, 23, 77, 118, 125, 230, 240; nonaggression pact with Germany, 201–3; and Finland, 208–11
Spanish Civil War; and ASU, 169–182; Communists and, 170, 176; as divisive issue, 162, 169–74, 189; and fascism, 169, 170–72, 175–81; pacifists and, 170–73, 175; Socialists and, 70, 170, 173, 176; student support for Republic, 149, 170–82, 262; student volunteers, 175–80. *See also* Neutrality legislation
Sports. *See* Athletics
Sproul, Robert G., 131–32, 207. *See also* University of California
Stalin-Hitler Pact, 201–3
Stalling, Lawrence, 26
Stanford University, 6
Starobin, Joseph, 137, 241, 244, 293 (n. 42)
State legislatures, 20, 204–5
State Teachers College (Murfreesboro, Tennessee), 126
Strack, Celeste, 137, 184–85
Strayer Commission, 101–2
Student activism: in England, 58–59, 120, 138, 178; right-wing, 104, 271 (n. 30); before World War I, 4, 32–39; in 1920s, 32–39; post–World War II, 233–235; in 1960s, 249–51, 261. *See also* Communism; Marxism; Pacifism; Socialism; names of individual schools.
Student activists: in 1930s, 42–47, 91, 94–95, 111–12, 131–33; suppression of in 1920s, 34
Student Advocate, 170, 177, 179, 198, 200, 253
Student League for Industrial Democracy (SLID), 39, 47, 53, 90, 95, 119, 122–23, 131; and ASU, 134–35; formation of, 38; in student peace movement, 14, 57, 112, 121

Student movements, 17, 254–56.
See also Student activism
Student Nonviolent Coordinating
Committee (SNCC), 250
Student organizations: membership
of in 1930s, 14–15, 134–35.
See also names of individual
organizations
Student Outlook, 47, 137
Student peace movement: arises,
3, 14, 211, 265 n. 1;
breakup of, 220, 226, 229–30;
unity within, 17, 123. *See
also* American Student Union;
National Student League;
Pacifism; Student activism;
Student League for Industrial
Democracy; names of
individual schools
Student publications: and academic
freedom, 36, 207–8;
censorship of, 35, 43–44, 142,
145; in 1920s, 33; and
peace, 30, 36, 108–9, 118; support student peace
movement, 119, 121, 243. *See
also New Student*; *Student
Advocate*; *Student Outlook*;
Student Review; names of
individual school papers
Student Review, 135
Students: characteristics of in
1930s, 21–23, 46, 101;
characteristics of in 1950s, 236–
37; common interests of,
21, 23, 37; relationship with
faculty, 99, 143–46, 149;
rights of, 35, 131, 142, 144–45
Students for a Democratic Society,
38, 250
Student strikes against war, 3, 27,
80–81, 211–13; in 1934,

95, 115–18; in 1935, 107, 121–35;
in 1936, 186–87; in 1937,
170–71, 186–93
Surveys, 21–22, 225
Swarthmore College, 32, 137, 156,
175, 177
Sweetland, Monroe, 38
Sweezy, Paul, 243–44
Syracuse University, 116

Tansill, Charles, 25
Teachers, 20, 142, 267 (n. 4);
unions of, 213, 214, 241
Teachers College (Columbia), 42,
118, 120
Teachers colleges. *See* Colleges and
universities, teachers colleges
Temple University, 21, 142, 174–
75, 225; ASU at, 207,
210–12, 286 (n. 37); antiwar
activity at, 123, 187, 211–
12; *New Horizons*, 142; *News*,
206, 223; religion and
peace activism at, 156, 161, 223
Testament of Youth (Brittain), 30,
148, 151–52
Texas Christian University, 126
Thomas, Evan, 222
Thomas, Norman, 41, 141; as
campus speaker, 42, 116,
123; and pacifism, 70, 230
Thorndyke, Edward L., 102
Three Soldiers (Dos Passos), 28,
31, 217–18
Trilling, Diana, 98
Trilling, Lionel, 98–99, 237–38,
256–57
Tugwell, Rexford G., 217

Union Theological Seminary, 41,
117, 120, 156, 222
United States Congress against
War and Fascism, 118

United States Signal Corps, 28
Unity, 154
Universal military training, 233
University of California,
    46, 107; Berkeley, 131–23, 177,
    247, 253–54; Los Angeles,
    46, 131–32; UCLA *Daily
    Bruin*, 46
University of Chicago, 5, 23, 116,
    177; *Maroon*, 105, 145
University of Cincinnati, 114
University of Idaho, 4
University of Kansas, 131
University of Michigan, 17, 21, 46;
    antiwar activity at, 126,
    158–61; *Daily*, 105, 109;
    expulsion of ASU members, 132,
    206–7
University of Minnesota, 31,
    129–30, 192–93
University of Oregon, 145
University of Pennsylvania, 106,
    113, 149, 225–26, 231;
    ASU charter revoked, 207; anti-
    war activity at, 118–19,
    123–24, 212; *Bennett News*,
    119, 124, 232; *Daily
    Pennsylvanian*, 52–53, 83, 119,
    157; conservatism of, 104,
    119; and Olympics controversy,
    50, 52–53
University of Tennessee, 114
University of Washington, 187
University of Wisconsin, 33, 46,
    105, 235; antiwar activity
    at, 126–27; *Daily Cardinal*, 127;
    extension, 129
Uses of the University, The (Kerr),
    237

Van Dusen, Henry, 158
Vassar College, 193, 204; and

student activism, 27, 116,
    149; World Youth Congress at,
    164
Veterans of Future Wars, 3, 186–
    87, 214, 253
Veterans of World War II, 233–35
Vietnam, 167, 251, 259
Vigilantism, 105–6, 117, 122, 126;
    at Harvard, 93, 95–96; at
    UCLA, 131–32
Villanova University, 165

Walker, Stuart, 28
Wallace, Henry, 229, 233, 235
Walsh, David, 22
War, 66; in art, 28, 262–63;
    economic causes of, 11, 25, 108–
    10; in films, 27–28, 218;
    in literature, 28, 30–31, 217–18,
    263; student attitudes
    toward, 23–25, 176, 179–80;
    resistance to, 159–60; support
    for, 88–89, 225; and women,
    150–51, 176, 227–28. *See also*
    Pacifism; Spanish Civil
    War; Vietnam; World War I;
    World War II
War Bride (film), 27
Ward, Harry F., 155, 241
War Department: manual on
    citizenship, 113
War Resisters League (WRL), 13,
    24, 70, 188, 193, 211,
    213, 259; opposes draft registra-
    tion, 222–23
Wayne University, 176, 187
Wechsler, James, 209, 219, 240–41;
    as editor of *Spectator*, 70,
    75–79, 94; as co-editor of *Student
    Advocate*, 137, 170–73;
    as peace activist, 115, 117, 120,
    133; and *Revolt on the*

Campus, 18, 99–100, 114, 140; in 1950s and 1960s, 243–45, 160, 291 (n. 23)

Wechsler, James, and Harold Lavine: study of war propaganda, 214–15

Weinberger, Casper, 84

Weinstein, Jacob, 27

Weiss, Max, 167–68

Wellesley College, 37, 116, 149

Wesleyan University (Connecticut), 122

West Point cadets, 48, 90–91

What Price Glory? (Stalling), 28

Whittier College, 156, 190

Williams College, 116

Wilson, Woodrow, 7, 65

Wilson College, 218, 226

Wilson Teachers College, 124–25

Wisconsin, 126

Wisconsin Idea, 26

Wise, Stephen, 154

Wittenberg College, 126

Women, 97, 166, 176; on faculties, 37, 147, 248–49; and peace, 37, 146–52, 261–63; and war, 113–14, 150–51; in World War II, 227–28; after World War II, 247–49, 257, 261–63

Women's colleges, 6, 10, 16, 146–51, 164; Catholic, 10, 164; and peace, 37, 61, 122, 148–52; in post–World War II period, 247–48. *See also* names of individual colleges

Women's International League for Peace and Freedom, 24, 37, 128, 148, 193, 259; and munitions inquiry, 108, 123

Women's movement. *See* Feminism

Women students, 9, 21, 146, 149; activism of, 148–52;

enrollment, 8, 248; and student movement, 149–50

Working class and war, 115

World congresses, 57–58, 67–68, 119–20, 164

World Moves On, The (film), 28

World Peace Fellowship, 37

World Tomorrow, 154

World War I, 19, 71, 155–56; artistic portrayal of, 25, 27–28, 30–31, 218, 263; and the churches, 155–56; and civil liberties, 25, 144–45; and colleges and universities, 25–26, 142; destruction of, 24, 66; economic causes of, 31, 108–9; effect on Europe, 24, 58; influence on student movement, 4, 65, 110, 124, 130–31; revisionist view of, 11, 15, 24, 26–27, 30–34, 56, 108, 164, 215, 224. *See also* Munitions industry; War

World War II: debate over United States entry, 202, 214–26; faculty and, 12, 214; students response to, 231–32; veterans of, 233–35. *See also* Collective security

Wright, Harry, 205

Yale University, 6, 8, 48, 83, 116

Yard, Molly, 137, 149–50, 185, 209, 219, 261–62

YM-YWCA, 57, 156–59, 163

Young Communist League, 75, 103, 129, 136, 198, 244

Young People's Socialist League (YPSL), 119, 136, 185, 213, 222

Youth Committee against War, 211, 213, 222